THE BIBLICAL VIEW OF SEX AND MARRIAGE

The Biblical View of Sex and Marriage

by

OTTO A. PIPER

CHARLES SCRIBNER'S SONS

New York

This is a complete revision of *The Christian Interpretation of Sex* by Otto A. Piper, copyright 1941 Charles Scribner's Sons.

A-10.60[H]

Printed in the United States of America

Library of Congress Catalog Card Number 60-14021

PREFACE

WHEN, some twenty years ago, I wrote *The Christian Interpretation of Sex* mine was a lonely voice in theological ethics. The situation has greatly changed in the meantime. There is hardly a book in the field that does not agree with the two basic principles laid down in my treatise: that the ethical treatment of sex should start not from the institution of marriage but from the nature of sex, and that the theologian had to derive his interpretation of sex from the Bible.

After considerable reflexion it seemed to me good not to have my old book issued indefinitely. While my basic views have not changed, the materials that experience had contributed during two decades no less than newly rising needs demanded a new book. The discussion with modern psychology required ample space. Problems of married life had to be treated in greater detail. However, I refrained, in this area, from discussing the problems of family life except as they are affected by sexual relations. Otherwise it would have been necessary to write a companion volume.

I am particularly indebted to a number of women who, through their books and orally, have made it plain that the problem of the sexes is considerably broader than the problem of sexuality, yet also that sexual problems cannot be adequately handled without constant attention being paid to the social problem of the man-woman relationship. Painfully did I realize to what extent men (including myself) take it for granted that there is only one valid perspective in matters of sex: from the vantage point of male superiority. I am glad I have now learned that the reciprocity of the two sexes applies to scholarship too.

For a characterization of my method I prefer the designation 'Biblical Realism.' With the older Biblicism it agrees that the Bible is God's Revelation and that we may therefore confidently turn toward the Scriptures in search for the ultimate truth concerning man's predicament. It differs, however, from the older Biblicism in one essential respect. There it was taken for granted that the words used by the Biblical writers had the same meaning that they have in our days, and that therefore the sense of a Biblical statement was immediately evident. It seemed, therefore, an easy task to select the appropriate verses from the Bible and to use them as a kind of catechism. The fallacy of that literalism lies in its neglect of the influence the mentality of an age and a cultural group has on language. No wonder, therefore, that with such a naïve use of the Bible the Scripture always happened to be in agreement with the theology of the interpreter or his group.

The difficulty we have in using the Bible for our ethical instruction lies in the fact that whatever it says on human life and conduct is derived from an image of man's nature and his destination that is everywhere present yet nowhere given by way of full description. The Biblical exegete has to use a method similar to that of the archaeologist, who attempts to piece together a number of fragments into what he thinks was the original shape of the vessel. Consistency of the parts with the whole will then prove the correctness of the reconstruction. But whereas the archaeologist can rely on extant specimens and analogy the exegete must grow with his material. Mere logical consistency has often been tried and has equally often faltered. It is only as, in the light of our spiritual experience, that image develops from within ourselves that it is in agreement with the intentions of the Biblical writers. That is the reason why no Biblical exegesis is possible apart from personal concern. In this connection, a word should be said about the use of the Old Testament, and in particular the first chapters of Genesis. I am fully aware of their mythical character but feel unable to find in that fact a reason for rejecting them. There is no other way but the myth to describe what we mean by human nature and its origin. They cannot be explained altogether, least of all in the naïve manner characteristic of the evolutionists of the last generation. But the riddle of man's existence does not dispense us from the obligation to define its ontic place and structure in the universe. I confess that in that respect more light has come to me from the wisdom of ancient times than from modern speculations.

In spite of the relative difficulty of the exegetical method its advantage in comparison with contemporary methods of Protestant ethics is obvious. Since he has to cling to the Biblical material the exegete is in constant contact with the facts of life, and does not stray around in the abstract spaces of an ontology, nor must he resign himself to the mediocrities and failures of a sinful world, for he sees man in the light of a purpose which God carries out through man in the Church of Christ. He is not doomed with the naturalists to betray his conscience by pretending that what is is what ought to be, nor is he compelled to share the idealist's delusion that the good will come into being merely because it is good. Rather, he sees himself verily as one who deliberately deviates from the path of righteousness, and who, in his struggle for a good life, finds himself severely hampered both by temptations resulting from his physical and mental setup and the spirit of the group whose member he is. In comparison with this realism many modern writers look like innocent babes. At the same time, however, he learns from the attitude God takes toward sex that it has its metaphysical dignity and is no mere shortcut to pleasure, and also that far from being unessential for the constitution of true life it is used by God as the means for the execution of his redemptive plans.

Otto A. Piper

Princeton, New Jersey

CONTENTS

INTRODUCTION

I. THE NEW INTERPRETATION OF SEX

THERE is hardly any other area of life in the Western world that has been so profoundly affected by the recent general upheaval of social, political, and economic conditions as our evaluation of sex, and yet, strangely enough, there is no other sphere of social relations in which such radical and revolutionary change has been accepted with such ease and so little opposition.

Two generations ago sex was still surrounded by the high fences of a Puritan morality which both protected and restricted it. The effects of these controls were felt far beyond the members of the churches. Although attacked from time to time in the name of individual freedom, this set of social standards was so deeply rooted in Western civilization that it was able, on the whole, firmly to hold its own. Of course these standards did not prevent immorality and licentiousness, but they swayed public opinion sufficiently to brand transgressions as serious violations of the social order. Lewd talk was confined to male company, literary description of sexual activities met with police repression, and any extramarital satisfaction of the sexual urge had to be done secretly.

The causes of this sexual revolution seem to be both physiological and moral. The twentieth century has witnessed a remarkable improvement in living conditions due to an ample supply of nourishing food, methodical care for the health of children and adolescents, and the wide spread of sports and other outdoor activities. One result of this development is to be seen in an increased vitality, and, coupled with it, in a growth of sexual energy which manifests itself among other things in the rapid increase of populations.

But this physiological change, which seems to represent a general rhythm in the life of nations, cannot explain what is most characteristic of the sexual attitude of our age, namely the general obsession with sex as the surest, shortest, and cheapest way to happiness. This new evaluation of sex was caused by two factors: the ascendancy of the naturalistic view of life, especially the way in which it has been popularized, and the positivism of the modern scientist. Until recently public opinion in the west was controlled by the Christian religion, and thus any world view which considered happiness and pleasure as the highest goal of life was effectively challenged by the Christian evaluation of man or its philosophical transformation, namely idealism. But at the turn of the century representatives of the materialistic outlook succeeded in capturing the older media of mass communication, especially newspapers and magazines, and in developing new types such as films, radio, and television. It is easy to see the economic motive behind this development. Those who craved happiness discovered that the easiest way to make a great deal of money quickly was to employ the media of mass communication for the spread of the idea that happiness was man's supreme good. By treating sex as the universally available source of happiness and by denying that, as a purely physiological function, sex had anything to do with the higher ends of life these agencies have succeeded in making their view of sex the one generally held in our days.

The positivistic trend in modern science, finally, helped to assign this view the appearance of a scientific dogma. The two Kinsey reports are probably the most conspicuous manifestations of that spirit; however, much of the modern psychology has taken the same position.

The two world wars have also decisively contributed to the final triumph of this view of sex. The close proximity in which millions of young people of both sexes found themselves in the armed forces and factories, and the absence of the social controls which had formerly effectively restricted bodily contacts, carried their effects and consequences into the postwar periods and communicated themselves to those, also, who lacked this special experience. Furthermore, the sexual indoctrination to which millions of young men and women of the armed forces were exposed was almost exclusively concerned with the diagnosis, avoidance, and cure of venereal diseases. Fortified by the prestige of the instructing officers, this naturalistic concept of sex almost nullified the endeavors of the chaplains to instill any ethical thinking about sex.

The movies and the magazines, in turn, have commercially exploited this change. By the glamorization of youth and vitality these media have presented sex as having a value in itself which often meant glorifying vice, crime, perversion, and vulgarity. All attempts of the censor to stop this trend prove to be futile. Because the portrayal of sex is financially highly profitable the dealers in sexual stimuli will constantly find ways, within the limits of the law, to sell their representations of "healthy vitality." As a result of the technological and economic primacy of the United States of America this outlook has now swayed the whole free world. Through the American film industry other nations and peoples receive the impression that sex, next to crime and money, is the only thing in which Americans are seriously interested. In turn, the demand for sexy films has given a powerful impetus to the film industry of countries whose censorship is less rigorous than that of the United States to produce "frank representations of illicit love," and the "wild and reckless" pictures meet obviously with the enthusiastic approval of the daily press.

We would be greatly deluded, however, in thinking that this aspect of the 'American way of life' which we try hard to sell to the rest of the free world, represented an universal phenomenon. The countries which are under the sway of communism manifest a remarkable restraint in the treatment of sex.

While Russian Socialism, in its earlier stage, propagated the Western ideas of free love, contending that monogamy and belief in sexual virtue were capitalistic inventions to solidify the rule of the bourgeois class, communism soon developed its functional interpretation of man to the point where marriage and sex merely vegetate on the periphery of a life totally dedicated to the State. The visitor to the communist countries is struck by the fact that in the East magazines and pictures that glorify sex are practically unknown. Apparently this new conception of life has captured the imagination of the communistic youth so thoroughly that they feel in no way frustrated in accepting it. Their lives seem to derive complete meaning from their jobs and political activities. Such an outlook may appear to our mind as dehumanizing man. However, the two modern views may come to terms. The idea that life unless dedicated to a great cause lacks meaning, may eventually appeal to the young people of the West who in the modern mass society have lost their individuality.

It would certainly be a mistake to explain the Western overemphasis placed upon sex merely as a result of the last war, or as the consequence of our generally undisciplined state of morality. One of the earliest roots of the whole change lies in the nineteenth-century fight for the emancipation of women. The patriarchal family, which had completely restricted the woman to household tasks and subordinated her in all things to her husband, had gradually disintegrated mainly under Protestant influence. The reformers' emphasis upon the personal nature of faith imparted to the woman in her relation to God a status equal to that of the man. This spiritual equality led to the idea of her complete equality as a person, and eventually the idealistic picture of woman's destination as a rational being became a reality in education. The demand for equal opportunities of intellectual training in high school and college was the inevitable accompaniment of this changed viewpoint. Other practical consequences followed, such as the campaign for equal economic, social, and political rights. Unavoidable as this development was its progress would have been definitely slower except for the rapid expansion of economic life. The equality of women had to be recognized because the demands of industry for workers became very acute, and the rapid rise in living standards compelled women to become wage earners.

Although passionately opposed in its beginnings by many men the emancipation of women was thus eventually achieved. The immediate result was a totally new and informal relationship on the job, between the sexes. Though originally this development lacked specifically sexual or erotic undertones, yet with the disintegration of the old social order, in which a definite place was assigned to women, the problem of sexual relationship would manifest itself in a new and pressing manner. It was obvious that the granting of social, economic, and political equality and rights had in no way abolished the difference between the sexes. Our sex determines profoundly the manner in which our self will manifest itself in daily life. Since practically all the job patterns have been created by men there exists today a great uncertainty about the function which womanhood is to perform in modern society. Of this perplexing search for new ways of life both sexes are painfully aware.

There is certainly much to commend the modern development. The legitimate motive behind the new attitude toward sex was the wish of the individual to live an integrated life of his own. Consistently interpreted such striving implies the demand that sex must be accorded a rightful place in adult life, and that it ought not to be considered as something only admitted into one's life with an evil conscience. Luckily the false unnatural attitude toward sex is removed today and the ground is laid for a healthier attitude. A further consequence has been the remarkable progress made in sexual hygiene. Finally, and most important, the natural relationship between the sexes in school and on the job has given an increased significance to the role played by personal affection in the sexual approach. Nevertheless, taken as a whole, the sphere of sexual relationships presents to the modern observer the impression of complete chaos. Obviously this generation has not yet succeeded in adjusting the striving for an integrated personality with the demands made by the reciprocal nature of the sexual relationship.

At a very early stage it was obvious that the modern revolution in sex was doomed to result in disappointment because it was carried on in the name of, or at least in the service of, the individual's search for happiness. This was precisely the goal that was unattainable. Happiness cannot be bought or manufactured. It is life's free gift, and he who deliberately strives for it chases a will-o'-the-wisp. Though today practically all the restrictions impeding the satisfaction of the desire for sexual happiness have been removed, and though the pursuit of ideal goals is generally considered as permissive rather than as imperative for a full life, yet the resultant happiness is not as great and sweet as was anticipated.

True, it is possible nowadays to pass unhindered from one woman to another, or from one man to another, or, in a conveyor belt fashion, enter into and terminate marriages, but the very fact of incessant repetition indicates that not much is gained thereby. Sexual satisfaction comes cheaply today. No sustained courtship and no period of long waiting is necessary. Because of contraceptives, means of abortion, clinics for sexual diseases, and the amazing demand for babies to be adopted no excessive risk is involved in promiscuous intercourse. Sex has become the most inexpensive general source of pleasure and is placed on the same level as eating and drinking. The sexual union, formerly considered the greatest happiness, has now become a mere pittance, and American youth in order to "get a bigger kick" has dashed headlong into narcotic addiction.

The ease with which women may be had for sexual gratification accounts for the queer mixture of romantic sentimentalism and cynical disregard for the other sex characteristic of the college boy and the magazines he patronizes, and this tension has been a reason for a steady increase in sexual neuroses. Formerly the mores of society had a considerable protective and therapeutic value, since a personal moral conflict could be resolved by complying with that order, whereas the conflicts resulting from the new unlimited freedom is manifested in a biological-psychological disturbance that needs a physician's care. Another serious consequence of the modern outlook is a crippling of the ability to love, a fact that, far beyond the erotic sphere, affects the social life of our days. Where sexual intercourse is but a biological function the partner counts only as a pleasure-yielding body while his personality is disrespected. It seems that the modern woman suffers more than the man from this new kind of equality. Simone de Beauvoir's attempt to restore the self-respect of the female sex will prove to be futile, however, since her suggestions start from the modern axiom of unlimited sexual freedom.

Even where the new order has freed people from certain inhibitions and tensions a sense of happiness is conspicuously lacking. While the modern author's desire to write a best-seller comes closest to fulfillment, when he has the nerve and the ability to describe in greatest realism and detail various types of sexual experience, his very realism requires him to admit that this is not the way to real satisfaction. The growing number of marriages ending in divorce seems even more indicative of the lack of happiness in sexual relations. Most modern marriages are not wrecked by adultery but by the spouses failing to understand that a genuine mutuality toward each other is the absolute prerequisite for a happy marriage. The desire to change one's partner is an evident symptom of a deep-seated misconception of sexual relationship.

What we consider the new view of sex represents the characteristic attitude of the Western world. It is not, as in former centuries, a rebellion of individuals against the pressure of mores or the order of a church-dominated society. We fool ourselves by saying that this is what people did in all ages and that the Biblical views of sex and purity were at no time identical with sexual practice. True as this objection is it overlooks the educative and restrictive influence of the then prevailing evaluation. The revolutionary change which has occurred in our generation is a state of mind which not only tolerates but engenders sexual practices from which people would formerly have refrained. Kinsey is right when he interprets, for example, the comparative prevalence of masturbation and sexual perversions in our days as being contingent upon their evaluation by modern society. For once the authority of objective standards has been abolished the only limitation which modern man will accept for his personal life and actions is the disapproval of the particular group to which he belongs. The perplexity of modern writers on sex proves that once the principle of unlimited sexual freedom has been adopted the practically inescapable conclusion is that all forms of sexual activity must be condoned, except perhaps where violence is used.

II. THE THEOLOGICAL PROBLEM

Our Perplexity

The amazing victory of the modern view of sex indicates that it carries with it an inescapable and irresistible urgency. It would be unrealistic to explain it as the sudden upsurge of uninhibited immorality on a gigantic scale. Rather it reflects modern man's understanding of himself. The image which a group forms of itself is the product of social conditions and historical events. We shall probably not be greatly mistaken when we consider the development of a mass society on a technological basis and the increasing secularization of modern life during the last two centuries as the principal factors in the making of modern man's mentality. Must we now say that Christianity was so intimately tied up with the feudal and bourgeois structure of the Western world that the technological and social revolution of our age has automatically eclipsed the faith of our fathers?

One thing is certain: mere complaints about modern corruption or condemnation of the public discussion and display of sex will be of no avail. It would be ludicrous, too, to hope for a sudden fundamental change in our economic and social conditions to which traditional Christianity could easily adjust itself, let alone to assume that the historical developments of the past fifty years could be undone. Even though naturalism is an inadequate interpretation of sex modern man, conditioned by the spirit of modern science, cannot be protected against this ersatz religion of our age by waging frontal attacks against it. Experience has already plainly taught modern man that he cannot find happiness on that road. Yet many of our contemporaries have acquiesced in the gloomy thought that man can find only an imperfect happiness in this world anyhow, and that wisdom should tell us to make the best out of a bad world. While this is poor comfort which too often ends in vice, crime, or alcoholism, we must admit, neverthless, that compared with this realism the Christian models of life seem mostly unrealistic, overdrawn, and utopian.

It would be futile, too, to approach our contemporaries with prohibitions and commands for they doubt the validity of all absolutes. They pretend that their views of sex are based upon the facts of nature which in their opinion bear a higher authority than philosophical ideals or Biblical commandments. We have no longer to fight for a particular issue of sexual ethics, e.g., the right or wrong of divorce. Today it is the Christian idea of man that has lost its power in public thinking.

The decisive question which confronts us is therefore this: is the modern understanding of man so exclusively the result of historical and social conditions that no deliberate change can be effected, or is it possible to challenge the present situation by a Christian view of man?

Modern man's understanding of himself is largely determined by the mass character of our social life. The mighty forces of modern industry, the concentrations of vast urban populations, the uniformity of public opinion molded by the press, radio and television, the increasing authoritarian character of the democratic state, and compulsory and protracted military service combine to make it almost impossible for the individual to live a self-determined life. Behaviourism has probably expressed this state of mind most clearly by denying that the faculties of the Ego are grouped around an autonomous self, and by asserting that its spontaneity is only a response to stimuli from without to which it reacts in the direction of least resistance or greatest pleasure. David Riesman has graphically described it in his portrait of the outer directed society. The average modern person, having experienced the bitter results of his revolt against these mighty levelling forces, is inclined stoically to accept the loss of his personal sphere and he considers adaptation and conformity as the better part of wisdom. Therefore, it is incorrect to speak of the Nihilism of modern man. Historically, Nihilism is the revolt of the individual, conscious of his power, against a senseless world. Modern man, however, does not want to be an individual because he has lost respect for himself as an individual. Existentialism is no remedy for him no matter how eagerly he discusses it. For in order to accept the challenge of reality, as Existentialism demands, man must first affirm his Selfhood. That is, precisely, what modern man is unwilling or unable to do. So Existentialism degenerates into mere dialectic with no driving necessity for action within it.

The preceding analysis has shown that modern man's interpretation of life is not exclusively the outcome of historical and social developments. While his life is largely conditioned by them he is not compelled to accept them in the manner he does. He does not lack Selfhood, but he does not consider it any longer worth while to be an autonomous person because the life of conformity, which the circumstances allow him to live, requires relatively little effort. Christianity's problem, then, is not how to engender Selfhood in man but how to confront him so effectively with the Christian view of life that he will consider it worth trying. Under less difficult circumstances Protestant ethics sought to achieve this goal in the nineteenth century by enlisting the help of Idealism. The individual was told that as a rational being he ought to submit his impulses to reason and to live within a civilized and organized community whose rational order demanded monogamy and a stable family life. This belief in an absolute reason is no longer held today. Modern man denies that the State, business, and social conditions are the products of reason. He is rather inclined to believe that the most plausible explanation of actual social life is to be found in the reckless and shrewd manner power is used for the satisfaction of one's desire for recognition, in his greed for possessions, and in his lust for pleasure. He doubts also that in human relations it is always the wisest and most cultured people who know best which way to pursue. How great is the mischief and confusion wrought by the "experts" on whose advice governments lean so heavily! Under these circumstances it would be anachronistic to select the idea of personality or the institution of marriage as the starting point of our sexual ethics.

The Biblical View of Man

Study of the Bible will help us overcome these methodological difficulties. The ultimate reason why modern man has lost his sense of Selfhood is his lack of faith. Of course, if it were true that the Ego had no defense and help against the forces of nature and history then it would be best simply to yield to their assault and give up every quest for Selfhood. Things are different, however, when the world in which we live is seen as pointing beyond itself to a higher and mightier Reality. We know that the God who created this world also directs all things according to His plan. It is His gracious will that man should not eke out a miserable and frugal existence at the mercy of cosmic forces but rather should have dominion over them.

On the other hand, since all other attempts at self-realization have only convinced us of their futility the Bible deserves to be given a second chance. In its light it strikes us as rather naïve when psychoanalysts like C. G. Jung and his school look for deliverance through the fairy tales and ancient myths of mankind! While these mental images express a longing for self-fulfillment the satisfaction for which they look belongs to an imaginary world. Unfortunately here on earth you do not encounter fairy-tale princes who gallantly take care of your troubles.

The Bible alone testifies to a God Who is as real as the things about us and Whose redemptive work in Jesus Christ is historically attested. By admitting man into fellowship with Himself the Creator helps His creature to attain real Selfhood. Modern man is prone to surrender his Selfhood to the mighty forces of this world even before he begins the struggle because he is sure that he will be defeated. But if we conceive of our destiny as fellowship with God we feel that it is worth living a life of our own because our faith in Jesus Christ implies the victory over the surrounding world. But how are we to convey this assurance of faith to others, who like us are confronted with the defeatist attitude of the modern view of man?

The presentation of the Christian understanding of sex must

adopt three axioms if we wish to speak to our time. To begin with, in spite of all advice to the contrary, we must start from God's redemptive work. Humanism has utterly failed to offer a satisfactory way of life. Our task is no longer to map out for the strong personality the way to perfection. The modern world requires an interpretation of sex which serves as a bread of life, supplying strength to weary and despondent people and encouraging them to continue in the pursuit of their goals. By consorting with sinners and harlots Jesus demonstrated that God's message does not address itself only to stalwart believers but also to people who, without religion or in spite of it, are so unstable or devoid of inner substance that they are unable to live a life of their own. While they may get along well in their businesses or professions their inner life is unbalanced and insecure and lacks a clear direction. Such people Jesus did not approach with commandments and reproaches but rather pointed out to them the help God was offering. Likewise modern man is unable to make sense of his life as long as he has not grasped a reality that can uphold him in his weakness and restore his self-respect. In vain does he try to regain his self-respect by identifying himself with the collective mass and by striving to live and act as all the rest. Developing fully the evangelical message of self-realization by faith would by far transcend the scope of this book. But the absence of a broad dogmatic groundwork should not mislead anybody into believing that the Protestant view of sex consisted of a set of ethical principles only. Apart from the practice of a living faith it is impossible to appropriate the power and inner reality of the Christian life. God is apprehended only by sanctified hearts and never without prayer. Unless these two factors are cultivated and given prominence in life our interest in a Christian solution of the problem of sex will remain a purely academic reflection.

The humanistic approach to sex—and all moralistic discussions remain in the human realm—is beset by peculiar dangers. If we investigate only the standards by which our sexual conduct is to be determined without paying attention to the context into which God has placed us we are bound to deceive ourselves and others. Since no man is blameless in sexual matters, not even the teacher of ethics, we are apt either to make exaggerated demands in order to shield ourselves against the reproach of our shortcoming by the greatness of the ideal, or in order to exonerate ourselves we exact too little of ourselves. This temptation may be avoided when we start from a serious contemplation of what the Holy Spirit wants to achieve in the believers.

Secondly Protestant ethics must be based upon the Bible. The Christian message cannot gain the attention it deserves if we content ourselves with repeating the conclusions which anthropologists, philosophers, biologists, doctors, psychologists, and sociologists have reached concerning the problems of sex instead of consulting the Bible. The Christian message will manifest its relevance only when it proclaims what no one else is saying, or is in a position to say. Biblical revelation offers that possibility. Today many people doubt that the Bible can speak authoritatively on a subject like sex because its views reflect the conditions and prejudices of a past age and an alien civilization. Yet the authority of the Bible rests upon the fact that notwithstanding its historical origin it presents a view of life that is of lasting truth. Measured against the great fundamental insights of the Bible the view of sex provided by modern science notwithstanding its valuable analytical descriptions of sexual phenomena is disappointingly shallow and shortsighted in its evaluations and interpretations.

The Biblical view of sex revolves about two fundamental ideas: reverence for the mystery of sex, and the sanctification of marriage as the God-appointed goal of the sexual relationship. These fundamental Biblical ideas retain their essential meaning even though we now use modern psychology to describe sex. To give an instance, there were many sexual taboos in the purification regulations of the Old Testament which the Hebrews held in common with their neighbors. Yet it is noteworthy, that unlike the pagan religions the Old Testament taboos had no independent meaning of their own, but were woven into the religious understanding of Israel's law. Similarly the fundamental principles of the Bible regulating sexual life are not dependent on the social conditions in which they were proclaimed. It is significant that the Old Testament law did not prescribe minute and detailed regulations for the social relationship of the sexes, although the Israelites, as all of their neighbors, must have had certain customs surrounding courtship, engagement, marriage, the birth of children, and much more; but none of these formed part of the Old Testament law. Regulatory laws are concerned only with those few instances where the basic Biblical idea of sex was endangered by the customs of pagan neighbors.

Even in those cases, however, Biblical authority does not require Christians literally to conform to these Old Testament laws. Their meaning and scope is to be recognized in the perfect light of divine revelation which has shone in Christ. The meaning of the mystery of sex and of human marriage has been disclosed to us in the idea of the Divine Marriage as this was understood by Jesus and His apostles.

Under the influence of positivism and historicism the theology of the nineteenth century tended to project Biblical events upon the same plane as those of world history. Thus, scholars were interested only in the question: Are they historical or unhistorical? And are they compatible with modern science? The exegetes did not realize that the records of the Bible were never destined to answer these questions but rather to give evidence of the divinely wrought foundations upon which the faith rests. Seen in that light, for example, the first four chapters of the Bible cannot be interpreted as a primitive hypothesis of man's beginnings, and the books of the New Testament were not meant to furnish documents for the study of the history of the early Church. Rather, the books of the Bible describe the way in which the natural life of man and the operation of God's Spirit were fused together in human history. Hence, the Biblical books must not be understood in a Platonic sense as though they revealed the eternal truth of what transpires within every man, but rather they exhibit the formative powers that are at work in believers and unbelievers, the reason why earthly conditions are what they are, and the divine goal and purpose which they help to achieve.

Thirdly, in order to be effective, the Christian approach to sex must be a realistic one. Modern people prefer to discuss their sexual problems with a physician or psychotherapist rather than with their pastor, because they assume that the former will take a more realistic view of them. While it would be fatal for the church and its members if the pastor substituted psychology for theology he must, nevertheless, know the facts of sex life in order correctly to interpret them. The modern scientific treatment of sex must bear part of the responsibilty for the self-depletion of modern man for his naturalistic view is the result of its Positivistic interpretation. However, we gladly acknowledge that by laying bare many important aspects of psychological and physiological relationships modern science has greatly helped to broaden and to deepen our picture of the nature of sex. The scientists have brought to light certain features of the Biblical view of sex which had been overlooked or ignored by the exegetes. Thus the theologian is able to show modern people how the Bible throws light upon the nature of their longings and desires. This correlation between experience and Biblical revelation can provide an interpretation of sex that is realistic and in agreement with the nature of this world yet leads beyond modern Positivism to a theocentric view.

A realistic approach demands, furthermore, that one proceed from a proper evaluation of man. Since the Bliblical standards of sex are to be realized, people must understand clearly that man is neither actually nor potentially good. The ethically minded contemporary is likely to share the serious mistake of thinking that man can attain the good by his own efforts; yet our approach is equally misleading if, while emphasizing his natural inability to do the good we do not also point out his dignity in God. He is a creature whose life completely transcends anything else found in nature. Men are called by the power of the Holy Spirit to grow towards their true life, even though they are persistently beset by personal weaknesses and failures and frequently lose their way. In order to do justice to these aspects of man's nature we will not confine ourselves in the following chapters to offering an interpretation of sex, but shall also discuss the reality of sexual experience, its problems and difficulties and last not least the victory which faith wins over them.

Part One

THE BIBLICAL VIEW OF SEX

III. THE NATURE OF SEX

THE older schools of psychology used to equate sex with a conscious intention of consummating the sexual act. Consequently, only those acts were considered as sexual that were either definitely directed toward sexual union or implied the desire of it, such as acts of self abuse. In recent times, however, psychology has greatly extended the area of sex including, for instance, the unconscious sexuality of infants and sucklings, and some will even hold that the subconscious mind in its totality is swayed by the sexual urge. While the Biblical concept of sex covers a considerably larger area than the older psychology assumed it, nevertheless, exposes the limitations and misinterpretations of the modern psychological views.

The Bible considers sex as a function of the body, but it designates by that term not the physiological life only but rather the Ego in its concrete entirety. While the Greek conception, still widely held in the Western world, conceived of man as a composite being formed of body and soul the Biblical writers underscore the integral unity of the individual. Physical and mental activities are different forms under which the Selfhood of the Ego expresses itself, and they condition each other mutually. Sex interpreted as a function of the Self is thus akin to the desire for life, the fear of death, and the surrendering or sacrificing of one's self, and it can, therefore, like them be directly related to religion. Accordingly the Bible teaches that sexual sins harm the body, that is to say they affect us in our total being. This fact constitutes the fundamental difference between sexual sins and other sins (1 Cor. 6:17). Because sex is a function of man's total self, not only of his sexual organs, a separation between a person and his sexual nature is impossible. Since masculinity or femininity is inseparable from our individual existence it is perfectly natural that he or she should experience sexual desires

(1 Cor. 7:7). If, as some hold, man were a mere spirit who only incidentally lived in a body the fact that he possessed sex would be irrelevant as far as the attainment of his true humanity is concerned.

The Biblical concept of sex makes necessary a differentiation between the acts and processes of sex, and sexuality itself. The development of the primary and secondary sex organs, the activity of the sex glands, menstruation, and emission are processes which evince sexual character; but they are not the basis of sexuality. Therefore, the manner in which the Ego experiences and controls his or her sexuality is almost entirely independent of the individual functioning of the sexual processes. Chastity and sensuality do not depend on the potency of the glandular secretions or the size of the sex organs.

Just as it is not the sexual organs or the sex glands which possess sexual desire, but the Ego or the Self, so sexual desire is not primarily directed toward the sexual organs of another person but toward his whole person as the bearer of a distinctive sexual character. This accounts for the urgency and the troublesome character of the sexual problem. It has nothing to do with functional troubles or diseases of the sexual organs. Yet as a difficulty besetting the Self it cannot be ascribed exclusively to the body or the mind. Although sexuality is not the only manifestation of the dynamic of the Self it is one of its essential functions. Hence every sexual activity and experience will not only influence one's own sexuality but also the other functions of the Self. Consequently, the processes of sexual maturation and recession are not confined solely to physiological and anatomical changes, rather the whole sexual cycle from the development into manhood and womanhood to the abatement and cessation of sexual activity affects profoundly the life attitudes and abilities of a person.

Since human Selfhood implies personality, the sexual life of man, unlike that of animals, is not governed by instinct only but is destined to give expression to his personality. Consequently, a person's attitude toward his sexuality will manifest itself in his whole behaviour, e.g., in the way he satisfies his appetite, his attitude toward work, the discipline or lack of discipline of his mind, and his manner of dealing with his fellow men. We can, therefore, agree with the assertion of modern psychology that apparently nonsexual dreams may be cryptic sex symbols revealing the true nature of one's sexuality. Yet, we part company with the psychologists who identify the whole unconscious life with sex, and presume to discover sexual motives in every dream or play of the imagination. Although sex is an integral part of the Ego it is only one of the manifold functions of Self, and should not be identified with the Self's total will for existence.

Because personal life is indivisible, however, sex must be practised and controlled in such a manner that the other functions of the Self are not thereby disturbed or hampered. A neurosis will ensue, for example, when a sexual desire or experience conflicts with the demands of the other functions or spheres of the Self. Such a conflict cannot be truly resolved when with Freud it is interpreted as resulting from demands arising from the outside, from a kind of super-Ego over against which the individual would have to assert himself because his sex is an integral part of his Self. Rather it is necessary to establish a harmony between the various functions and appetites of the Self. This explains the harshness of Jesus, who in dealing with sexual desires, says: "If your right eye causes you to sin, pluck it out, and throw it away: if your right hand causes you to sin, cut it off, and throw it away: for it is better for you to lose one of your members, than that your whole body should be cast into Hell" (Matt. 5:29ff, cf. also Luke 11:34-36). Such demands are not meant to be understood literally, rather the members of the body symbolize the various desires of the Self. Such imperatives are reasonable since the various desires of the Self affect the whole individual. Stern discipline is necessary though it is not an end in itself. It is required because only by withstanding the desires in a concrete way is it possible to regulate and control sex itself.

IV. THE UNITY OF THE TWO PERSONS

LYING at the very center of the Biblical interpretation of sex we find the brief but significant sentence, "The two shall be one flesh" (Gen. 2:24). Three ideas in particular are expressed thereby:

1. Sexual intercourse establishes an inner union between the two persons concerned.
2. That union is a "unity of the flesh," i.e., it affects the vital wills of these persons.
3. This union can never be dissolved.

THE UNION OF MUTUALITY

Sexual intercourse is never a passing affair. On the contrary, in each case it establishes a lasting union between the two persons. In turn, it is characteristic of the sexual relationship that it can never concern more than two people at a time, even in cases when more than two people are in the same place and engaged in sexual activities. The Bible calls the resulting union a unity of the flesh, and this idea forms the basis for the understanding and the ethics of sexual life in both Testaments. The sexual unity of husband and wife is their exclusive mutual possession which neither of them can share with a third person. It is on this basis, not on account of legal considerations, that Jesus condemns divorce because it violates the unity of the flesh (Matt. 5:32 and parallel passages, and Matt. 19:6ff). Paul, too, states emphatically that the individual spouse is not the master of his or her body, but that both of them in a spirit of mutuality must agree on their sexual relations in each case (1 Cor. 7:4ff). This demand cannot be derived from the ancient marriage laws which doubtless granted a superior role to the husband, rather the mutual control of the bodies is established upon the Biblical idea of sexual unity. It is a significant fact that Paul applies the idea of the unity of the flesh not only to the husband-wife relationship but, in a forceful appeal to Gen. 2:24, also uses it as a description of the relationship of Christ to the Church.

Since this Biblical idea of the unity of the flesh was misunderstood or neglected in Christian theology, misconceptions of the nature of sexual relationships arose in the ancient church and were shared both by Catholicism and Protestantism. For apart from the unity of the flesh sexual life is shorn of its independent meaning and value, and needs, therefore, to be justified as a means for superior ends, e.g., marriage or propagation. Such utilitarian views unfortunately were a serious obstacle to the understanding of the deeper meaning of sex. Though it is true that in modern Catholic ethics the mutual relationship of the couple is considered a positive value it remains an isolated feature which has no connection with the procreative end of sex. Since, according to the Bible, this unity of the flesh is the reason why there is a differentiation of the sexes not only homosexuality is sharply condemned but also all attempts on the part of women to assume to themselves male prerogatives. The Biblical idea of unity does not imply a disregard for the sexual differences; on the contrary it stresses them. However, it is not a difference in kind, as philosophers have repeatedly asserted all the way from Aristotle's theory that men and women have souls of a different kind to Schopenhauer's and Nietzsche's Anti-Feminism, but rather a difference of function. The Bible admits no psychological or physiological superiority of one sex over the other. The Biblical account of Creation in Genesis chapter 2 emphasizes their common origin. Nevertheless, in view of their different functions, we deem it a miracle that a man and a woman can achieve unity.

That the sexes are correlated has been noted outside of Biblical religion, too, but in a sense entirely foreign to the Bible. In his

"Banquet," Plato offers an interpretation which has retained its attraction for poets and psychologists alike to the present day. The Athenian thinker introduces the myth of the bisexual nature of man. Human beings, the story goes, were originally creatures with two faces, and were mostly double-sexed; however, some were doubly male and some were doubly female. Because of their disobedience, Zeus split them into two halves, and now each single unit must go through life filled with unsatisfied desire until he has found his other half. By the nature of their orgin some will find their happiness in homosexual relations while most of them long for the other sex. While with this idea of the correlation of the sexes Plato apparently comes close to the Biblical view he actually discloses his individualism in this myth. He does not think that people yearn for the other person in order to achieve a reciprocal unity, rather the partner is loved because the individual wants to find self-realization through him. The original bisexual character of man serves no creative end, while according to the Biblical conception persons existing separately are united by sex in order to achieve a higher type of human existence.

C. G. Jung and his school, who have started from this Platonic myth, have seemingly corrected it by considering each individual bisexual having a masculine animus and a feminine anima. But thereby Jung does not transcend Plato's individualism. He too holds that the partner serves only as a stimulus of one's own animus or anima. No real unity of the two individuals is thereby brought about. This should hardly surprise us, since according to the Bible this unity of the flesh is not the natural outcome of the sexual differentiation but rather the work of God implied in the special destination given to man.

The Bible nowhere states that the individuals who have been united through their sexual relationship were from eternity predestined for each other. It is only the functional correlation of the sexes which is from the beginning. As Eve was taken from Adam so man and woman always have the desire for each other and the capability of being united. The actual union, however, is in each case individually conditioned and established through the sexual intercourse of these two people. While the Bible denies that any person is destined from eternity for a certain definite person of the other sex it assigns a divine meaning to sexual intercourse. The sexual relationship is not the initial stage of the lifelong development and growth of the erotic faculty, as Plato held, but it has its fullest meaning within itself as the act through which the union of the couple is accomplished.

Unity of the flesh in the Biblical sense depends exclusively on the consummation of the reciprocal sexual relationship. It is not qualified by, nor is it contingent upon, any other personal elements such as race, social position, or religion; nor is it merely a union of wills. Likewise personal affection at the time of intercourse is not vital to the creation of this unity since, according to Paul (1 Cor. 6:16), even a man who has sexual intercourse with a prostitute or who commits rape becomes one flesh with the other person. On the other hand, this unity achieved in sexual intercourse is different from all those other relationships in life which arise out of mutual agreement and common purpose, such as a business association, or the relationship between teacher and pupils, or between neighbors. It is also unlike those unifying relationships into which we are born, e.g., unity of the family, of race, or of mankind. Its nature is so unique that it can actually be in conflict with all other relationships: "Therefore shall a man leave father and mother, and shall cleave unto his wife" (Gen. 2:24).

Unity of the Flesh

Why is it that this unity is called a unity of the flesh? According to the Biblical usage it designates a unity that embraces the natural lives of the two persons in their entirety. It is strange that two persons of separate wills and individualities should succeed in achieving real unity. According to Existentialism and Individualism sharing one's self with another is impossible. Even the modern theores of Holism, which have so effectively demonstrated the insufficiency of Individualism, are not fit to explain the Biblical view of the unity of the flesh, for the sexual union is essentially different from one's belonging to a nation or race. Membership in those entities presupposes a reality that precedes and engenders the individual, whereas the unity of the flesh is not brought into being because the two belong to the same human race but because as two persons of different sexes they have had sexual intercourse. Thus, paradoxically, they become one in spite of the fact that they are and remain different individuals. The Biblical interpretation of the union of the couple gainsays Simone de Beauvoir who contends that the active part played by the man in sex causes the woman to lose her Selfhood and reduces her to the status of a mere object. Therefore the French author is anxious to find a new way by which the woman may retrieve herself and become a subject in the sexual relationship. This writer overlooks the fact that by giving herself to the man the woman is not altogether passive, for the man is as dependent upon her as she is upon him. It is precisely in this interdependence that the true unity of the two persons manifests itself.

The correlation of both sexes is noticeable already in sexual desire. Although the longing for the satisfaction of sexual desire may well be described as a purely subjective process taking place in an individual, the fact that the glandular secretions are connected with sexual desire canot be explained either from the nature of the glands themselves or from the Selfhood of the individual. Sexual desire is possible only because each individual belongs to one of the two sexes and is capable of turning his desire to the other sex. However, this general longing cannot develop into a conscious desire until a definite person of the opposite sex has been chosen as the possible source of satisfaction. If the other person did not attract me (perhaps unconsciously so), then my instinct would not select her or him as the object of my desire. Thus the other person has the power to make me sexually dependent upon her or him, and this power may be so formidable that people lose their self-will or are in sexual bondage. However, there can be no actual relationship unless a mutual attraction is exercised by both parties. Therefore, sexual unity is primarily mutual sexual dependency. This explains why sexual desire is experienced as an awful and incomprehensible urge whose pressure cannot be alleviated by explaining it scientifically. Since the other person has the power to refuse or allow sexual relationship he or she can determine whether one's life will be happy or miserable. Personal antagonism and quarrels cannot destroy this dependence as is proved by the fact that sometimes persons suing for divorce continue to have sexual relations with each other.

Oneness of the flesh will be attained only when the mutual desires of both persons lead to sexual intercourse. While emotional relationships or intellectual exchange may create deep and lasting fellowship they do not bring about that unity. Only through the actual bodily contact can the union be so consummated that this man and this woman belong to each other. This explains why one of the principal causes for psychic disturbances is the willful interruption of the sexual act. When the man withdraws himself from the body of his wife at the very moment when the desire for unity and union is strongest an unresolved tension is called forth. One way in which the unity of the flesh manifests itself is in the fact that in their intercourse the two people place their bodies at the disposal of each other. Sexual attraction is not directed solely to the sex organs; it is the whole body that tends fervently toward the other in the desire to achieve an intimate union. Whereas normally, out of bashfulness or modesty, we conceal portions of our bodies from the view of other people we make no secret of our body for our sexual partner. He or she is granted an unrestricted knowledge of the appearance of one's body and its particular manner of experiencing and expressing one's sentiments. It is true that in terms of time the sexual act occupies a very small portion of the lives of both partners. But the feeling of happiness which even the gentlest touch of the other person may produce proves that once the union has been achieved every bodily contact can release essentially the same experience of oneness as that produced in sexual intercourse. In turn, a true sexual relationship requires the physical presence of the other person, and all of one's bodily and mental experiences are more or less conditioned by his presence or his absence.

Sexual desire is misunderstood, nevertheless, if it is interpreted only as a yearning for bodily contact, or if the actual sexual relationship is interpreted as being nothing more than an act of highly intensified physical contact in which the tactile nerves are stimulated to highest sensitivity. It surely is not a misdemeanor only but rather a perversion when a man seeks sexual excitement by means of touching women or otherwise making contact with them in the congestion of a public conveyance or in the press of a crowd, because by this one-sided kind of sensation the desire for union with another person can never be satisfied. On the other hand, sexual unity is not confined to physical union. Flesh, in the Biblical sense, denotes not only the body but one's whole existence in this world; and the attainment of oneness of the flesh, therefore, creates a mutual dependence and reciprocity in all areas of life. One is ready to sacrifice his life for the other person, one feels that life is valueless apart from him, and one wants to be and to act like him. Without previous examination one is able to share his views. This fact is especially remarkable when his or her opinions are tinged by emotions, for instance, when they concern his world view or his social and political outlook. The reason is that these are matters in which one is "existentially" involved because they affect our concrete existence in the world.

For sexual dependence the social position, intelligence, and education of the other person do not matter. Knowing that another person is a criminal or involved in other undesirable relationships may deter some people from involvement with him or her, but such knowledge proves impotent in a case of sexual dependence. Indeed, the latter may become an irresistible stimulus to crime if there is hope thereby to win or maintain the other's affection. Sex is able to wield such a tremendous power over us because our mental and physical life condition each other since both are manifestations of our Self. Unity of the flesh means, therefore, that two persons arrive at a unity in all of life's natural manifestations.

However, the Bible sounds a warning against the idealistic fallacy which expects all of life's meaning from love and sex. The term 'unity of the flesh' denotes that this mutual relationship does not extend beyond the field of natural life. Flesh in Biblical understanding designates the natural mode of existence which man shares with the surrounding world. Since sexual intercourse imparts an overpowering feeling of happiness people have been tempted from time to time to believe that thereby they had achieved union with the source of life, the heart of the world, or even with the Divine. But not only is this unity confined to the two persons involved but also it is not by itself unity of the spirit.

Indissoluble Union

Nevertheless, the unity established by the sexual relationship is not simply a momentary subjective experience, it is an objective and indelible feature of our Self which we cannot get rid of again. This is the reason why Jesus frowns upon divorce (Mark 10:2-12; Matt. 19:3-9). His rigorism would be meaningless if that union were nothing but an emotional or legal tie. Paul uses the same argument in order to show that a Christian must not have intercourse with prostitutes (1 Cor. 6:16-20). Paul refutes the frivolous conception that sexual relationships are but fleeting and transient affairs of the body. A sexual experience is not only existential, being related to one's Self, but also brings about an ontic connnection with the partner.

Some psychologists think that as a rule the first sexual experience does not leave any lasting impression on a person's mind unless the conditions surrounding this occasion were unusually painful or repulsive and, therefore, produced a psychical injury or trauma. Yet, on account of its unique character, the first sexual experience even though taking place under normal circumstances is one of the few constitutive factors in the making of one's personality. The effect which it has upon our self-consciousness will be the same no matter whether or not the persons concerned afterwards parted company, never to see each other again. No matter whether the original occasion is later on remembered or not our self-consciousness is thereby as radically and lastingly affected as in the case of other events of vital significance which ordinarily occur only once in a lifetime, such as some serious danger to our lives, the loss of our parents, or the birth of the first child. In the case of a girl this radical change is described as the loss of her virginity, yet our modern language has no specific term for what the male adolescent in primitive society experiences as sexual initiation. In neither case, however, does our terminology denote the element of union with the partner implied in this experience.

V. CHILDREN, A DIVINE BLESSING

Sex and the Will to Propagate

So far, sex has been discussed only from the standpoint of mutual relationship without any reference to propagation. This is not due to an arbitrary bias, but corresponds rather to the Bible's viewpoint. Although the Biblical writers are aware of the intimate connection between sex and propagation sex is not regarded primarily as a means for the procreation of children. The reason that the woman was created is that God saw that it was not good for the man to be alone (Gen. 2:18). By giving man a female rather than another male as his companion God indicates that sexual differentiation and the resultant sexual desire have meaning apart from procreation, and that the partnership of husband and wife must be regarded as life's chief blessing.

By this view the Bible backs natural experience. When people look for sexual partners it is not primarily done with the will to propagate but rather out of the desire to find satisfaction in the sexual union with the other person. Nevertheless, we would be unrealistic if we ignored the close connection that exists between sexuality and reproduction. But what exactly is the nature of this connection?

A preliminary psychological consideration will be in order. First of all we must distinguish between the will to propagate and the wish to have children. Deeply embedded in every person there is a longing to pass on to another generation the life he has within himself. It is, however, differently motivated in the two sexes. In the case of the man it is conditioned mainly by the thought of his own death, and so becomes a wish for an heir. The heir may be considered as the recipient of the father's hereditary biological qualities, or, from an idealistic viewpoint, as continuing the father's work. In the case of the woman this longing is conditioned by her ability to bear children, and manifests itself as a wish to rear the fruit of her own body lovingly.

Both the desire for sexual unity and the wish to have children belong to human nature much in the same way as our individual existence and our membership in the human race. Because I am by nature a solitary individual I stand in need of fellowship with others, and this desire is most powerfully expressed in the sex impulse; and because I am a link in the chain of the generations I want to be a father or a mother. Since both aspirations are deeply rooted in our nature they may manifest themselves simultaneously, but springing from different roots they often appear separately. The Bible does not lose sight of either feature. While it is aware of the fact that sex includes the possibility of procreation yet it does not equate the sexual desire with the wish for progeny.

Secondly, the wish to have descendants must be distinguished from the intention to beget children. Although the Roman Catholic moralists have attempted to make sexual desire ethically acceptable by tying it together with the intention to beget children, their rationalization is based on a complete misunderstanding of the psychological facts involved. A sexual act may be connected with the wish to have children and with a complete readiness to accept them as a result of sexual intercourse. But it is unrealistic to believe that the intention to beget children would be sufficient to stimulate sexual excitement in a person.

As early as the marriage law of the "Book of the Covenant" (Exodus 20:22-23, 33) sexual intercouse was considered one of the duties of married life (Ex. 21:10), and when Paul speaks of marriage he adopts the Old Testament viewpoint. The Apostle, who could hardly be charged with moral laxity, very characteristically discusses sexual intercourse in marriage not from the standpoint of reproduction but as a mutual obligatory service which the spouses owe each other, and whose limits are not set by the purpose of procreation but by the necessity to respect the partner's habits of prayer (1 Cor. 7:3). The first Epistle of Peter expresses a similar attitude. In discussing marital relations it is silent about the intention to propagate whereas it demands that sexual intercourse should take place "according to knowledge" (1 Pet. 3:7). This means, as will be indicated in the next chapter, with an awareness of the mystery of sexual relationship.

All that the Bible has to say concerning sexual life is incomprehensible if we try to understand it as based on the will to propagate. In that case, Jesus would not have warned against the objectionable nature of lustful glances but would have fulminated against sexual desires devoid of the will to propagate. Similarly, in the Old Testament the death penalty would have been imposed in those cases only where the existing right to propagate was interfered with by a third party. Likewise, we would expect to find at least one passage in the Bible prohibiting sexual intercouse where propagation was not intended. The story of Onan (Gen. 38:8ff) cannot be adduced as evidence, for his sin consisted not in wanting sexual pleasure without propagation but in shirking his duty towards his deceased brother for whom he was obligated to beget an heir by his widowed sister-in-law.

The Divine Blessing

In matters of sex the Bible is more natural as well as more devout than the rigorists. Instead of regarding procreation as the rationale of sexual union it proclaims that above and beyond the pleasure derived from the intercouse children are an added divine blessing. When sex is subordinated to the intention to propagate the begetter is regarded as the cause of progeny and the child as the necessary consequence. While not contesting the causal connection between sexual intercourse and conception the Bible denies that the effect is inevitable or that parents have the power to bring about conception. The Bible preserves a deep respect for the mystery of fertilization, and urges a sense of thankfulness to God by emphasizing that the gift of a child is a divine blessing.

By saying to the first couple, "Be fruitful and multiply" (Gen. 1:28) God obviously does not give them a commandment (as if any person had the power to call forth life), but just as in the parallel passages (Gen. 1:33 and 9:7) a blessing is pronounced by God (Psalm 127:3; "children are an heritage from the Lord," cf. Ps. 128:3). The correctness of our interpretation is confirmed by the fact that within the same passage in Genesis 1:28, and almost in the same breath, God promises man dominion over all creatures. Although God's primary purpose in creating the woman was to let man have a companion, God bestowed a special blessing upon their union by enabling them to live on in their children. It is one of the marvelous wonders of Divine love that implied in the unity of the flesh we find the promise of descendants. Therefore, motherhood appears as a sign and wonder even to unbelievers; not because of the physiological fact that the female glands form ova and the male glands semen but because a new person is formed through the union of ovum and semen. This blessing was not revoked as a result of man's Fall, but only restricted. Fertility was coupled with the pains of childbearing (Gen. 3:16).

As long as man living in communion with God possessed true life he felt no desire for descendants and was content to have a helpmeet and companion (Gen. 2:18). After his expulsion from the Garden, and when the pains and labors of child-bearing were imposed upon his wife, he no longer called her "woman," i.e., the "she man," but Eve—the living one, the mother of all (Gen. 4:1). Only after his life was threatened by death did the possibility of propagation and the consequent perpetuation of life enter his thinking. As Eve, the woman is not only his companion and counterpart but also the potential mother of his children.

The high regard which antiquity accorded the fertility of woman may originally, in Israel as elsewhere, have been motivated by the economic advantage of having children. Of more importance for the Israelites, however, was the idea that by means of descendants the People of the Covenant would be kept in existence and thereby the blessing given to the man and to the woman would be perpetuated. For this reason the childless woman felt forsaken of God (Gen. 30:23; 1 Sam. 1:3-9; Isa. 4:1), while the woman who had borne a child would praise God for His blessing (Luke 1:48-50).

The "Right to Motherhood," recognized by the Old Testament

is incomprehensible except as it is based upon belief in the divine promise of children. This right could be appealed to by women who, through no fault of their own, were deprived of the possibility of bearing children, as in the cases of Lot's daughters (Gen. 19:30-38) and of Tamar (Gen. 38:11-26; cf. Isa. 4:1). The regulation of the Levirate marriage (Ex. 21:10), which insured issue to a childless widow by her brother-in-law, is based upon the same divine promise of children.

VI. THE HIDDEN MEANING OF SEX

THE sexual act leads to a new and deepened understanding of oneself which is characterized by three features: it is an intuitive knowledge given in and with the sexual experience; it discloses what was thus far hidden from the individual; and its subject matter is one's Self seen in the mutual relationship in which it stands with the partner's Self.

Sexual Knowledge as Intuitive Self-Understanding

While it is possible to understand the idea of the unity of the flesh without sexual experience the sexual act, nevertheless, conveys a knowledge apart from which the full meaning of that idea cannot be comprehended, because, except for the sexual encounter, the meaning of sex and of our sexual differentiation would remain hidden from us.

Characteristically, sexual union is commonly designated in the Old Testament by the verb "to know," and this expression is used interchangeably of the man and of the woman (the latter usage in Gen. 19:8, cf. Luke 1:34). This strange expression points out that there is a hidden element in sex which does not come to light except in the intercourse.

In order to understand this terminology we have to start from the difference between objective knowledge, i.e., knowledge about something, and comprehending knowledge. In the first instance we describe an object in its relation to other objects. When I know, for example, what name a man has, where he lives, what he does, then I have a knowledge which allows me to look him up or to write to him; for the place he occupies in social life has become known to me. This kind of knowledge, because it describes its object in terms of relationship to other objects which can be known by other people, can easily be transmitted. For the most part, human knowledge consists of such statements of relationship. They form the basis of education and civilization. Entirely different, however, is the comprehending knowledge which is possible only when an object is directly given to the self. Take, for example, the way in which I understand my friend's anxiety as distinct from my knowing about it. Though in the case of sympathetic understanding my friend does not cease to remain a distinctive individual, differing both from me and from all others, my understanding, nevertheless, implies that I am able, as it were, to look into his heart from the bottom of my Self. Apparently, we are capable of so identifying ourselves with another person that to some degree we understand him from the center of his own being.

Knowledge gained in sexual intercourse is of this latter kind, and thus differs in essence from the knowledge offered in the books on the psychology, physiology, and anatomy of sex. This fact explains the sexual troubles of young people. They are not caused by a lack of knowledge about the facts of sex itself—the normal adolescent in our days has gained abundant information—but are rooted in his inability to understand the joys, the fears, and the disillusionments of his sexual impulses as long as he has not yet achieved actual intercourse.

Far be it from me to disparage the usefulness of instruction in sex, for ignorance of the facts of sexual development and of reproduction is apt to surround this area with an appearance of immorality whereby the sensational interest in them is unnecessarily heightened. However, the disturbing symptoms of adolescent sex life would not be experienced if familiarity with its biological aspects were sufficient to comprehend it. In turn, however, it is not mere ignorance of these facts that does produce fear and anxiety, let alone sexual neuroses.

Both the advocates and the opponents of instruction in sex usually overlook the fact that what young people are actually longing for is not information about the nature of the sexual processes. They are vexed by their inability to understand their sexual emotions and desires. Yet there is no way of teaching them such understanding objectively because it can be gained only by means of personal experience of the sexual relationship. The existential inability of parents and teachers to convey to the young people the kind of sexual knowledge that would really satisfy them constitutes the basic problem of education in sex. The period between the awakening of sexual impulses and the time of marriage is therefore one of special difficulty and temptation. In turn, the person who has attained physical maturity will in the sexual act receive a real understanding of his masculinity or her femininity. This is an experience of far-reaching consequences. The philosophers who identified the Self with the ability to think intelligently denied that the Self as given in direct self-consciousness possessed any further characteristics. In the sexual experience we discover, however, that there never is such an abstract Self. Rather each Self is either a masculine or a feminine one, and thus in the intuitive awareness of myself I also apprehend the function of my masculinity or femininity. They are not tacked to Selfhood but belong to its essence. Physical maturity is obviously a prerequisite of such knowledge.

Though sexual sensations can be aroused in children by stimulating their sexual organs the child's immaturity precludes a specifically sexual experience and thus the acquisition of a genuine sexual knowledge. While sexual maturity depends on physical development it requires also a corresponding psychical maturity by which the individual is enabled spontaneously to respond to the sexual advance of the other person. For the same reason, any inhibition which prevents a person from actual contact with the other person will preclude sexual knowledge even in an adult sexual relationship. It may lead to sensations of the sexual organs but does not engender sexual self-understanding. However, an immature sexual experience is never simply a passing physiological incident. The seduction or rape of children is a case in point. Though no genuine sexual knowledge is evoked thereby the memory of the experience may, through further associations, lead to a sexual inhibition in later life which will manifest itself as a sexual vice or perversion or as a neurosis.

As an act of self-understanding sexual knowledge is highly personal and cannot, as such, be communicated to another person. In this respect it resembles the feeling of strangeness and abandonment one has when arriving by oneself in a foreign country. Directly communicable are only past sexual experiences and the pattern of one's sexual life. Beyond this a trained observer may also be able to ascertain whether one's sexual understanding produces happiness or depression. But no one except myself can really know what my masculinity or femininity means to me.

The Discovery of the Hidden Meaning

Sexual knowledge is further characterized by the fact that in sexual intercourse a secret is revealed to me. I learn to understand why it is that in order to be myself I must be of the male or the female sex. Since this awareness coincides with the first sexual experience it is frequently misunderstood. But it cannot be completely ignored. Adult behavior indicates in many ways the realization that sex contains a secret, and even small children have obviously some intimation of that fact. They try to conceal acts of infantile sexuality from their adult environment.

The fact that many parents recoil from giving information on sex to their children, notwithstanding the essential difference between sexual knowledge and sexual understanding, also points to their awareness of the secret implied in sex. Whereas in the acquisition of objective knowledge we simply pass from ignorance to recognition we are aware that in the attainment of sexual understanding we have entered into the possession of something formerly inaccessible to us. This fact is evidenced in the sexual pleasure felt, especially by men, when they perceive portions of the female body which are normally covered. But since the unclothed parts of the body do not by themselves stimulate sexual feelings—the nude in Art is beyond the realm of sex—it is obviously the unveiling or unclothing that arouses the excitement. This experience indicates that the covering is meant to conceal from other people's sight what by its very nature is a secret. The effect is therefore independent of the size of the portion of the body covered. The studied sex appeal of the cover page illustration of many magazines is obvious for the picture of a girl is not simply printed in order to show her beauty but is so posed and arranged as to impress the beholder with the realization that parts of her body commonly concealed are now specifically bared for his eyes. In the strip tease this effect is admittedly intended.

The instinctive intimation of the mysterious nature of sexual knowledge is observable, too, in the manner the sexes make advances toward each other. The shyness in a young man's first approach to a girl is not so much caused by a lack of self-confidence as by an awareness that he is confronted with a secret which demands a delicate and sensitive courting. A certain reserve on the part of the woman expresses the same instinctive feeling. This restraint differs characteristically from the female attitude in the erotic contest in which the woman's apparent refusal is merely meant to give the man an opportunity to show his superiority. The girl's reserve indicates her unwillingness to allow anyone to penetrate her secret who does not properly appreciate what he is to experience. This reserve will disappear once the secret has been discovered whereas the erotic contest may be repeated at any time during their sexual relationship. Though the mystery of sex has been disclosed in the first sexual encounter people do never fully lose the awareness of its secret. No matter how long they may be acquainted with each other they feel their mutual strangeness in the very happiness of sexual union. While realizing that their Self encounters that of the partner they sense nevertheless the miracle that something so unknown and unknowable as another person's self should be united with their Self.

The inner secret of sex is a mystery not merely something previously unknown or withheld from us. Secrecy presupposes a purpose for which something is withheld from general knowledge; but such a secret may be made public when the purpose for which it was kept secret has been realized. On the other hand, the sexual mystery is a secret whose disclosure is solely in the hands of the two persons concerned. They are not only unable to share it with a third person but must also guard it against profanation. Because the sexual secret is a mystery it never loses its sublimity. It may be profaned and disgraced—and heaven knows how often this occurs—but everyone feels guilty when he allows it to happen.

The mystery of sexual knowledge is therefore something uncanny. Some educators are so naïve as to believe that if young people could only be taught to consider sex as something clean and natural then all of their sexual problems would be resolved. That, of course, is a delusion. One can say, on the contrary, that the only assurance of relieving young people's perplexities lies in making them aware of the enticing and uncanny nature of sex itself. This quality clings to sex throughout life, and its attractive power cannot be equated with the insatiable character of the sexual instinct. Sexual knowledge remains forever concerned with an enchanting secret of abysmal depth.

The Content of the Mystery

What then is the secret that is revealed to us in sexual intercourse? All sexual desire is basically intent upon solving the question: Why is it that I am not simply a person but rather a human being either of the male or female sex, and therefore one who is sexually attracted to persons of the other sex? This is not the scientific question concerning the nature of sexual differentiation but rather the existential problem of the purpose of my own life as a man or a woman. The enigmatic character of our masculinity or femininity is disturbing until the solution is found. Therefore, the potent development of the sexual instinct adds an impatient urgency to young people's restlessness and makes them desirous to discover the meaning of their lives. How absurd that modern naturalistic ethics should contend that sex as such has no problem in the face of the intimate connection between the sexual instinct and the quest for the meaning of personal existence! In vain do people hope to get rid of the vexing enigma of sex by denying its problematic character and by focusing all attention on the pleasure it provides. How much more realistic is the recognition that beyond the pleasure derived from sex the meaning of my sexually conditioned nature is revealed to me in sexual intercourse.

What is the experience sustained by the partners in sexual union? Generally speaking, it is an experience of happiness caused by the fact that the original antagonism implied in sexual differentiation is resolved when at the peak of the union all consciousness of difference vanishes. This experience moves through a number of stages each of which makes its own contribution to sexual knowledge. First of all, the man concentrates all his desire on the possession of the beloved woman which is met by her willingness to surrender herself. Even when she deliberately sets out to win a man the roles of the sexes are reversed as soon as he accepts her challenge because then he becomes the active one who demands. This creates a conflict of wills. The woman, though characterized by Goethe, as the "one easily seduced," does not surrender her individuality without resistance, and only during the progress of love-play and the erotic contest will she submit to his urging and desire. She offers opposition yet hopes that he will break her resistance so that she may experience his superiority. Although the female sex seems to be defenseless against the man's wooing the part the woman plays in sexual relations is not entirely passive. Yes, he takes eventual possession of her body but not until she has surrendered it to him. She is as active in receiving as he is in giving.

A distinctive feeling of well-being suffuses both persons at the completion of the sexual act. The man experiences release from tension and a sense of satisfaction because finally the restless striving of his will and desire has found its respite through this person. The woman too feels enriched by the assurance that she has encountered the person who gives meaning to her womanhood. Both partners are happy in the joyful certainty of mutual blessedness and of belonging together. This sense of belonging together implies on the part of the man the jealous wish to possess his partner for himself alone; while on the part of the woman there is the desire to bind him to herself in permanent union. Furthermore both take pride in their procreative ability. Although the desire to propagate is not the motive of sexual union mature persons know that sexual intercourse implies the possibility to create new life. Thus they realize not only their distinctive qualities of manhood and womanhood but become, in their sexual intercourse, also aware of their fatherhood and motherhood.

Thus the unity of the flesh is experienced as a fusion of the two individuals into a mutuality of existence, a common destination for reciprocity of life and experience. In sexual intercourse both partners come to understand what it means that their Self is a masculine or a feminine one, namely that to be a man means to be destined for a woman and vice versa. While the biologist, who studies sex from the outside as an objective observer, may be inclined to deny that there is such a thing as masculinity or femininity, and that the term sex merely denotes a differentiation of physical organs and functions, sexual experience teaches that both partners need each other.

People who are primarily intent upon experiencing sensual pleasure in the sexual union will be inclined to interpret sex in purely psychological terms by holding that the sexual desire only strives after the sensation of physical contact with a person of the other sex. In fact, however, there is interdependence which extends over the whole life of the two people, because sexuality is a quality of the Self.

The individual, far from being a self-contained entity is, and must remain, a fragment unless his partner enables him to attain to completeness. Therefore, the solitary person is a riddle to himself. This explains the deep perplexity of young people when sexual impulses make themselves felt in their lives and keep them under pressure. Sex will not allow any self-centeredness and self-contentment; a partner must be found. Since the meaning of the whole person is involved in such experience young people easily fall victim to desperate methods in their search for the answer to the mystery, such as masturbation, reading obscene literature, and associating with prostitutes. The great number of suicides in the seventeen- to twenty-one-year-old bracket is another tragic commentary on the disastrous result of this consuming perplexity.

Sexual intercourse supplies knowledge of our selves as sexually determined bodies. However, this is not simply an objective knowledge of our corporeality but rather it tells us why our existence in this world is tied up with a physical body. We also comprehend why no person is able to solve this mystery for himself since sexual partnership is the prerequisite of its solution. In this way we arrive in sexual relations not only at a general understanding of the function of sexual differentiation, but also discover the unique and incomparable significance the other person holds for us. It is not the partner's personality, however, that renders him or her so important for my life, but rather the fact that through him (or her) for the first time I have learned to understand what the aim of my sexual longings has been. This basic experience can never be repeated. While in the course of life my sexual knowledge may be deepened by further experience, it is only once that one crosses the threshold that leads to that understanding in which sex's hidden meaning is disclosed. Because of this unique and momentous significance which the sexual partner has for one's understanding of oneself the Old Testament considers it right and natural that a man should leave his father and mother and should cleave to his wife (Gen. 2:24), which view is unreservedly adopted by Jesus (Matt. 19:5).

Further, by the unity experienced in sexual intercourse we are not only made aware of our mutual dependence but also of the fact that our masculine and feminine natures supplement each other. It would be meaningless to assign to either of the sexes a superior role. Notwithstanding their anatomical differences and the different psychological and physiological functions performed by them, or rather because of them, each person needs a partner of the other sex in order to live as a man or a woman. When Mme. de Beauvoir contends that in the sexual relationship man is the originator and the woman but his product, she obviously overstates what is given in sexual understanding in order to have a foundation for her sociological hypothesis. Since the sexes depend so completely on each other in their sexuality it would be absurd to place one above the other. Unwillingness or inability on the part of one of the partners to co-operate (e.g., because of sexual frigidity), prevents a sexual relationship.

Apprehending the Reciprocity of Sex

Though substantially the same for the two partners, the experience of mutuality has a different meaning for each of them because it implies also the realization of their different functions. The man must admit: "I am yours in all my being and activity," while the woman confesses: "Because of you and through you I am what I am." Sexual intercourse furnishes a goal for the man's manhood while it provides the content for the woman's womanhood. Therefore, while unity of the flesh denotes a harmonious relationship between the sexes, it is not a symmetrical one. Though a complementary relation it derives its character from the fact that the deficiencies to be filled up by the partner are not the same in either sex.

In the sexual relationship the woman performs a threefold function. She is the one who loves the man, who serves as his companion, and who is a child-bearer for him. However, there are no directly corresponding functions in the man, such as lover, companion, and begetter, as would be the case in a strictly symmetrical relationship. In fact the man is the one who bestows honor upon the beloved, he is the guide of his companion, and the guardian of the mother of his children. While it would be a misinterpretation to say that a man does not love, or does not desire companionship, or is averse to the assumption of fatherhood, these attitudes do not clearly indicate the unique nature of his function in this reciprocal relationship.

First of all, the woman who has given herself to him becomes for the man an object of high regard. In German he calls her his "Schatz," i.e., his treasure whom he honors and reveres. Characteristically, however, we do not think of a woman as honoring a man, except in a nonsexual sense. Paul calls the woman the glory of the man (1 Cor. 11:7) by which dignity and true meaning are given to his manhood. It is no accident that we speak only of feminine sexual honor or of its loss but not of a corresponding male quality. A girl's honor is not an abstract value; it is implied in her bodily existence. It resides in her being destined for a husband. The measure of the honor, in turn, in which he holds her is gauged by the way he treats her honor. His sexual honor is therefore a special form of his personal honor. In order to be a man of honor a man must not only refrain from extra-marital sexual relations but also recognize that his manhood is destined for one woman.

A man who deprives a woman of her honor by treating her merely as an object for gratifying his lust thereby loses his own honor. This is perhaps not true in a social sense for today a man rarely loses the respect of his fellowmen by such conduct and often may even enhance it. Since sex is a quality of Selfhood sexual honor is intimately connected with one's personality. The measure of honor a husband accords his wife is revealed by her appearance, and the nature of his love for her manifests itself in his behavior, for honor is a lustre that radiates from the whole personality. The reciprocity of the sexual relationship actualizes itself in this sphere too. The woman must be intent upon protecting her honor as the honor of her husband, while the man has to take seriously the fact that it is in his power to divest her of her honor. In other words, the sexual honor of a couple is not solely determined by one of them but by their mutual concern for it. It is up to her so to influence their sexual lives that the honor of both is preserved. Modesty, which has nothing to do with frigidity or prudery, is, therefore, a natural quality of a woman's sexual life. If she is indifferent to the honor of her womanhood, and regards a man only as a dispenser of pleasure, she destroys the meaning of sexual union for herself. Feminine pride is not only a pride in belonging to the fair sex—let alone a feeling of superiority over the other sex—but a woman's pride in her ability to love a man so deeply that he is bound to feel reverence for her. Seduction or rape are not the only ways by which feminine honor may be violated. A man's lascivious look may give a woman the feeling of being defiled because it indicates that he considers her only as an object of lust, or as a mass of living flesh, but not as a person. Nevertheless even such experiences cannot be adduced as proving that woman is only a passive object in the sexual relationship. It depends entirely upon her whether or not she will accept such insulting challenge.

Corresponding to the woman's function as a companion we find the man's function as her guide. According to Paul the man is the head of the woman (1 Cor. 11:3). This designation does not indicate superior social status or mental excellency but refers to the sexual relationship. In a living entity like that formed by the unity of the flesh there can be no concerted action unless one of them is recognized as the leader. But just as the body is nothing without the head so in turn the head is as nothing without the rest of the body. Only when the two are united and work conjointly is a body constituted. However, there are various functions of the body, therefore, the man as the head is normally the one who takes the initiative in the sexual relationship. We speak of the seduction of a girl but never of a man, for he can only be tempted or enticed into immorality (e.g., Joseph and Potiphar's wife, Gen. 39). This difference does not imply that the man is morally stronger than the woman rather that either plays a different role in the sexual relationship. A woman's nature cannot express itself apart from her sex because her whole body is determined by her sexual function. In order to be the man's companion she gives herself to him and thus becomes dependent on him. Whereas the man is the determining factor in their relationship the woman alone has to accept the biological consequences of their union. As a result of conception she is unalterably bound to this man while he, to all appearances, remains free to consort simultaneously with other women. This dissimilarity shows clearly that their mutual relationship is not one of identical functions. Nevertheless a woman's dependence upon the man must not be construed as though as a person the woman were inferior to the man. Her dependence is actualized within the realm of sexual relations, and is naturally confined to it. She demonstrates her instinctive awareness of this dependence in a thousand ways. By means of coquetry, by the way she plans the strategy for his courtship as well as subsequent erotic contests, by teasing him, and by challenging him to show his abilities she stimulates him to prove his superiority.

However to be a consort means also to have and cherish common recollections, to work together, and to share each other's interests. In this respect the sexual relationship of man and wife differs fundamentally from friendship. Paul considers it natural that in married life the woman should be the one to ask questions and the man the one to give the answers (1 Tim. 2:11). This principle does not mean that he should do the speaking all the time and she should content herself with listening. Both her right to ask and his duty to answer are grounded in the fact that God created both of them. Only when both persons participate in each other's life can there be an enduring state of question and response. The male sex is prone to accept the actual conditions in which the couple lives as a matter of course since they have been largely created by men. On the other hand, it is not surprising that the wisdom and the right of these conditions should be questioned by his wife since they have come into existence without the active participation of women. In married life the mutual relationship of the sexes is permanently on trial. Since both husband and wife are indissolubly united the husband cannot escape his obligation to give reasons by which to justify these conditions, while the wife must constantly learn to adjust herself to them.

The ontological difference between the sexes explains the distinctive role which the man and the woman have in conditioning the structure of social life. As head and master man represents the general features of life, the common interests of society, law, and order; while the woman in her self-giving emphasizes the significance of individual life. Individual existence has no meaning in itself but only as the individual manifestation of the general life of mankind. True to her nature the woman will be inquisitive about that which gives meaning and significance to life. It is not by chance that laws and philosophical systems have been established by men. But in the name of the individual life woman will challenge their validity and demand proof of their authority. So vital to their relationship is such exchange of thought and purposes between man and woman that their absence is an indication that something has gone seriously wrong in their sexual relationship.

Finally, the woman's part as child-bearer has its complement in the man's part as protector. The act of propagation is far from having the same all-pervasive influence upon the life of the man that child-bearing has upon the woman. Begetting is a single act whereas motherhood is an enduring condition. Nevertheless, since the man makes the first advance in sexual intercourse, he carries the responsibility for its consequences whereas the woman expresses her belonging to him by her willingness to bear him children. However, except for the biological sphere, sexual intercourse establishes no direct relationship between the father and the children he has begotten. Rather it is through the mother that this relationship is set up indirectly. While being manifestly her children because they are literally bone of her bone and flesh of her flesh they are his children only by indirection, namely, as the children of his wife. The fact accounts for the matriarchal forms of society in which unusual privileges are extended to motherhood. Though proud of the fact that it is exclusively her body by which the newborn child has been produced the woman nevertheless expects the man to be the protector of their mutual relationship, and he is under obligation to ward off all difficulties and dangers from her and her offspring.

Therefore, both knowledge of the unity of the partners and awareness of the differences between the sexes are implied in the mystery of sex. The assurance that in spite of their strangeness they have merged into unity gives the partners a feeling of happiness. Yet despite their unity in married life man remains man and woman woman, and thus a hidden source of permanent tension is constantly with them. The sexual differentiation may become the cause of hatred between the sexes, because the individual in being so terribly proud to be a Self resents the loss of his (or her) ability to lead an independent life, and he turns against the other person upon whom he depends if he is to solve the riddle of his existence.

VII. THE DEVELOPMENT OF SEXUAL KNOWLEDGE

Presentiment and Knowledge

Being a basic and unrepeatable experience the first complete sexual intercourse is of decisive importance to the self-understanding of both partners. It endows them with a new understanding of what existence means for them and by this disclosure radically transforms their awareness of themselves. The encounter with the other sex changes former possibilities, dispositions, and desires into realities. So momentous is this change in self-consciousness that life can no longer be lived without one's being constantly aware of the presence of the other sex. This effect reveals the superficiality of the naturalistic view according to which the sexual relationship is on a level with the satisfaction of hunger, or the quenching of thirst, that is to say the satisfaction of the demands of bodily organs. The advocates of that view overlook two things, however, namely, the personal character of sex and the union thereby established with another person, and the concomitant changes in self-consciousness. These differ radically from the succession of experiences connected with the anatomical and psychological development of sex. It is natural that in view of the far-reaching changes which take place in the adolescent girl she should be more deeply affected than a boy by the growing pressure of sex. Notwithstanding the fact, however, that the onset of menstruation is colored by deep emotional stirrings, this experience is not as basic as the alteration of understanding of one's personal Self accomplished by sexual intercourse. Therefore, the Bible, in contradistinction to the customs of many primitive religions, does not assign any particular importance to the beginning of the menstrual period. Though the woman's experience of dependence upon the man, which is contingent upon the first sexual union, has no direct counterpart in his life the changes in the male partner nevertheless are no less great; for he leaves a life of independence to assume responsibility for a person with whom he is now closely united. This change may seem to be less apparent in his life because today a man can easily disavow this acquired responsibility, but he will not do so without serious consequences for his character. Loose sexual indulgence will result in indecision and fickleness.

The political and social outlook of an historical group is more intimately conditioned by the sexual tone and attitude of its members than is usually assumed. The man who disavows responsibility in sexual matters will almost inevitably display irresponsibility in other areas of his life too. An unpredjudiced, i.e., unprincipled, concept of sex leads, perforce, to a disintegration of the social and political structure. This was particularly evident in National Socialism where the officially propagated indulgence in sex had to be counteracted by the rule of force or a dictatorship in public life. Similarly it is absurd to extoll our democratic institutions when public opinion supports at the same time concepts of sex that undermine a young man's voluntary acceptance of responsibility in sexual relations.

The Old Testament, in recognizing the lasting importance of the first sexual experience, gave special protection to the girl. The seducer of a virgin had to bear the consequences of his action and was duty-bound to marry her (Exod. 22:16; Num. 22:28-29). Correspondingly, when a man, by the act of engagement, declared his willingness to be bound to one woman he also could rightfully expect that prior to her marriage no other man had irresponsibly taken advantage of her (Deut. 22:13-21, 23.24). A comparison between these regulations and those of modern law is most instructive. The Old Testament upholds the respect for the unity of the flesh as it is created in the original sexual experience; modern criminal law is only interested in protecting the individual girl in her inexperience and weakness. While it is true to say that in motherhood the woman has a further basic experience which has no counterpart in a man's life, it is overdrawn to maintain that as a result of pregnancy the woman ceases to feel as companion and sweetheart. Though during pregnancy the woman's life is less determined by her interest in the man, the new relationship with the child is of a totally different character and does not, therefore, affect the sexual relationship with her husband. When after pregnancy an alienation in the sexual relationship between wife and husband occurs the reason lies in her resenting the burden or dangers of pregnancy rather than in her excessive love for the child.

In order to be complete the basic sexual experience requires that the two people who meet in sexual union should be mature persons. However, since unity of the flesh is the goal of the sexual differentiation it is not surprising that there should be some presentiment of that goal from earliest childhood. But this does not mean that sexual knowledge is a natural result of an increase in age or that it can be gained independent of sexual union. Although in onanism or homosexual acts sensations of the sexual organs may be aroused which resemble those of sexual intercourse, yet the absence of a partner of the other sex leaves the riddle of bodily existence unresolved because unity of the flesh has not been achieved. To be sure, such pseudo-sexual experiences, too, will influence one's self-understanding. Whether they are integrated in the normal sexual consciousness or remain as disturbing elements in sexual life will depend entirely upon the nature of the first genuine sexual intercourse.

Knowledge and Experience

We have emphasized the decisive significance which, according to the Bible, the first sexual intercourse has for the self-understanding of the partners. To this interpretation it is objected that in many instances the first sexual intercourse provides a partial and imperfect experience only, and that in cases of sexual incompatibility the encounter will not mediate an adequate understanding at all. While such happenings cannot be denied they do not refute the Biblical view. They only indicate that sexual maturity, which the Bible considers as the prerequisite of sexual intercourse, implies normality. Such experiences cannot be adduced, however, as justifying divorces nor can male impotence and female frigidity ever be recognized as legal causes for divorce. For where these conditions are caused by inexperience they will soon disappear; and in cases in which physical malformation or deformities are obstacles to successful cohabitation they can be corrected surgically. More serious are those instances in which a partner has powerful inhibitions against sexual intercourse. There may be various reasons for it—fear of the discovery of premarital sex experience with another person may be one—but in no instance would divorce and remarriage bring about a satisfactory condition. Spiritual counsel or psychotherapy is here indicated as the means of restoring the couple's union. It is true, of course, that the very nature of the woman accounts for considerable variations in sexual attractiveness depending upon temperament, age, and physical beauty. Consequently, under some circumstances, a man may derive greater pleasure from a sexual relationship with some woman other than his wife; but the degree of pleasure in sexual relations does not affect the nature of sexual knowledge or the unity of the flesh.

To be sure, considering the great number and variety of sexual types, each of which requires a different approach, sexual intercourse with many persons of the opposite sex may give a more expert knowledge in the field of sexual behaviour than is acquired by people who remain faithful to their first partner. However, such expansion of experience makes no relevant contribution to the true understanding of our masculinity or femininity.

Of course, much disillusionment and embarrassment could be averted if, at the time of marriage, young couples possessed dependable knowledge of the basic anatomical, physiological, and psychological facts of sex. Similarly, since before marriage people move mostly in circles of their own sex and don't meet the other sex in critical situations, newly wed couples are surprised to realize that the other sex has its specific ways of reacting to the situations of life. Usually it is only through a continued series of quarrels and conflicts that they begin to realize the mystery of the sexual union in which they are united. It is a fallacy, however, to think that frequently changing the sexual partner would deepen one's understanding of sex and thus would assure increasing happiness. In actual life the advocates of such views are not so much interested in an harmonious marriage as in opportunities to apply their knowledge of the feminine mind to the seduction of inexperienced girls and morally unstable women.

Sexual and Personal Knowledge

Because the sexual instinct is frequently felt as an overpowering force, and sexual intercourse transports persons into an ecstatic state, the suggestion is sometimes made that sex has nothing to do with the personal nature of the Ego. By asserting that sex is a purely physiological function, naturalism hopes to deliver sex from all moral fetters. The same view is used by idealism for contending that sex is ethically justifiable only when it is supplemented by nonsexual personal acts, e.g., by living a married life, by caring for children, or by sharing intellectual or spiritual interests. There is also a sexual mysticism which pretends to experience in the sexual impulse the instigation of a divine force, i.e., a cosmic impulse imposing itself upon the Self rather than one originating within the Self. This perplexing multiplicity of viewpoints can be integrated only by earnestly accepting the Bible's interpretation of the unity of the Self.

Every human being is destined to become a person. For, being created in the image of God, he is qualified to enter into personal relationship with God. Though this destination does not prompt us always to conduct ourselves according to God's will it imparts to us the power of free choice in confronting our destiny. Thus every manifestation of a sexual impulse demands a moral decision on our part.

Unlike the majority of physiological processes in our body, such as the countless optical impressions on the eye, which are of little significance for our personal life and are therefore not consciously perceived, the basic sexual experience is so decisive that it carries with it the urge to become aware of the changes effected in our personal life. Though a physiological act, sexual intercourse establishes a relationship not with an impersonal object but with another person. A woman who submits her body to a man gives her personal self in and with her body. Rape is a crime not because it may do bodily harm but rather because a man forcibly intrudes upon the personal being of a woman. Similarly, what renders prostitution reprehensible is the fact that the woman who sells her body thereby denies that she is a Self and that in turn she is dealt with only as a physical object and not as a person.

Since the sexual union calls forth a unity of the partners, sexual understanding implies not only understanding of one's self but also of the partner. It would be a mistake, however, to believe that such comprehension of the partner is the natural outcome of the intercourse. It is true that the release of the mutual tensions which results from sexual intercourse implies a readiness to disclose one's entire individuality to the other person. However, once the ecstasy of the union has abated other factors may enter their mutual relationship by which any further self-disclosure is obstructed. Hence it is that sexual relations affect self-understanding in varying degrees all the way from those in which sexual intercourse is simply a passing sensual excitement to those in which sexual knowledge has become the crowning of personal life. The Self which is thus disclosed to the partner is not an abstract principle of spontaneity but rather our Selfhood which has guided us through our whole life. People have not attained therefore to the kind of knowledge which corresponds to their being a couple as long as they attempt to conceal from each other their sexual past. This does not mean that I must receive a detailed report of my partner's sexual life and experience and vice versa. Nevertheless, the oneness of the partners suffers if, and as long as, there is a justified suspicion that he (or she) is hiding pertinent information from the spouse. In turn, the unity of the flesh into which they have entered requires that both of them are willing to accept the partner's past as a part of his existence. Through the mutual self-disclosure of the lovers depths of the Self are probed which are not attained even in the most intimate friendships of our adolescence. A genuine mutual frankness and openness is generated that affects the whole character of the spouses. Conversely, the desire to conceal certain facts of our life from the partner destroys the ability to communicate, and the constant fear lest sexual matters of our past might come to light is apt to cause a neurosis.

Masculinity and Femininity

The Biblical record of the Creation indicates that the sexual differentiation of mankind and the destination of the sexes for mutuality form the foundation of human history. Hence there can be no human activity that is completely independent of the man-woman relationship. Thus we reject the various attempts to form ideals of manhood or womanhood separate, i.e., apart from their mutual relationship. Though recent attempts on the part of women to construct a new image of their sex have, to some degree, helped to correct the conventional ideal of womanhood, which heretofore has almost exclusively been formed by men, these attempts are nevertheless as patently prejudiced by the female viewpoint as the former ones were by the male perspective. Similarly, the traditional ideals of masculinity, e.g., man as warrior, explorer, or worker, actually describe one sphere of masculine activity only. Hollywood no less than the sagas of antiquity rightly introduce women and sexual relations into the picture of the ideal man.

Simone de Beauvoir completely distorts the picture by interpreting the sexual relationship according to the Socialistic axiom of the equal rights of the sexes. Considering the great number of women who are employed in remunerative work it is natural that in a traditionally male-governed society these women should feel some economic pressure in competing with men, and it will require special efforts on their part to win full recognition of their achievements. Such claims, however, cannot be based on any specific masculine or feminine qualities but only on actual or possible performance. Likewise, when the Communists derive the equality of the sexes from their ability to work rather than from their place in the mutuality of sexual relationship they start a trend which clashes with the specific needs resulting from the particular character of the female body. By requiring women to work under the same conditions as man, and by assigning to the wife the same share of financial responsibility for the support of the family as to the husband, they lead the hypothesis of the equality of the sexes *ad absurdum.*

VIII. LOVE AND SEX

The Nature of Love

The isolation in which sex has been discussed in the preceding chapters may have appeared abstract and unrealistic to many readers. What about love? Can we completely ignore the fact that for the common people love and sexual sympathy are synonymus? Or that numerous persons in our days will hold that except for love sex places us on a level with the brutes? Does not such outstanding a scholar as Freud consider both sex and love as manifestations of *libido* and thus as correlated? It is the erroneous belief in the identity of sex and love, or in their genetic relationship, in which love appears as an evolutionary outgrowth of sex which prompted us to postpone the discussion of love and its relation to sex until the nature of sex had been fully analyzed.

In view of the various ways in which the term is used in modern parlance love may be defined in general terms as a form of sympathy for something or someone based on a sense of belonging together. This mutuality is due to the fact that God not only made all existing things but also destined them for each other. All people sense this to some extent and therefore strive for an existence beyond what they are by themselves and for contact with others. Yet, love would not be so much desired and so highly prized unless people realized that under the conditions of this world they were dependent on others. In spite of our mutual destination for each other this is a world in which enmity and opposition are common occurrences. The individual, therefore, is poignantly aware of his own fragmentary existence. For as an individual he can realize only a limited number of human possibilities, and in addition he shares the limitations of his sex in being either a man or a woman. Since love is experienced more or less consciously against this background of one's natural loneliness and limitations, to love, and especially to be loved, is such a deeply enriching and happy experience. Aware of his dependence on others the lover strives for the assurance of belonging to some definite individual. Thus when there is no voluntary response to one's wooing and courting all forms of pressure are attempted. If one could be absolutely sure of belonging to another person love's happiness would not alternate with faithlessness, melancholy, or despair.

As far as sexual relations are concerned there are three forms of love which demand our special attention: sexual passion, erotic attachment, and personal love. These kinds of love differ typically from other forms of sympathy, such as friendship, kindness, helpfulness, or pity. While these, too, are sometimes found in sexual relationship they are not specifically connected with the man-woman relationship.

Forms of Love

To begin with, sexual passion is a form of sympathy directed toward another person because with him or her a sexual relationship seems desirable. The sexual passion, in itself, is not contingent upon beauty but upon the fact that on account of youthful vigor and health, sensuality, sexiness, buxomness, or physical strength the other person has sex appeal, i.e., promises sexual satisfaction. This explains why people are sometimes powerfully attracted to persons of other races or of lower levels of education with whom they have nothing else in common. Unlike mere desire sexual passion implies an element of choice, yet the values aimed at are always physical qualities of the partner that make him sexually desirable. Sexual passion is therefore apt capriciously to shift from one person to another if the latter happens to be more attractive or promises greater sexual satisfaction.

Frequently, but incorrectly, erotic attachment is equated with sexual passion. It, too, is directed towards a person of the other sex, but whereas the passion desires the act of cohabitation erotic love seeks the happiness which is derived from the presence and physical nearness of the other person. This requires of course that the physical appearance of the other person should be pleasing. While with an ugly person a friendship is conceivable erotic love would be impossible. Since it finds its fulfilment in the presence of the other person the absence or separation is felt painfully. In erotic love lovers will therefore conjure up the absent one by means of a picture or some other souvenir. Separation from the beloved person may lead to despair or even to crime or suicide. Erotic love, more so than sexual passion, takes hold of a person like an inescapable fate. Just as it cannot be called into being so there is no defense against it. Its violence causes one pain because it robs us of our Selfhood; but at the same time it carries with it a feeling of happiness previously unknown. With the presence of the beloved person the world is bathed in a strange new light, and life becomes a process of mutual giving and receiving. The man is anxious to prove himself worthy of the beloved's presence, and he makes every effort to secure the uninterrupted continuance of this happiness; while the woman underscores the value of her presence by embellishing her dress and appearance.

The physical presence of the other person fills a basic need of individual existence, for each of us longs for company as a protection against personal loneliness and the hostility of the outside world. Therefore, erotic love, although not in itself sexual, implies the desire to give physical expression to one's affection by all forms of tenderness. This can be seen in the fact that whenever young people of both sexes meet in an informal way they indulge in hilarity, teasing, pushing, and wrestling with each other, and they joyfully express their appreciation of physical attractiveness and beauty. The happy feeling of mutual suitability experienced in dancing together is also a manifestation of erotic love. Similarly many friendships between older and younger boys, and also between girls and women, are erotic in nature. But the psychologists who pretend to discover a latent sexuality in these associations fail to notice that erotic love has its satisfaction in itself. It contents itself with the agreeable and pleasurable experiences of momentary physical contact, whereas sexual love implies the desire to possess the other person, or to surrender one's self to him. However, this type of love is compatible with sexual experience and particularly in modern times it has often been considered as the necessary prerequisite of sexual relations.

A comparison of the erotic literature of antiquity with modern love stories will show that the forms of erotic love vary at different times under different circumstances. When, in the eighteenth century, the old formal concept of society gave way to the notion of individual freedom erotic love was assigned the central place in the relations of the sexes. The happiness received through the beloved person was highly prized, yet simultaneously there was a growing desire to assert one's personal freedom in the right to dissolve the erotic relationship at random. The modern mass society in which the individual is but a cog in the wheel of the economic process has created its own form of erotic relations. Today, no great importance seems to attach to the personality of the person loved provided he or she is and looks nice. A case in point is the pin-up girl, whose charm is transferred by tens of thousands of boys to the girl with whom they go.

Personal Love

Finally, personal or dedicated love is an affection for another person called forth by the fact that he represents certain objective values, such as intelligence, education, or character. Such love creates a genuine participation in those values and a sense of belonging together in the depth of one's personality. This fellowship finds expression in an exchange of thoughts and in common creative work. In this type of love the physical qualities of the other person are practically irrelevant and his presence is not absolutely necessary. Such love is possible between mature personalities only.

A mutual giving and receiving is found in all three forms of love. There can be no love that receives only, for the happiness of love, after all, does not depend upon the affection one has for the other person but upon the partner's spontaneous reciprocation of one's affection. For the same reason there is no satisfaction where love confines itself to giving. Loving union requires on either part receptivity for the gifts of the other person. Reciprocity only can make the happiness of love real. The uncommunicative person who is selfishly encased within himself can never experience love's happiness.

Lack of differentiation between the three forms of love, as well as the false opinion that they represented a scale, have caused considerable confusion. In reality, the three forms of love referred to are three independent possibilities of expressing one's sympathy for another person. Except for sexual passion they are not directly related to the sexual desire yet are not adverse to it either. Even personal love, for instance, does not by its nature exclude sexual relations. The love stories and love songs of mankind offer ample evidence that erotic love and personal love may co-exist. The distinction between real love and its opposite has nothing to do with the distinction of the three types of love, however. The expression "genuine love" should not be used as a means of discriminating against one or the other of these forms of love. None of them is genuine if pseudo-sexual substitutes are allowed to enter the dream image of the lover or the ideal of one's self or if the lover is immature and thus incapable of being in earnest about his partner as he actually is and directs his affections instead towards an imaginary partner. In these instances the partner in sexual passion is used only as a means of self-gratification; and in erotic love one raves about a person while no effort is made to live in his presence; and in personal love the other person is taken in earnest only in so far as he agrees with the values prized by ourselves. Thus understood the differentiation between real love and any of its counterfeits is highly important. What is decried today as a widespread lack of the ability to love is, in fact, a lack of genuine love caused by pseudo-sexual substitutions or by sexual immaturity.

The fact should not be overlooked that erotic love, as it is commonly understood today, is a comparatively recent phenomenon, and in spite of its popularization by the motion picture industry is restricted only to the middle classes. Since it presupposes an economic position in which there is room for leisure and play it is no wonder that erotic love is rarely found where the struggle for existence makes large demands upon life. Therefore, many young people in the Western world, no less than under Communism, view erotic love as trifling and unnecessary. It is to be feared, however, that in the West such male attitude will lead to disillusionment in many a marriage since as a rule women cherish the romantic viewpoint that erotic love is an essential part of the sexual relationship. Many girls dream and hope that the motion picture's portrayal of love will be re-enacted in their own experience with their man. Therefore, although a man might feel a healthy sexual passion for a girl yet she will be prompted by her different idea of love to complain about his lack of love.

Interrelation of Love and Sex

Love and sex have this in common that they establish some kind of interdependence between two people, yet the dependence is experienced differently in either case. In sex it is my masculinity or femininity that makes me look out for a person of the other sex; whereas in love it is the loneliness of the solitary individual which propels him toward another person. The reciprocal connection between sex and love results from the fact that the sexual relationship though primarily directed toward the sexual nature of the other person nevertheless encounters him as this individual, and that love, in turn, because of the sexual differentiation cannot be oblivious of the other person's sex. This is particularly obvious in the relationship of erotic love and sex. Since in love I yearn not only for the physical presence of the other person but also want it to be granted me as a special privilege, tangible evidence of his sympathy is essential, even if it is only a handclasp or a touch. Sexual desire on the other hand is intent upon possessing the other person's body and is never content until this end is achieved. Whereas erotic experience intensifies and elevates one's sense of vitality sexual experience makes us aware of our incompleteness, and this depressing feeling is only temporarily allayed by the happiness of physical union. Since antiquity a great deal has been said and written on the sadness following cohabitation. While modern writers are inclined to dismiss it as a relatively rare and pathological phenomenon one must in fact differentiate between a constitutional or acquired despondency contingent upon sexual experience, on the one hand, and the realization of one's fragmentary nature on the other. It is the latter awareness which has inspired the most beautiful poems extolling the tender sadness implied in the happiness of love.

Sexual desire is basically intent upon nothing but its own gratification. Its source is not to be found in one's individual existence but in the self's being rooted in the life of the species, and therefore it is never a conscious volition but a compulsive drive by which the individual is placed in the service of the species. When a normal satisfaction of the sexual desire is impossible the intensified pressure may lead to pseudo-sexual manipulations with other objects or even with animals, or satisfaction may be sought from an imaginary partner, as in onanism, or the individual may be driven to an act of criminal rape. Hence it is wrong to hold that the objective of sexual desire is the pleasure connected with its satisfaction. If this were so sex would be more easily controlled by the conscious will or by substituting other enjoyments for sexual pleasure. Rather the urgent demand of the sexual desire aims at relieving the tension incident to the differences and the separation of the sexes. Since the problem with which the sexual desire is concerned lies in the fragmentariness of our own nature we can understand its insatiable hunger and the ever-recurring need of its satisfaction, as well as the serious mental problems of those persons who after having enjoyed sexual relations for some while have been deprived of their partner.

The fact that erotic personal love and sexual desire are not necessarily connected causes some modern women to look upon sexual intercourse as a degrading experience. They charge that in the sexual relationship they serve only as the means of satisfying a man's sexual appetite. However, this experience is not a universal one. There are women who find full contentment in the fact that they should be physically fit to satisfy a man's passion. On the other hand, it is not accidental that in our days this feeling of degradation should be found especially among educated women with an articulate sense of personal value who engage in extramarital sexual relations. Having experienced success in business or the professions they have a high regard for themselves, and although they do not instinctively resist sexual advances yet on reflection they regret to have yielded to a role which in their view could have been assumed by any other woman. However, in many of these instances the sense of degradation is not attributable to sexual intercourse itself but to the use of contraceptive methods rendered necessary by the absence of the marriage bond. Though sexual desire is not the will to propagate or the will to beget children nevertheless it implies the man's burning wish to take complete possession of the woman's body. He wants to make her willing to receive his seed into her body in an act of unconditional surrender which implies her readiness also to accept the results of the sexual act. That this analysis of the sexual intercourse is correct can be learned from the fact that such a large number of children are born out of wedlock. That phenomenon cannot so much be ascribed to the carelessness of the man as to the actual complete surrender of the woman in sexual intercourse. In turn, then, where the results of the union are basically rejected by using means or ways of preventing conception sexual intercourse has no deeper meaning than any other gratification of one's desire for pleasure. No wonder that in such a case intelligent and thoughtful women should feel bitter. However, sex ought not be blamed for this result as though sexual intercourse in itself were meaningless, nor is the fault to be found in man's pretensions of superiority but in a self-imposed limitation of the function of sex on the part of those women.

What gives meaning to the sexual intercourse is the unity of the flesh thereby created. Although any sexual relationship will provide some intimation of this unity yet the full awareness of it is only attained when sex is coupled with love. Love has a twofold function in that respect. It makes one aware of the significance of one's existence as an individual self, and it assures one of one's own value because one has been accepted by another person. Loveless, promiscuous sexual activities or intercourse with prostitutes are therefore bound to appear worthless aside from the momentary pleasure. Such relationships not only cause people to hold the other sex in disdain but frequently also bring about an increasing disintegration of one's personality that will result in alcoholism, narcotic addiction, or a callous striving for money, power, or social position.

To differentiate between love, particularly erotic love, and sex is of great practical importance. Especially in Christian circles all premarital and extramarital erotic love has frequently been frowned upon because it was equated with sex; while on the other hand, the failure to recognize the difference between sex and love, for instance, by considering 'heavy petting' as a manifestation of erotic love, has obscured the seriousness of sex with the result that the couple drifts unintentionally into sexual relations. Erotic love is playful and relaxed and neither of the partners is thereby seriously endangered in his Selfhood. Infatuation is an indication of a low degree of Selfhood rather than of its loss. On the other hand, the sexual approach is always serious. It is a struggle in which possession and surrender are the stakes. Erotic love-play, even when it engages in romping and contests, seeks the sensual pleasure of pain or the joy of competition; whereas in sex one contends with the loved one in order to break down any mental and physical opposition against the unity of being a couple. It is by the wish to possess and to be possessed that the sexual approach differs from erotic love.

In our age the combination of sex with erotic love has gained special importance because thereby a personal element has added to the choice of the sexual partner. Though wooing and love-play are found in the animal kingdom, too, the sexual partner is there simply a representative of his species without any real choice being made. A human being, however, is aware of his personal nature and so desires freedom of choice. Nevertheless, not only throughout the ancient world but also in a great part of the Orient today the choice of a spouse is a family concern with no participation of the young people themselves. In such circumstances the only avenues open for the exercise of freedom of sexual expression are prostitution and adultery. It is, therefore, not accidental that in the Western world once the individual had become aware of his value the concepts of personal freedom and of erotic love also emerged side by side. In erotic love the individual is offered an opportunity to direct his attention toward a person of his choice in the other sex. Since love is conceived of as a game in which both persons enjoy not only the right of choice but also the right and the possibility of change, the first love and love at first sight are as a rule nothing but exhibitions of erotic love, and because of their playfulness should not serve as a basis for marriage.

The Problems of Sex

Since it is primarily through erotic love that people are made aware of the meaning and nature of their sexuality one might assume that all the problems of sex would disappear in the union of love and sex. But this expectation is not corroborated by experience the reason being that the significance the sexual intercourse has for either sex differs greatly. Take the woman. The more she realizes her individual nature the less she is content to be accepted merely as a sexual being. Beyond the temporary satisfaction which sexual intercourse provides she seeks fulfillment of the sexual union in the security of her home, in her place in the civil order, and in the community's recognition of her worth as a married woman. Because she needs the man to achieve these ends she will, therefore, use every means to bind him to herself as firmly as possible. However, by shifting her life's center of gravity from her husband to the security of home and marriage the significance of the erotic relationship is bound to diminish. Thus, unless personal love binds husband and wife together in the pursuit of common interests and service a crisis in their married lives is inevitable. Sexual passion may temporarily conceal the gravity of the crisis but cannot prevent it. The discontinuation of sexual intercourse enforced by pregnancy and the wife's dwindling sexual attractiveness explain why in such cases the sexual passion of the husband terminates, usually after ten to fifteen years of married life, and makes him or her frequently seek a divorce.

Home and civil order have a different significance for the man. In the case of the woman their importance outweighs any sacrifices she makes for them. While he, too, will normally cherish the comfort of his home yet it is only one of his centers or resting places. Office or shop on the one hand, and club or tavern on the other, are of equal importance for him. This difference of outlook is rooted in the fact that his sexuality does not preoccupy him physiologically and psychologically so completely as the woman. In his case, the sexual approach is meant to impart meaning to his sexual appetite and thus it tends towards possessing her. This yearning manifested already in love-play reaches its goal in the first intercourse since therein the wife surrenders herself to her husband. But it is precisely on account of that victory that he may doubt his superiority; because only by striving in their sexual relationship to overcome her feminine opposition can he prove his male superiority. As long as there is erotic love it may help him retain his sense of superiority because it stimulates him to act as the guide of his companion, or as the protector of the mother of his children. Where the erotic side of love is not coupled with personal love, however, this sense of superiority will gradually develop into the wish to prove his importance and significance outside the sexual sphere, especially on the job or in exclusively male circles. For the same reason some husbands become family tyrants or grumblers; others try to assert their superiority by pennypinching in household expenses, or attempt to keep their wives in submission by scoldings and even by blows. I would not be surprised if in many instances it was the husband's doubt of his sexual superiority that lay at the root of his marital unfaithfulness. By seeking to win the affections of another woman he wants to convince himself of his male superiority. Such unfaithfulness will not ordinarily disrupt his marriage because it is not motivated by real love for the other woman but merely by his sexual doubts. Experienced wives will therefore deal casually with this unfaithful conduct saying: "I won't mind his vagaries, he will come back to me soon enough." Of course, there are cases when a married man becomes involved in genuine erotic love for another woman. Since he ages more slowly than his wife he is anxious to continue with the youthful expressions of erotic love in sport, dance, and love-play for a longer period of time than his wife. In such instances the marriage is in real danger.

In spite of all contentions to the contrary, there is no natural harmony between the sexes nor can sexual intercourse or any of the forms of love effect more than a temporary and passing concord. Although modern women are unwilling to recognize man's superiority, yet the possessive character of male sexuality speaks in no uncertain terms. The resulting tensions are evident in all their relations, including the erotic play. He wants to win the prize, be it only a kiss or a passing touch. In turn the girl wishes the boy to feel that he is dependent upon her. In the love-play allurement and denial will constantly alternate. Similarly behind the gaiety of the game the man secretly wishes to humble her by reminding her that at bottom she is only the "little woman" who should not be taken too seriously by the superior sex.

Modern women get irritated as a rule when the man's sexually conditioned superiority is mentioned. In fact, however, though unconsciously, they admit it. Yet it is done grudgingly, and that breeds a secret hate between the sexes. The Biblical account of the Fall (Gen. 3:1-13) elucidates this point. Having transgressed the Divine command Eve tempts Adam too. She is angry that as a result of her transgression she has become inferior to him. Hence in order to reduce him to her own level she attempts to persuade him to follow her in her wrong-doing. The divine curse: "He shall be your lord," (Gen. 3:16) shows, however, that she has failed to reach her goal. But the desire to humiliate the man remains the permanent counterpart of the woman's sexual surrender. It manifests itself most conspicuously in the many cases in which women incite men to commit crimes, but more frequently in their pleading with him for the sake of pleasing her to give up the things he cherishes most. The Bible illustrates this, instructively, by the stories of Samson and his Philistine wife (Judges ch. 14-16) and of Herod and Herodias (Mark 6:17-29; Matt. 14:3-12, cf. 1 Cor. 7:33).

But let nobody think that man is above this hatred of the sexes. On his part it expresses itself mainly as the wish to subdue the woman. This easily calls forth the desire to seduce her. Except in cases of relations with prostitutes sexual intercourse never occurs by simple mutual agreement. Rather the man must woo the woman and overcome her opposition. This fact irritates him because momentarily his superiority appears to be placed in question. Instinctively aware of this situation he feels that in order to break her superiority and to take possession of her body he must induce her to go farther than she knows is prudent and to deprive her of her most precious good. So he contrives to make the girl "hitherto untouched" surrender herself completely to him without any assurance that he will assume the responsibility for any consequences of his act; or he attempts to seduce a married woman to yield to his entreaties even though she belongs to another. Modern psychology has shown how even men who would never permit this desire to be satisfied are, nevertheless, experiencing its urge. Nowhere more conspicuously than in the modern literature of sexual confessions does this come to light. For the detailed description of sexual scenes painted in lurid colors rarely depicts the actual experiences of the author. Rather such books show how powerfully the writer's imagination is agitated by his desire to deprive women of their sexual value and worth.

These conditions engender a feeling of bitterness and contempt for the other sex in men and women, and humanity would be rent into two widely separated camps but for the fact that the sexual appetite breaking constantly forth from the depths of their nature would compel the sexes to be joined together again.

Sex and the Divine Curse

The foregoing analysis confirms what every sexually experienced person already knows, namely, that in spite of the enticement of the sexual relationship and the feeling of happiness produced by sexual intercourse yet no lasting satisfaction is found in sex. No less important is the fact that whereas people expect a measureless bliss from love all its passion and tenderness are not able to resolve the tensions involved in sex; not because most people's love is half-hearted, shallow, or egotistical, but because even great love does not yield the happiness anticipated. According to the Bible it is God's will that sex should produce a limited measure of satisfaction only. The curse pronounced by God upon the first couple (Gen. 3:16-19) applies particularly to their sexual relationship. In the case of the woman the blessing of motherhood is to be associated with the pains and dangers of childbirth, and her amorous longing for the man is in unrelieved tension with the oppressive experience of his lordship over her (Gen. 3:16). In the case of the man the joy of having a lifelong companion is marred by the necessity to provide and care for his family at the price of neverending work and toil (Gen. 3:17-19).

No wonder, therefore, that after the first joys of the honeymoon a young couple soon discovers the many unavoidable reefs and rocks on which the boat of their married life can be wrecked. Unless the cause of this unexpected risk is discovered to lie in the sexual relationship itself rather than in the partner's character or nature the couple will get ready for a divorce after a short time.

The bitter curse of God, however, far from nullifying His good work in Creation merely renders precarious the unity which results from the sexual encounter. This may explain many of the seeming contradictory factors in the man-wife relationship. For instance, it is a well-known fact that many women patiently endure the blows and mistreatment of their husbands because they interpret them as a confirmation that he still loves them and is still conscious of their belonging together. Likewise, it frequently happens that a married man who had left his wife to escape the responsibility of maintaining her later returns because he feels comfortable and at home with her.

The account of the divine curse in Genesis chapter 3 does not imply that sex itself is a curse laid upon mankind but only that the evil results of sin are particularly conspicuous at the very center of human life, that is to say, in the sexual relationship of man and woman. In order to counterbalance this curse it is necessary that both partners should accept marriage as the God-appointed form in which the unity of the flesh is to find its appropriate expression and upon which God's blessing rests. Thus the Biblical viewpoint is not only opposed to Neoplatonism and to all Faustian natures and romantics who attempt to cope with the inadequacies and limitations of sex by constantly searching for the true partner, but it is also against the utilitarian views of those who see the meaning of marriage in the service it renders to the life of society or the State.

IX. SEX AND THE DIVINE MARRIAGE

The Paradox of the Divine Marriage

Of all the things the Bible says about sex probably the strangest for modern people to grasp is the metaphor of God's marriage with His people. For the God of the Old Testament, unlike the gods of Canaan and Mesopotamia, is not a deity of fertility or procreation. The God of the Bible has no sex. He operates in a conspicuously nonsexual manner through His Word. Yet there is a close historical connection between Israel's strict view of marriage and its exclusive monotheism. Where earnest attention is given to the knowledge of the unity of the flesh and the indestructible nature of sexual union a new understanding of the meaning of faithfulness and obligation is generated that also expresses itself in religious matters, and the divine demand to keep faithfully the Covenant has its inevitable repercussions on the regard people have for their marriage contract. The prophet Hosea is the first in Biblical literature to elaborate this metaphor when he compares God's relationship to Israel with his own unhappy marriage to an adulterous prostitute. Another reference to that marriage is found in Isaiah 5:1-7, where, for the first time, Israel is introduced as the "Virgin of the Lord," whose covenant relationship with Yahweh is destined to be divinely blest with a son. Jeremiah frequently uses the metaphor of the Divine Marriage when he decries Israel's adultery in her relationship with God (Jer. 3:8ff, 5:7; 9:2; 13:27; 23:10; 29:23). Deutero-Isaiah presents both sides of this picture—the shame of Israel's adultery and also the joy of reconciliation with her spouse (Isa. 54:8; 61:4-5). The Song of Songs, which originally must have formed a collection of secular love and wedding songs, would hardly have been accorded a place in the Old Testament canon except that at an early date its description of love's bliss had been applied to the Divine Marriage (cf. Ezra 5:23-26). The Divine Marriage is conceived of very realistically. It is God Himself who begets the virtues of marriage (Hos. 2:19-20) and the knowledge of Himself (Hos. 2:22). The issue of this marriage is the Protector and Heir whom God raises to His people and the land of Israel (Isa. 62:4-5; also 9:6-7). Referring to Israel's role, the two metaphors of prostitution and adultery appear side by side; the latter, according to Old Testament law, was a violation only on the part of the woman. Rarely does Israel appear in a masculine role, as in Malachi 2:11.

The New Testament has retained this group of metaphors. When Jesus calls the generation of His contemporaries adulterous (Mark 8:38; Matt. 12:39; 16:4) He is not referring to their sexual transgressions but to their breach of the Divine Marriage. Going a step beyond the Old Testament He hints at His being the bridegroom (Matt. 9:15; 25:1-29; Mark 2:19-20; Luke 5:34-35), and points to the approaching marriage (Matt. 22.1-14). This terminology was continued in the early Church (John 3:29; Rev. 12:1-17; 19:7-9; 22:17; cf. 14:4). While Paul discusses the implications of the divine marriage especially in Ephesians 5:23-33, yet he refers to this "mystery" (Eph. 5:32) in most of his letters. He will, for instance, apply the sexual expression "to cleave" to the relationship of the believer with Christ (1 Cor. 6:16-17); or say that by this union with Christ we shall know as we are known (1 Cor. 13:12). A new feature in the New Testament is the thought that in the present the people of God are only betrothed to the Saviour while the wedding is to be consummated in the future. Paul paradoxically connects this thought with the idea that formerly the whole of mankind had been married to sin (Rom. 7:14) and had begotten children from this relationship. The Church is plainly that part of mankind that through Christ's victory has been delivered from that ignominious union and has been miraculously restored to virginity (2 Cor. 11:2) by the power of Christ's triumph over sin (Rom. 7:3). From the New

Testament viewpoint God's marriage with Israel was only a provisional relationship for the real Bridegroom is the Saviour, Jesus Christ (Eph. 5:32; Rev. 22:17).

Over against the idea of the Covenant and the election of Israel as the people of God—which the Israelites understood selfishly as an unconditional human prerogative—the metaphor of the Divine Marriage draws attention to three neglected aspects of God's relation to his people, namely, God's lordship as the husband, the unity and the exclusiveness of God's union with His people, and God's seeking and forgiving love. In their light it was obvious that Israel's relation to God had been indifferent, thankless, unworthy, and faithless.

The picture of the Divine Marriage as used in the New Testament not only illumines the redemptive work of Christ but also discloses function and purpose of human marriage. Owing to the vehemence of the sexual desire, its ability to produce both happiness and to make a mess of life, and its incomprehensible mystery people at all times have had an instinctive feeling that sex must point beyond itself, and, therefore, they have variously related it to religion. Even the modern psychology of sex seems unable to manage without mythological ideas. It is therefore entirely legitimate to employ the idea of Christ's Marriage as the supreme standard and the complete illumination of the sexual problem. Through the metaphor of the Church as the Bride of Christ we perceive the great God-given potentialities implied in the sexual relationship; and from the actual attitude of the Church light is shed upon the gravity of the wrong we commit when in our sinfulness we disregard the true meaning of the sexual relationship. While even those who do not believe will experience the disclosure of the Self imparted in sexual intercourse they will be prevented by their limited insight from probing the depths of the divine relationship implied in the life of faith.

Christian Love

From the metaphor of Christ's marriage to His people we attain to the full understanding of what is meant by love in the New Testament. Bishop Nygren's fine study on *Eros and Agape,* unfortunately, has confused the New Testament meaning more than elucidated. By his exclusively theological discussion of the problem he has created the impression that the two kinds of love are mutually exclusive and that erotic love is essentially irreconcilable with a truly Christian life. The New Testament, however, knows only one kind of love, and it uses the same expression for natural and for Christian love (Matt. 5:46; Mark 7:6; Luke 6:32; John 3:19); but it distinguishes plainly between the motives and objectives of a sinful love and those called forth by the Holy Spirit. In this connection the account of the woman who anointed Jesus is highly instructive (Luke 7:36-50). Although some kind of erotic love seems to be implied in her action yet she merits Jesus' praise for not thereby asserting herself or selfishly seeking her own happiness. Through her loving deed she gave recognition to Jesus as her Saviour in a manner appropriate to her nature and abilities.

By his deeds and teachings Jesus revealed a new level of love, namely, love of the neighbor for God's sake. The neighbor is not to be loved because of his abilities or accomplishments—that is done in personal love—but because God so loved man that Christ died for him. The ultimate objective of Christian love is therefore to enable the other person to appropriate the benefits Christ has won for him. When that happens the other person shares in the Body of Christ, and thus in meeting him one encounters not only a fellow-man but also in him Christ Himself. We can see now that the attitude of responsiveness toward each other, which is such an essential part of the sexual relationship, attains its fullest meaning in the Marriage with Christ: "Behold, I stand at the door and knock; if any man hear my voice, and open the door, I will come unto him" (Rev. 3:20).

Since these two ideas of concern and responsiveness apply to all circumstances of life they operate within the sexual relationship too. Accordingly, when Christian spouses have love for each other it is not an effect apart from sexual love or substituted for it. Paul points out, for instance, that since the spouses have become one flesh it would be absurd if they hated each other because they would then be hating their own flesh. Thus the sexual relationship helps to clarify the Christian meaning of love for the neighbor (Eph. 5:22ff). Beyond the demand of the Golden Rule, according to which we should treat our neighbor as if we were in his place, the Gospel tells us that he and we are one. Hence I am going to harm myself if I do not treat him with love. Our loveless and hateful attitudes fall back upon ourselves disintegrating our inner life.

He who loves his marriage partner as his own flesh thereby solves the mystery of life both for himself and his partner. For the understanding of the enigma of human existence depends upon the manner in which the two partners approach each other. A self-centered person, selfishly concerned with his own pleasure, impedes his sexual partner in attaining to comprehension of his existence. The reports of psycho-pathologists reveal, for instance, how the seduction of children or the rape of modest girls has a lasting and deep going effect upon the self-consciousness of the victims, since in this first instance of sexual experience the only purpose of sex seems to be the satisfaction of the sexual desire of the other sex. The result is a distorted view of sex in general and of the other sex in particular.

Similarly there is nothing else that, like Christian love, is able to impart to the woman in her self-surrender an enduring consciousness of feminine dignity and honor, as Mozart has brought out so beautifully in his *Magic Flute*. Such love makes the sexual partner realize that the natural correlation of the sexes and the intimate union made possible thereby is one of God's greatest gifts to mankind. It is out of His commiserating grace that God has given man a companion (Gen. 2:18).

We conclude that Christian love while an affirmation of the divine meaning of sex yet makes the partner feel that the fellowship of the sexes is not limited to the flesh. In a higher sense the two partners belong together as members of the Church, the Body of Christ.

Part Two

THE STANDARDS OF SEXUAL LIFE

X. DIGNITY AND VALUE OF SEX

Divine Marriage and Sexual Ethics

From the way the Bible treats sex it is obvious that sex is considered the basic phenomenon by which the place of husband and wife in social life, the institution of marriage, and the relationship of the spouses are determined. This role of sex presupposes that the Biblical writers discovered in sex certain intrinsic standards or regulative principles. Seemingly the same view is taken by those Protestant theologians who start in sexual ethics from the will of the Creator or the orders of Creation. But by choosing marriage as their point of departure, and thus disregarding the foundational role of sex, they actually distort the Biblical view. One reason for this fundamental change is the fear of following naturalistic ethics by which the sexual desire would be elevated to the position of supreme standard; another reason is the intention of establishing Christian ethics exclusively on the basis of divine revelation. Even though Karl Barth in his *Church Dogmatics,* Vol. III, Part 4, is willing to accord a just place to sexuality he finally decides to make the nonsexual relationship of man and woman his point of departure. By combining it with a romantic concept of the image of God in man, and a highly speculative view of the Christ-marriage, he denaturizes his original idea to the point that sex is reduced to something of secondary importance.

Over against these tendencies we are firmly convinced that the standards of sexual relationship must be developed in accordance with the Bible by proceeding from sex itself. Naturalism cannot be overcome by prematurely introducing speculative ideas but only by emphasizing the teleological relationship in which sex stands to the Divine Marriage.

The consummation of the Divine Marriage has been the God-intended goal for mankind from the very beginning. Therefore, the History of Salvation proves to be the gradual realization of this purpose. The relationship between God and His people grows more intimate as time goes on, and a steadily deepened understanding of the nature and goal of the mutual relationship of the sexes is thereby attained. On the other hand, the history of sexual relationships in mankind is evidence that the Divine Marriage operates everywhere as the basic pattern of sexual life.

The historical development of sexuality tends toward monogamy and Christianity has considerably deepened and purified this institution. This process indicates that God's redemptive work manifests itself in the molding of the natural area of sex too. This is true not only of the institution of marriage in general but also of individual marriages. By accepting his partner, and the unity established with him, as a gift of God the believer experiences the blessings of marriage as divine acts by which God constantly reminds him of his power to transform human lives. Similarly, the loss of a spouse is not simply a sad natural occurrence but, as will be shown later, it is a divine intervention by which a marriage is terminated so that the surviving partner may devote himself fully to the service of God in the Church. Therefore, every stage of the individual's sexual development both depends on his being subject to the law of God and is also a partial execution of the divine plan of redemption. Much more than the development of a set of moral standards is thus needed for a true understanding of marriage; a metaphysics or theology of sex is just as necessary.

The Dignity of Sex

Apart from its religious evaluation sexual pleasure is generally regarded as the highest physical enjoyment, and the poets outdo themselves in singing the praises of sexual love. Unless this view prevailed in the Old Testament also it would be difficult to explain the inclusion of the "Song of Songs" within the Biblical canon. Nevertheless an entirely different appraisal of sex is conceivable. Those who believe that sex is meant to serve the purposes of God and not those of individual men and women will also be ready to notice the darker side of the sexual relationship. Only a step separates this thought from the conviction that sex is a heavy burden that God has laid upon mankind. This step appears to have been taken by Paul and by John in Revelation. Paul expressly states that it is good for a man not to touch a woman (1 Cor. 7:1).

However, our generation recoils from such views and prefers to discard them as pathological or as remnants of a pre-evangelical and dualistic spirituality. We have been so greatly influenced by modern man's self reliance that the first question we raise concerning the meaning of our life is: what shall we do about it? But the life of faith is not meant to serve the realization of values in the same way as cultural activities do. Above all, faith is an attitude of receptivity. God approaches us with promises, gifts and blessings that need to be accepted and acknowledged. Realizing that God confronts us as one who imparts good gifts, is of utmost importance for our handling of sex on account of its deficiencies. Though the Bible is characterized by a positive attitude toward sex, the Biblical writers, nevertheless, have also a keen eye for sin. Therefore, they distinguish clearly between human sexuality conferred by God in Creation and the sinful use mankind makes of it. Sexual sin may be likened to a gold ring in a pig's snout (Proverbs 11:22). Just as a jewel loses none of its value when it is worn in an inappropriate place, so it is inconceivable that sex should be divested of its dignity and meaning on account of abuse or misuse. For it is related to God's purpose, and not a mere part of nature.

What is usually called natural is never just mere nature because the Creator is at work in everything that exists. For instance, God uses the natural instinctive drive of sexual attraction to entice the solitary person out of his loneliness, and compels him to establish a relationship with another person.

When, at the very beginning of the Bible, God says, "it is not good for the man to be alone" (Gen. 2:18) he thereby reveals the danger inherent in man's individuality. Nothing in God's Creation exists for itself alone, all things are created for each other. Man finds it more difficult than any other creature to live according to this principle, he not only is individually differentiated from all other persons, but also, more significantly, he has the power of conscious choice and self-determination. This ability implies both the temptation of a self-sufficient individualism and the complacent boasting of man's very greatness. This danger is increased by the existence of the two sexes. The individual's natural tendency toward isolation is intensified by sexual differentiation, for when the individual becomes aware of this fact he adopts a shy and retiring attitude toward the other sex. It is not just accidental that at the onset of puberty boys feel uncomfortable in the presence of girls. They prefer to play with boys only, and feel particularly happy in the company of men. This same attitude prevails in the lives of girls. However, the pressure of the sexual impulse makes young people overcome this shyness. To be sure, there are other instincts too which move the individual to associate with other people, but as a rule the sexual attraction proves to be the most effective one. Naturally, a person who has felt the charm of sexual attraction is, nevertheless, free to revert to himself again and live a solitary life of seclusion. But, as the Bible states, it is not good for such a person. For by refusing to co-operate with the divine plan, he acts contrary to what is human in himself and thus blocks his own growth. God has endowed us with our nature so that we should develop life's possibilities to the greatest extent. Normally these imply our sexual characteristics.

Therefore, the misanthropist's absolute withdrawal into isolation, as well as the exclusive association with members of one's own sex, finally poisons the springs of personality. In many instances the spinster, the bachelor, and the habitués of bachelor clubs are types of atrophied humanity. They are unlikable and humanly unproductive not because they have not married but because they have cut off their manhood and womanhood from the other sex. This is confirmed by the fact that there are unmarried persons of both sexes who are highly enjoyable because they have retained their ability informally to mix with people of both sexes far into old age.

Furthermore, in addition to establishing intimate fellowship sex preserves life in a world where all things pass away and die. When Paul refers to Christ as the Saviour of the Body, he thinks not only of the Church (Eph. 5:23) but also throws light upon human sexuality. For it is the earthly Body of Mankind, symbolized by the union of Adam and Eve, which forms the object of Christ's redemptive work. The propagation of the human race is not a matter of course. From a biological standpoint one might play with the idea of what might have happened if the progenitors of the human race had been but hybrids of a lower species. Devoid of the gift of reproducing itself the new race would never have gotten beyond the first pair. According to the Creation story, it was God's special grace which endowed mankind with the gift of sexual propagation.

We read that Adam and Eve having eaten of the tree of knowledge were subject to death (Gen. 2:17). Mortality, which could have been warded off by constant obedience to God's commandment, then became their inescapable fate. When Adam later on "knew" his wife he acknowledged, however unconsciously, the perishable nature of individual life. For mortal beings only need reproduction. By entering into sexual relation with Eve he was able, in spite of his and her mortality, to keep in existence that life which pulsated in them. Thus mankind was saved from destruction notwithstanding the eventual death of the first pair, and the place which God had alloted to mankind in Creation remained occupied. In this way the body was preserved though no longer as the individual bodies of Adam and Eve but as the body of mankind. Sex has therefore not only made possible the subsequent history of mankind but also provided the opportunity both for the Incarnation and also for that body which the Saviour forms for Himself in the Church.

The sexuality of mankind has therefore a dignity of its own. Sex is good and noble because as a biological function it has played a decisive part in the execution of the plan of redemption. Of course, only those who know of God's purpose for mankind can clearly perceive this connection. However, it is the privilege of human beings not only to possess sexual life but also to be able to understand its meaning. Inasmuch as they experience sex people are also intuitively conscious of its dignity and its right to exist. Christians do not, therefore, need a special theory of sex in order to bear their sexual nature with a good conscience. Like all of God's creations sex is good and may therefore be thankfully received (1 Tim. 4:4ff).

Violence is done to the story of the Fall when it is interpreted as teaching that sex is essentially bad or sinful. While this interpretation has become traditional, on the authority of Augustine, both text and context demand a different interpretation. Far from stressing sexual pleasure as the good offered to Eve, let alone intimating that Eve had sexual intercourse with the serpent, the narrative rather emphasizes that in order to obtain a pleasurable experience Eve brazenly transgressed the divine prohibition to eat of the tree, and was followed therein by Adam.

In like manner, neither the story of the Virgin Birth nor any other New Testament passage can be construed as teaching that sex is bad or sinful by nature. The records of the Birth of Jesus in Matthew and Luke do in no way suggest that it was the sinfulness of sex which made it necessary for the Redeemer to enter into mankind in a nonsexual way. On the contrary, the Biblical stories of the Virgin Birth accentuate the feminine ability to bear children. Luke speaks emphatically about Mary's great sacrifice (Luke 1:38), and Matthew refers to the ensuing loss of her social respect (Matt. 1:18-19). The mother of Jesus realizes that the foregoing of sexual conception, as is demanded of her, is in accordance with the fact that the coming of the Saviour exacts complete dedication on the part of men. The very fact that Mary's sacrifice is so tightly joined to her womanhood underscores the high value assigned to femininity, and thus to sex. Matthew makes this idea plain with reference to Mary's spouse. However much Joseph may have come, later on, to love Jesus and to treat Him as his son his manly pride and his desire as a suitor must have suffered severe disappointment when God demanded of him to have a son quite independent of sexual intercourse with Mary (Matt. 1:18-21). There is no Biblical support for the monastic attitude which heaped contempt and condemnation upon sex. Since the practice of ascetic life rests upon the belief that the material world is intrinsically evil, the reference to the 144,000 saints who were virgins and were not defiled with women (Rev. 14:4) cannot be cited as the first appearance of a depreciation of sex in the church. For the Revelation of John does not share the dualistic view of the universe. These saints were persons who had not loved the world (1 John 2:15).

The Temporary Function of Sex

Seen in the perspective of the divine plan of redemption sex possesses an inalienable dignity. However, that dignity is confined to the present conditions of life. Sexuality will be absent from the world to come. "In the Resurrection they neither marry nor are given in marriage" (Matt. 22:30; Mark 12:25; Luke 20:34-35). All people instinctively feel the lack of ultimate meaning inherent in sex. That after sexual intercourse people should frequently experience a strange admixture of sadness with their happiness is not a pathological condition, and it defies any physiological explanation. Rather it gives expression to the deep-seated awareness that the pleasures of sex are unable to yield final satisfaction. What seems to be the climax of life and perfect union is, at the same time, a reminder of our mortality and of the precarious character of the oneness of the flesh. Likewise, only a very superficial view of life can consider abnormal the radical repudiations of sex which seem to occur periodically in human history. They express, though often in a distorted and vague way, mankind's awareness of the temporary function of sex. Man realizes that during his earthly existence he cannot fully attain to his destination. Since sex plays such an important part in our natural lives, yet never supplies complete satisfaction, it is the sexual instinct which in those ascetic movements is erroneously blamed for man's feeling of nonfulfillment.

In turn it is not surprising that man's sense of the dignity of sex has at various times caused people to believe in its redemptive power. But those who hold that man is destined for fellowship with God will reject such a suggestion because it underrates the gravity of man's predicament. In his natural condition man is not only alienated from himself but also from God. While sexual intercourse and sexual love may enable the individual to fulfil his Selfhood, they have no power to redeem man or save him (1 Cor. 7:16). Though deified in a number of religions, sex is a cosmic power and not God's own creativity. To be sure, a person who has faith can become a saviour for another person by way of sexual relationship; a thought that has been given powerful expression by Tolstoy in *Resurrection,* and in *The Brothers Karamazoff* by Dostoevski, to mention only two outstanding works. However, sex serves then only as a means of Christian love without being the cause of redemption.

The temporary function of sex is further indicated by the fact that notwithstanding its dignity it also has its limitations. Since it is neither absolutely good nor absolutely bad it must be approached with misgivings because it is apt to delude people. Unaware of its temporary nature they will seek the perfect meaning of life in sex itself. For this reason the Bible, although not treating sex as a dirty or ignominous thing, yet does not cease to warn of its latent dangers.

However, the sex impulse's intrinsic longing for unlimited expansion, and its frequent disregard of boundaries, must not lead to an ascetic denial of all sexuality. The many serious warnings sounded against sex in the Bible, and particularly in the New Testament, are only limiting qualifications of a fundamentally affirmative attitude towards sex. They are intended to remind the believer that there are situations and times where the boundaries of sexual life must be drawn in bold lines, because with all the marrying and giving in marriage people are prone to forget that this earthly life is not an end in itself. Man is called upon to be God's servant in the execution of His plans in history. There are instances in which in the service of God celibacy is the right thing to choose for a person. However, any unequivocal negation of sex is in opposition to God's redemptive work and celibacy as a general demand for all people is therefore branded as a doctrine of the devil (1 Tim. 4:1-3). When, in 1 Corinthians 7:5, Paul advises temporary sexual abstinence he does not intimate that sex is unclean, subhuman, or sinful yet that, nevertheless, it should be tolerated because concessions must be made to the weakness of human nature. On the contrary, Paul affirms the rightful place of sex in the marital relationship, yet he also reminds the spouses that sex must not detract from the spiritual duties.

It is true that the Bible evinces a high regard for virginity. In Judaism the girl was required to retain her virginity until marriage because she was to give herself with all that she had and was to her affianced husband; therefore, chastity as respect for marriage, but not physical virginity in itself, was the meaningful element. This view is as far removed from the pagan practice, which demands physical intactness of the bride because her husband claims the privilege to initiate her sexually, as from the Catholic thought that lifelong sexual abstinence is more meritorious and God-pleasing than sexual relationship even when practiced in married life. Paul clearly states that in God's eyes the value of a person is not dependent upon his married or unmarried state (1 Cor. 7:38).

Bondage and Freedom

The important role which God has assigned to sex in the development of mankind explains why the emergence of the sexual impulse is such an inescapable fate in the life of the adolescent, and why, as a rule, the sexual drive is the most powerful of all human instincts. The Bible takes these facts for granted, and it abounds with examples showing both the power of the sexual impulse and the ease with which it transgresses its natural limits. In the New Testament the power of sex is not so much illustrated by stories as directed by means of moral instructions for men and women. According to Paul the ability to disregard the pressure of the sexual impulse is a special privilege granted by God (1 Cor. 7:7); and when Jesus refers to people "who have become eunuchs for the Kingdom's sake" He has the same condition in mind (Matt. 19:12). In view of the fact, however, that under normal conditions an adult person cannot suppress the instinctive desire for sexual satisfaction, Paul warns against the dangerous experiment of spiritual alliances in which young couples attempted to live together without sexual intercourse, and he recommends marriage as a more satisfactory solution. Though the apostle does not mean that people living in those alliances are absolutely unable to forego the satisfaction of their sexual desire he is also aware of the dangers for moral and mental health implied in such union. For once the sexual desire has made itself felt toward the partner the passions will mount feverishly and the wish to have sexual relations with that person can never be completely dispelled (1 Cor. 7:9). Thus the very end for which the couple entered into that alliance, namely, to support each other, spiritually and personally, would be defeated.

The experience of sexual desire must be taken seriously because God Himself uses the sexual impulse like all the urges and needs of our physical life to make us aware of our destination. Among animals the appearance of sexual desire is, as a rule, immediately followed by the sexual act. A similar situation would prevail in human life if man were destined only for physical life. But man feels instinctively that his life transcends the physiological functions, and revelation teaches him that he is made for fellowship with God. This fact implies that he is destined to be free and that it is up to him to realize this in his life. Like other desires, sex does not derive the right of its satisfaction from the fact that it makes itself felt, but in each instance the individual person must determine if and when a desire has a right to exist. By means of the pressure of the impulse and the perplexity which it causes in us God wants to impress upon us the necessity for decision. The exercise of this choice is the evidence of our being truly human, i.e., creatures fashioned in God's image, while the nonethical view of Naturalism is based upon a false and inconsistent concept of man's nature. For those who infer from the power of the sexual desire that man not only has in illimitable right but perhaps even the bounden duty, for reasons of physical and mental health, freely to indulge in sexual acts contradict their own self-consciousness, and they conduct themselves not as free beings but as nature's slaves.

True freedom respects the limitations set to sex in human relationship, and it manifests itself both in deciding whether or not one should enter into a sexual relationship with a certain person and, for the sake of Christ, in altogether denying oneself the right to have a sexual life of one's own. Thus Paul can paradoxically admonish married persons to live as though they were not married (1 Cor. 7:20), obviously meaning that a Christian should constantly remember that he is living in the shadow of the End. Unlike the life of pagans that of the Christian can never be lived in unconcerned abandon from day to day because we know that whatever we do has its weighty consequences both for our own future and that of mankind. This viewpoint ought perpetually to undergird our lives. Likewise, marriage, notwithstanding its dignity, must never be considered the supreme value in our lives, nor should the union of the flesh ever result in the lover's losing his personality in that of the beloved. At this point, there emerges a serious problem for the Protestant ministry whose urgency has traditionally been concealed by extolling the blessings that the Protestant parsonage has brought to the Western world. In this regard the accomplishments of the Catholic clergy and the members of the monastic orders which were rendered possible by their celibacy have not always been given just consideration by Protestants. But, in the Protestant churches under Communistic rule the problem of a celibate clergy will probably soon reassert itself with new urgency. The sacrifices demanded of the minister and the constant risks of conflict with the political powers will make it inadvisable for the pastor to be hampered by his regards for wife and family.

Passion and the Spirit of Adventure

How to reconcile the inescapable pressure of sex with the limitations set to its satisfaction is a problem for the Christian which cannot be solved by cool ratiocination. Since the dignity of sex is not confined to its sublimated forms, but to sex in all its manifestations, passion occupies a rightful place in life and no Christian needs to be ashamed of it. However, when given free rein passion will press on to the furthest limits of the allowable, that is to say, to the dangerous point where sex may lose its dignity and its right of existence. While in the realm of sex, as in other spheres of life, many people will walk considerately on the smooth paths of convention, there will also be some daring souls who throw caution to the winds as they clamber along the steep slopes of the mountain gorge to pluck some rare and precious flower. Since Peter and Paul and Jesus Himself have given the Church outstanding examples of adventurous living the right of an adventurous spirit in the area of sex cannot be denied. However, there is a particular danger involved in sex such as does not threaten the adventurous proclamation of the Gospel. While the messenger of the Gospel may endanger his body his endeavour remains subject to the will of God. Sexual adventure, however, may lead to sin.

Passion has a rightful and important place in all areas of life, for its potentialities can be fully realized only when individuals, moved by a great passion, advance to the very limits where injury and suffering may be sustained. Human existence itself is a dangerous thing because of the tensions between the longing to be an individual person, on the one hand, and its corresponding limitations on the other. In sexual matters passion begets erotic love. The motto here might well be: No Eros without the readiness to play the game, but also no Eros without risk. The erotic game will remain a harmless and innocuous play only as long as the protective walls of custom and convention keep it from becoming an earnest involvement. But passion will always be on the lookout for places to play its game for the highest stakes, even though they may lie outside the precincts of social custom and order. The erotic game is then threatened by the possibility of gliding into sexual reality before the involved persons are aware of overstepping the limits, or are able to anticipate the consequences of their acts.

Should then the adventurous spirit be altogether exiled from the realm of sex, and the right of a daring attitude be contested? It is neither a part of Biblical wisdom, nor is it a universally accepted truth, that the person who exposes himself to danger must necessarily perish. The circumspect person of negative virtue will, of course, never be threatened by the dangers of sexual passion, but neither will he ever plumb the depths of sex or explore the outlying and uncommon areas of life. He'll remain a prisoner to his own caution, and the sublime wonder accomplished in the union of two different persons will but dimly dawn upon his mind. It would, therefore, be absurd to lay down certain general limits for love, or to define in advance what is harmless and allowable play and what is not. Since the dignity and the limits of sex are determined by the divine plan for mankind no general ethical principles nor rules of moral restraint can define for each case what the relationship of these two elements must be. The decision rests with faith that trusts the guidance of the Holy Spirit. He alone has the power to transform our ideal and our dream-image of the beloved so as to agree with a true evaluation of sex, and to call forth a genuine respect for the mystery of life and the dignity of the partner, and unlike our unaided reason and will the Holy Spirit is able to restrain our passions from precipitating us into the abyss.

XI. MAN AND WOMAN

The Differentiation of the Sexes

Although everybody is aware of the obvious anatomical and mental differences between man and woman yet many attempts have been made to treat them as accidental. As compared to the basic unity of human nature they are said to have but a subordinate significance. Granted that this humanistic view is plainly superior to the purely biological concept, according to which the organic and functional dissimilarities of the sexes make for an absolute differentiation, the Biblical interpretation, nevertheless, stands in sharp relief over against both of them. The second account of the creation of man in Genesis 2:7 is in its present context meant to serve as a commentary on the first one (Gen. 1:26-30) by stressing the difference of the sexes. Accordingly, woman's legal status among the Hebrews was quite different from that of the man. The Bible attaches such importance to the differentiation of the sexes that the full destination of man cannot be attained except by means of it. In order to be a human being I must live my life either as a man or as a woman.

For this reason, sexual differentiation is not simply a natural datum of life. Rather it is divinely destined to make a positive contribution to man's redemption. Since both sexes exist for the sake of an united and reconciled mankind their differences, far from being purely divisive, have also a positive value. By her eagerness to please the man the woman introduces charm and color, harmony, joy, and the spirit of light-heartedness into human life, no matter how critical the man may be of her love for adornment, her vanity, talkativeness, superficiality, and fondness for amusement. On the other hand the man by his desire to rule establishes order. He makes room for creativity, transformation of nature, and human accomplishments, yet will be told that with all this he is greedy of power, officious, pedantic, and overly ambitious for fame. Nevertheless by making the sexes so different God directed them toward each other so that they might supplement their specific nature in the unity of the flesh.

The question is frequently raised whether, aside from biological differences, women has really any definite characteristics and abilities. The advocates of equality appeal to statistics in support of their contention by calling attention to the many men who are, for example, cooks, tailors, and teachers, and on the other hand to the countless women who are actively engaged in industry, trade, or the academic professions. Nothing is proved thereby, however, except the fact that there are no specifically masculine or feminine jobs or callings. Both sexes seem capable of performing any kind of work necessary to maintain and advance the human race. It is little short of ridiculous or self-seeking, therefore, to bar women from certain professions and jobs. Yet it is true that a woman has a different way of reacting to certain life situations and fortunes, and when in the same position with a man she may do the same job yet will do it differently.

Because the sexes exist for each other their relationship needs definite forms of social life particularly during adolescence. This explains the educational value of leagues and organizations for youth of both sexes. If the time and place for young people to get together is left entirely to chance or their own discretion, the operation of the law of supply and demand will tend to direct their mutual relationships to occasions which serve the sexual desire to possess and to surrender. This has the serious disadvantage that under such conditions their personal Self is not at all involved.

The idea that a woman has no existence of her own, and is but an appendix of man, represents another rather common self-appraisal of man and woman. However, even if this idea were true in sexual relationship it would, nevertheless, completely disregard the part woman plays as mother. Man has a twofold aspiration toward the female sex: it provides to him the companion whom he wants totally to possess, yet it also gives him the mother toward whom he likes to withdraw for security, and into whose lap he yearns to return even in death. It is no accident that many religions use identical symbols for the grave and for the mother, for instance in Job 1:21. Since the woman knows about this deepest secret of the male heart she is in her love never solely anxious to love and attract and tempt him in order to bind him to herself as she surrenders to him. At the same time there is a motherly element in her love. She discovers that man, who is her master, is open and unprotected against an hostile world, vulnerable, uncertain of himself, unable to arrange his life pleasantly and comfortably, and anxious at times to forget the exacting demands of life and to play like a child. These two attitudes are so closely intertwined in married life that the woman is scarcely aware of her dual function. She combines in herself the roles of sweetheart, home maker, and companion. It would seem that outside of the strictly sexual sphere the woman is best able to engage in fruitful relations with the other sex through the medium of motherliness.

Whenever, apart from it, women enter into public or social life, and by asking questions or expressing doubts attempt to set the plodding male institutions into motion, they appeal, in the last analysis, to man's belief in his sexual superiority. No wonder that with the growing participation of women in the discussion of social and political problems in the eighteenth century a spirit of eroticism suffused French society. Women used their equality as a stimulus of male attention. On the other hand, when, in an objective and nonsexual manner, the woman enters into the man's business or professional circles he will reject her as a competitor or tell her that on account of her feminine mentality she is only moderately competent. Things are quite different when she allows her maternal instinct to tinge her activities. If only by bringing a flower to the office, or by addressing a sympathetic question to a fellow-worker or colleague, she is able to contribute to her group something for which men instinctively long yet are unable to provide for themselves. Probably there is no better definition of motherliness than the formula given by Ursula Laessig: the sheer necessity to provide joy for others. This evidences that man is as greatly dependent upon woman as she is upon him.

The Bible corroborates general experience by calling the woman "the weaker sex" (1 Pet. 3:7). Since this appraisal concerns the very nature of femininity, her greater seductiveness is inferred from the account of the Fall (1 Tim. 2:13-15, cf. 2 Cor. 11:13). In 1 Thessalonians 4:4 she is called the vessel into which the man deposits his seed.* This evaluation refers not simply to man's superior physical powers but also to the way men actually rule in public life. Undoubtedly, this Biblical view has contributed greatly to fortify the male prerogatives in the marital arrangement and it survives in the matrimonial law of the modern state. The woman is required to admit her dependence by taking the man's name. Whether there have ever been matriarchal societies in which the women had pre-eminent direction of legal and social matters is a question still under debate. Biological and legal differences, however, can never form the ultimate basis of evaluating the two sexes. For their dignity does not depend upon natural and historical factors but upon the places the sexes assume in God's plan for mankind.

The Dignity of the Sexes

In 1 Corinthians 11:3 Paul points out that this whole world is arranged in an hierarchical order. As the lordship of Christ over all men derives from the lordship of God, so there is a system of superiority and subordination among all creatures but specifically among mankind. But this hierachy is not an aristocratic structure of rank in which the upper class looks down upon the lower class without any upward relationship on the part of the subjects. The reciprocity within the order is emphasized in the Creation story. The man not only expresses his lordship by giving the woman her name (Gen. 2:23) but he also acknowledges her similar nature by calling her "flesh of my flesh." Accordingly, Paul emphasizes

* Some expositors refer this passage to the body of the man, however; but in that case the apostle would use a strange and confusing kind of expression.

the fact that all human relationships represent an organic connection between the body and its head. Hence it follows that not only all the members exist for each other, and are interdependent in the unity of the body, but also that superiority and inferiority have only a relative meaning. While in temporal matters, for example, the man is the head of the woman (1 Cor. 11:3) nevertheless in the light of Biblical understanding the difference vanishes: "There is neither male nor female, for ye are all one in Christ Jesus" (Gal. 3:28).

Only by giving earnest consideration to the two viewpoints of hierarchical order and equality in the Body of Christ can we arrive at a true Christian understanding of the dignity of the sexes. Adopting any other basis people will hold antagonistic and irreconcilable views, with the misogynist and the anti-feminist at the one extreme and the suffragette and the champion of mother's rights on the other. Temporary compromises may then be tried but to the satisfaction of no one, because neither of the sexes has any independent right to exist.

Under the influence of idealistic philosophy masculinity and femininity are usually understood as ideals which have to be realized by a personal effort. But interpreted in that way the individual would never realize himself because he lacks the degree of goodness which, according to this view, would make life meaningful. According to Mme. de Beauvoir, for example, it would be the perfect man who would deliver the perfect woman from her inferior status. In the Bible, too, masculinity and femininity are not considered meaningful as such. In order to realize their destination, however, it suffices to acknowledge two facts, namely, their reciprocal relationship in the unity of the flesh and their being destined for the upbuilding of God's people. This goal can be reached by all people.

Accordingly masculinity means the individual's willingness to be a man for a woman, and womanhood consists in a woman's readiness to exist for a man. Hence in order to have harmony of the sexes there is no necessity for ignoring the sexual differences because each sex acquires its meaning through its distinctness. Yet, what is more important, by faith the sin-bound and reluctantly-borne relations of superiority and subjection can be transformed into privileges because superiority becomes a responsibility and subjection a service of love. In that way the sexual relationship partakes of the life of God's people.

Thus, in describing the Christian life, the New Testament writers emphasize two aspects of the sexual relationship, namely, that the dignity of the sexes is based upon their mutual recognition and that by doing so the two partners attain to true selfhood. Paul will, for example, call attention to the fact that the wife is the honor (*doxa*) of her husband (1 Cor. 11:7). The husband's position of superiority becomes apparent only if his wife recognizes this fact. This means that a married woman who renounces the external evidences of her married status heaps dishonor on her head, i.e., her husband. Likewise, the husband is required to treat his wife "in sanctification and honor" (1 Thess. 4:4). Rejecting all attempts to ascribe the husband's superiority to any natural male qualities, Paul reminds the Corinthians that the man holds this position solely by divine appointment, and the man's inability to reproduce himself is a clear indication that by God's will a definite limitation has been imposed upon the natural state of masculinity. All men were born into this world by mothers (1 Cor. 11:11-12).

What we call the dignity of man and woman consists of an objective excellence which originates out of the divinely arranged correlation of the sexes and the destiny of mankind rather than merely subjective or conventional appraisals. Hence the individual possesses that dignity quite apart from engaging in sexual relations. Witness of its objective character is the fact that people sense it instinctively. Respect for the dignity of the female sex is expressed not only by the high regard in which the sweetheart is held but, above all, by the reverence shown for womanhood and motherhood. The special politeness with which men used to treat women in past generations was not a prejudice inherited from feudal days, but rather was the fruit of deep insight into the nature of life. On the other hand, modern men debase themselves by their indifferent and unchivalrous attitude toward women. Though allegedly meant to place woman on the same level with the man, such conduct deprives man of his superiority. When men today exhibit so much egotism and complacency toward women the women find it difficult to admire men.

Of course, modern women must accept some share of the blame

for this development. Their aspirations for economic and political equality have led them to a denial of the primordial correlation of the sexes. From a vocational or economic viewpoint the results may be satisfactory, but what a price women must pay for gaining these objectives! Abandoning the claim for respect of feminine dignity women have exposed themselves to humiliations in vocational and public life, and deprived themselves of the protection by which mores and customs had formerly emphasized their dignity. Modern man is prone to interpret women's equal status as implying that he has every right to hunt them as fair game for the satisfaction of his sexual desires.

The Biblical revelation illumines the regard in which the sexes hold each other instinctively. Because of the interdependence of the sexes the superior position of the man as head does not reduce woman to a condition of slavery. In no respect is femininity more slave-like or servant-like than masculinity; rather man's superiority consists in his obligation to take the initiative and to assume the responsibility for their common life. Whenever heterogeneous elements are united responsible leadership is required for the smooth functioning of the whole. Unless we realize that the relationship of the sexes is determined by God's plan for mankind it must seem objectionable to modern people that the woman is told to "fear" her husband (Eph. 5:33) and to be subject and obedient to him (1 Pet. 3:1; 1 Cor. 14:34). These demands are not the remnants of an obsolete social order of antiquity but rather derive from the fact that God contrived to redeem mankind by a man rather than by a woman. To be sure, this does not mean that the husband must be obeyed only if he himself is obedient to Christ as his head. The objective nature of the Divine plan demands general acceptance of the commandment. If, to the present day, women have not succeeded in becoming man's equals, the reason is not to be found in any immoral or tyrannical lordship of men over women but rather in the fact that God created two sexes and assigned them different goals.

The structure of this world is a three-dimensional one, not only in the physical universe but also in social relations. It has a top and a bottom, a front and a back, and in it some must direct while others will be led. Why God assigned to the male sex the superior position is a moot question, since the sexes may not choose the place they will occupy. Even though the husband may not care for his superior position yet God will hold him responsible for the success or failure of his marriage; and the wife who rebels against her husband's role as the responsible head must give account for her sin.

The wife naturally expects her husband to assume leadership in their married life. However, the mutuality of their relationship demands on his part consideration for her womanly nature and qualities. Though he should not always yield to his wife's whims and moods, yet he must realize that she is full of contradictions and frequently unable to understand her own inconstancy. All the more, she expects him to direct their mutual relationship in a definite and consistent manner. However, since the man's position of superiority is not based upon his natural qualifications its exercise does not go unchallenged. By his achievements in social and political life he must prove his right to the position he occupies. Not only in their love-play must he contend for his wife's recognition and conquer her but his marital position will suffer if he does not constantly prove his right to superiority instead of taking it for granted. Therefore, man is seriously concerned about his sexual virility, whereas there is no such thing as female impotence but only frigidity. Except as a phenomenon of old age sexual impotence has always mental causes. It may result from a husband's sense of inferiority which makes him doubt his ability to assume the male function as head; in some instances it is caused by moral scruples concerning his pre- or extramarital sexual life which prevent him from asserting himself in relation to his wife. Since the husband is the head he has a more direct relationship to matters of law and order than his wife, and thus finds his greatest satisfaction in political, economic, and technical achievements. However, the establishment of order being an act of generalization, man will, as a rule, show greater interest for the general than for the particular. This tendency of his mind sheds some light on the so-called polygamous disposition of the man. If we are to believe Goethe a man's unfaithfulness is not so much the result of his desire to possess a number of women at one time as of an innate deficiency of his sexual impulse. He is concerned with the feminine sex, as such, and only indirectly with some specific woman. Hence if a man does not feel personal love for the woman of his choice the fullness of life will elude him. The kind of knowledge which he acquires through promiscuity may inform him concerning various sex habits, yet he never thereby realizes that Selfhood and true life can be found in personal relations only. The situation is quite different for the woman. In her self-surrender she is bound to relate herself to one specific man and her surrender is conditioned by the particular situation. Thus the woman is by nature directed toward individual things. In turn, it is only indirectly, namely, by the regard for her husband, that she is enabled to establish an intrinsic order in her life. Apart from it order means for her outward neatness and tidiness.

Since, in the New Testament, the mutual relationship of both sexes is seen in the light of God's plan the emphasis placed upon the man's superiority does not imply any humiliation or disparagement of the woman. Just as the redemptive work of the risen Saviour could not have been perpetuated unless He had a body here on earth, namely, the Church, so the man's title of lord would be as empty as that of a king in exile if the woman had not been assigned to him as a companion. It follows from the asymmetrical relationship of the sexes that her companionship does not consist in her assuming a share of the work that he ordinarily performs. Of course she would not be his helpmate if she refused altogether to participate in his work, and hence there is always some division of work between husband and wife, though their respective obligations vary greatly at different times and in various sections of the world. Even though in our days the two sexes perform pretty much the same tasks in agriculture, in the factory, in the office, in commerce, and in the professions yet this does not mean that thereby the modern wife has become a better companion to her husband than in former times, when her work was in the main restricted to the kitchen and to the home, while he toiled in the fields or in the workshop. The woman's dignity as companion is not determined by the kind of work she performs but rather by the fact that both sexes work together for the attainment of a common goal.

The Fall of Man and Equal Rights

Some modern theologians have interpreted man's superior position as a particular punishment inflicted upon the woman for taking the initiative in the original Fall of man. Accordingly it is held that with the redemptive work of Christ her penalty is over. From an exegetical standpoint this view is untenable. It is true that, along with the other results of the Fall, God pronounces His judgment over Eve in Genesis 3:16: "He shall be your lord." However, the context does not indicate that this lordship is by itself an evil. Rather the evil is found in the fact that the woman desires for herself a partner, yet when the desire is fulfilled the partner turns out to be her lord. Thus, through her very femininity, she is brought from her state of freedom to one of subjection, and her hope to enjoy independent freedom by the side of her husband is, by the facts, unmasked as a dream. Neither does the New Testament refer the origin of man's superiority back to the Divine curse but considers it an implication of man's creation. It is derived from the fact that the woman was created out of man and for him, but not vice versa (1 Cor. 11:8 cf. 1 Tim. 2:13). Besides, in Christ's being the Head of the Church, Paul finds a revelation of the true meaning of the sexual relationship (1 Cor. 11:3). In other words, the superiority of the man, and thus the subjection of the woman, is a fundamental phenomenon of human life. That this mutual relation should often cause pain and displeasure in married life is not due to man's position of lordship but rather to the fact that sinful men and women are not willing to accord loving consideration to their partner's interests. So the husband's sinful unconcern for his wife's dignity causes him to exploit his lordship in sexual as well as in social relations. Whereas he has claimed for himself complete freedom in matters of sex he has been unwilling to make a similar concession to married women, and he shows contempt for their licentiousness, although he enjoys it. What vexes women in this respect is not so much the denial of freedom—for most women know that the freedom of the prostitute and the woman of easy virtue is of doubtful value—as the lack of respect for female dignity. The wife expects not only polite and chivalrous treatment from her husband but above all she wants to be assured that her presence makes all the difference in his life. Even though the husband's lack of reverence for his wife's dignity may not always cause a neurosis yet it profoundly affects her sense of self-respect.

In turn, however, women are apt to blame the male sex for the many difficulties resulting from their femininity. Unmarried women, resenting their loneliness, will ascribe their condition to the stupidity and callousness of the men who ignored their existence. Similarly the married woman, confronted by the chores of family life and marital frictions, envisions a different life for herself if only she had remained single. The independent modern woman, if we were to believe some women authors, would anticipate complete happiness from a life in which she allowed a man to enter into a sexual relationship with her while remaining economically and socially independent of the other sex.

In general a woman has greater difficulty in making satisfactory adjustment to her sexual nature than a man because sex permeates and conditions her daily life so forcefully and completely. It is therefore difficult for her always to assert her sense of womanly dignity. Although women are no longer regarded as impure during the menstrual period, as in Old Testament times and among many primitive peoples, yet the onset of menstruation greatly upsets a young girl and its regular recurrence is a source of disturbance and discomfort to all women. Furthermore, there are the additional dangers and difficulties of pregnancy, which in the Bible are considered as special burdens and punishments for the woman's part in the Fall (Gen. 3:16). The countless women's troubles and diseases, from puberty to the menopause, all of which are outside man's experience, frequently have, according to gynecologists, mental causes. Many women are fed up with all the physiological manifestations of their femininity and hate this burden. No wonder, then, that these undesirable conditions often affect the mutual respect and appreciations of the sexes. In order to avenge what seems to her a disregard for her person the woman will employ every feminine enchantment to enslave the "lord of creation" and keep him in sexual bondage.

To conclude. Although sin did not bring about the superior position of man, human sinfulness nevertheless obscures the true meaning of superiority and subjection in the sexual relationship to the extent that genuine respect for the dignity of sex is easily lost. By acquiring a particularly beautiful and intelligent woman for himself a man may merely satisfy his vanity. He may be more concerned about other people's approval of his choice than he is about his wife's personal worth and dignity. Or, a wife may make a bid for her husband's continued attention by a carefully chosen wardrobe, exquisite jewelry, or discerning make-up, though she may have no regard for him personally and take no interest in his life.

Jesus' personal attitude toward women taught his disciples what the true and ideal relationship between the sexes must be like. Unlike the rabbis', his message did not disparage women and some of them were among his followers and close associates (Luke 8:2-3). On one occasion He took a stand against the prevailing view that adultery was a special male prerogative but a crime on the part of a woman by telling the Scribes and Pharisees that no man who disdains woman's creaturely dignity has the right to condemn a woman for disregarding her husband's dignity by committing adultery (John 8:1-11). Even more particularly plain was the lesson He gave His disciples at the well at Sychar (John 4:4-30). When they were surprised to find their Master talking with a woman, He told them that the whole question of sex must be solved on the basis of the Gospel. God, Who is the Creator of both man and woman, desires the salvation of both, and, since salvation depends on personal faith, the Gospel must be addressed to both sexes without discrimination. Jesus was concerned about the fact that the Samaritan woman consorted with men yet was indiscriminate in her relationships. She rightly perceived that by taking her womanhood seriously Jesus had rendered her the kind of redemptive service she needed.

The equality of the sexes presupposes both the joint privilege of having the Gospel proclaimed indiscriminately to both sexes and their common duty to bear witness to it (John 4:16). In this respect, the story of the "woman who was a sinner" (Luke 7:37-50) is especially enlightening. Jesus can hardly have missed the erotic element in the woman's act of anointment, yet He not only defends her against His host's harsh and mean insinuation but He even assures her of God's forgiveness. By His statement that "her sins which are many are forgiven, for she loves much" (Luke 7:47), Jesus does not condone her doubtful love affairs let alone proclaim them the basis for forgiveness. Rather He accepts her action and her tears as expressions of repentance for her past sins, and as true womanly evidence of her love for Him as her sole helper. Her repentance and love prove the divine transformation of her heart, and in turn this gracious gift ratifies her forgiveness. Jesus' recognition of the real meaning of her act confirms her both in her humanity and her womanhood.

Though God's plan aims at the formation of His people, that is to say a collectivity, faith has never ignored the differentiation of the sexes in the process of redemption. This is made very plain in 1 Timothy 2:15, "The woman shall be saved in (or rather, through) child-bearing." Thereby Paul shows how realistically saving faith must be understood. Since the divine curse laid upon a sinful mankind manifests itself in the woman through the pains of childbirth and all the burdens connected with womanhood, repentance on the part of the woman is her readiness to accept that condition as placed upon her by God's just will. Similarly, however, she ought to recognize the divine grace by which she is enabled to preserve the human life through childbirth. Thus it is not the act of giving birth to a child by which the woman is saved—Paul is far from promising her a way of self-redemption—but rather the faith by which she accepts her womanhood and all the inconveniences and troubles connected therewith in the light of Christ's redemptive work. The correctness of this interpretation is proven by Paul's concluding statement, "if they (i.e., both spouses) continue in faith and charity and holiness with sobriety."

In view of the common service rendered to God by both sexes, Paul can also state that there is neither man nor woman in Christ (Gal. 3:28) because both are equally privileged in their being members of God's people. They work for a united mankind under divine rule. However, Christ's saving work does not destroy or abolish their sexual differences. To mention only one instance, Jesus chose men but no women as His ambassadors, not because of woman's unfitness for the task but rather because, in view of the Jewish prejudice against women such an appointment would have been inappropriate and ineffective. A change of attitude was needed before women could assume their place in the Church.

In the light of the Biblical teaching it can be said that any arrangement in public life by which women are granted special rights will invariably do more harm than good unless the dignity and interdependence of the sexes are thereby safeguarded. Although women not only outnumber men in the population of most countries but have also been given equal voting rights with men, yet men determine almost exclusively how the mighty and dreadful technological discoveries of today shall be utilized, and what trends future research must take. So it happens that in our national life the political, military, economic, and athletic interests outweigh in importance all other considerations. This state of affairs shows clearly that the universal suffrage was not granted for the defense of the specific interests of wives and mothers but rather for the increase of support the male representatives of the nation are coveting. However, in a healthy social order the future of the nation must not be determined solely by men but by families, and the welfare of families must take precedence over considerations of security. For what is the use of security when the family perishes? Since God gave the dominion over nature to both sexes (Gen. 1:28-29) no social progress can be made if the interests of one sex are promoted at the expense of the other.

XII. RIGHT AND DUTY OF SEXUAL RELATIONSHIPS

The Obligation to Sexual Relationship

If the sexual union is an indispensable means for the execution of God's redemptive plan has anyone the right to remain unmarried? Or is every sexually mature person obligated to seek out a partner of the other sex? If with the Lutheran theologians we consider marriage as an "order of Creation" an unconditional duty to marry seems to be the implication. On the other hand, the Roman Catholic Church's requirement of a celibate priesthood and the belief in the meritorious character of the vow of virginity indicate some definite restrictions. Where are we to look for the truth? The answer is not to be sought in the nature of sex but rather in the significance of human relations.

Whenever I meet another person it is Christ who offers me thereby the opportunity of finding Him. The other person is destined to help me transform my life into that of a child of God. Man's natural egotism engenders the wish to shape one's life exclusively by means of one's personal gifts and talents. To counteract that tendency God sent Christ into the flesh. By living our human life He reveals that we must enter into mutual relationships and learn to understand each other if our lives are to be changed into true humanity.

The fact that the other person is God's gift to me places an obligation upon me. Since Christ has led me to this other person I dare not depend upon my own discretion to determine how I will treat him. I would be guilty of despising God's gift if I did not deal with him as I would with Christ. A general attitude of friendliness and love will not do. Since the other person is an individual in his own right, and has come out of a definite set of circumstances, I am now bound to take these factors into serious consideration in order to work together with him in a spirit that befits God's people. This obligation extends also to sexual relationships. The sexual impulse is not by itself a temptation of the Devil, but rather God uses it to arouse me to a sense of my vocation as a male or female. This call demands a response. I have no right simply to disregard the existence of all persons of the other sex. However, my response to this call need not necessarily lead to a sexual relationship, either. In most instances this is precisely the form my response ought not to take. The nature of my response must meet two demands. Inasmuch as the other person is an individual, the response must be determined by the individual task assigned to me as well as to the other person as members of God's people. The very fact, however, that we are all sexually attracted by persons of the other sex requires also my preparedness to marry when the occasion arises. The virtues of virginity and celibacy do not have a greater value than the sexual relationship, though, as will be shown they have a considerable educative value in the history of mankind.

Paul's advice that it is good for a person not to marry has nothing to do with the bachelor's desire to find an easy and comfortable way of life by shunning marriage. Such attitude, far from fulfilling God's will, expresses a selfish and unthankful spirit toward God. The Bible teaches that marriage is the rule for adult life.

The Temptations

It should not be denied that this general positive affirmation of sex is fraught with considerable dangers. Since God treats us as adults the life of faith is anything but child's play. It is a battlefield on which we must contend against the powers of evil.

We cannot affirm the claims of sexual desire without also granting erotic love the right to exist, for it is the normal and most effective way to bridge the gap between myself and another person by whom I am sexually attracted. But erotic love implies the danger of entering into sexual relations before it has been decided whether or not this is the partner God has in mind for me.

There is still another danger implied in sexual attraction. A person may be ready to obey the divine call, but his faith has not yet attained a proper understanding of the true dignity and destiny of the sexes. Thus he wants to enter into a lifelong inviolable fellowship, yet he marries for no higher reason than to acquire a housekeeper, a bed fellow, or a servant. Likewise a woman may enter matrimony for purposes of economic security, or social standing—such marriages, even when contracted by Christians, are an abomination to God. Even though both partners may remain faithful to each other in sexual relations they will never attain that personal fellowship which alone imparts real meaning to marriage. Others confuse the Christian respect for the dignity of their partner with the ideal image of a sweetheart or lover that they carry about with them. These Faustian characters and Don Juans are so obsessed with the ideal image of their Helena that they never take any one woman seriously as a person. In love with their wish-image they are inevitably driven from one woman to another only to languish in the surfeit of their desires. The response to the Divine call, on the other hand, is a simple readiness to live with and for the other person and to promote the development of his faith to the best of one's abilities.

This two-fold responsibility must be assumed under all circumstances, however. We cannot enjoy the other person's affection and appreciate it as a divine gift unless we are willing, in God's stead, to accept responsibilty for him. For lack of a common spiritual basis marriages between Christians and non-Christians, and even between Protestants and Catholics, are seriously handicapped. As a rule it is impossible in such unions to share in the partner's spiritual life, and thus God's purpose for their lives easily vanishes from sight. Since the other person has not been accepted as a Divine gift more is lost than is gained by such a marriage.

Reasons for Celibacy

From a New Testament viewpoint, the inner conviction of a divine call must determine whether or not a person should marry. Because of the temporary function of sex the Bible does not impose an unconditional duty to marry.

Age is a decisive factor. Since marriage requires personal fellowship, it must not be consummated until a partner has attained to maturity both physically and psychically. In order to get married a person must be able to assume the responsibility the spouses have for each other. Even though in some states the marriage laws allow marriage at an age when people have hardly reached sexual maturity, Christians should be taught to refrain from early marriages. Adolescents are hardly good parents, and immaturity in personal relations is one of the principal causes of wrecked marriages.

But even adult people are not under absolute obligation to marry. Sexual union is not the supreme value in life. However, since sex is indispensable to God's plan of salvation only the most compelling reasons, in accord with His redemptive purposes, can release a person from the duty to marry. No one may act arbitrarily in this matter.

Jesus gives three justifiable reasons for the celibate life (Matt. 19:12). First of all some people have been made incapable of sexual life by castration or sterilization. However, such surgical operations are not necessarily barriers to marriage or to sexual relationship, particularly in the case of women. The resultant barrenness is no obstacle to a genuine personal relationship. Nevertheless, marriage, in such instances, is advisable only if both spouses understand that there can never be any children of their own. In recent times physicians have advised sterilization for social reasons in cases where, otherwise, hereditary deficiencies might be transmitted and the offspring is likely to be a financial burden for the community. Yet all these cases require the greatest possible care. Sterilization should be confined to persons who are mentally unfit to act in a responsible way, and to instances where the transmission of mental illness or permanent invalidity would preclude the child from living a genuinely human and self-sustaining life.

In the second group are those who by nature are unsuited for sexual life, either on account of physical deformations or because they are incapable of sexual stimulation (Matt. 19:12). We shall note later on that these persons are not unqualifiedly unsuited for marriage.

The third group is composed of those persons who, for the sake of work in the Kingdom of God, feel constrained to silence the call of sex within themselves. Such decisions must not be made arbitrarily but must issue from a sense of personal dedication to God's cause. Only by persons who identify themselves with God's intent for mankind, and who are clearly aware of a divine call for full-time evangelistic work, may the duty of sexual relationship be disavowed. However, the simple fact of being a Christian and thus under obligation always to do God's will is in itself not a valid reason for renouncing marriage.

Paul deals with this group of 1 Corinthians 7:27. He holds that he who is able to live without a wife should do so, for a Christian is principally called to the propagation and realization of the Gospel. But Paul points out that this is by no means a general commandment. On the contrary. If sexual continence only increases sexual desire this is a sign that such a person has not been granted the special gift of virginity. Paul's exposition of 1 Timothy 5:11ff, concerning the remarriage of young widows, follows the same line of thought. We miss Paul's meaning if, following the theologians of the Middle Ages, we interpret it as meaning that marriage is but a medicine or a palliative for unchastity. The apostle does not deal with immorality in this verse but rather with the problem of channeling sexual vitality in an appropriate way. No one can know in advance whether he is better fit for marriage or for celibacy, experience only can tell. For instance, if sexual desire so persistently and forcefully impels a person toward the other sex that even his readiness to work for the sake of Christ is unable to suppress it (1 Cor. 7:37) then permanent celibacy would be contrary to God's will. For even if he refrained from sexual acts such a person would commit sin, because he refused to exercise his God-given freedom to enter the estate best suited to him. Experience provides ample proof that in such circumstances celibacy impedes the development of spiritual life. Most frequently the frustration of the sexual desire leads to overindulgence in eating and drinking and induces a materialistic conception of life.

Quite different is the type of person whom Jesus describes as those who have made themselves eunuchs for the Kingdom of God's sake. They may be strongly attracted to the other sex, but since they have dedicated themselves completely to the service of God marriage ties would be a hindrance to their full devotion. Jesus never said that all work and service in the Kingdom of God demanded celibacy. In some circumstances the messengers of God must marry because their conduct in marriage will demonstrate that man's natural life is no obstacle to the Kingdom of God but rather its foundation. From this point of view, the decision of the Reformers "to free the office of the pastor from the bonds of celibacy" was the right response to the historical situation. When, for so many centuries, the theology and practice of the church had treated sex as sin and thus at best as tolerable, when practiced in marriage, the leaders of the new movement had to show by their example that there was nothing wrong with sex as such. In times, however, when people worship physical life and its pleasures as the highest value it is necessary to indictate by way of example that our life transcends itself. Under such circumstances it may be necessary for God's messengers deliberately to renounce sexual life. This fact is clearly illustrated by Jesus' life. Had Jesus been devoid of sexuality He would hardly have made reference to the lustful look (Matt. 5:28) for such insight is not attained by theoretical deliberation, but is born out of victory over desire. Jesus renounced the happiness of sexual love for the sake of His mission, therefore He was able to give mankind an example of genuine love instead of its customary simile in sexual or erotic love. Surely, Jesus' life also proves the error of a literal interpretation of such words of His as Matthew 19:12. The Lord does not require self-mutilation, as Origen wrongly surmised, but renunciation of the desire for sexual relationships.

However, people who are unmarried, or have never known the joy of sexual relationships, are not therefore better than those living in marriage. When His disciples were perplexed about the risks of sexual life and the rigorous requirements for marriage (Matt. 19:11ff) Jesus impressed upon them that voluntary renunciation of marriage and sexual life is necessary only when the specific form of service in the Kingdom of God explicitly demands it.

There is no justification for the Roman Catholic view that life in the monastic orders with its voluntary lifelong celibacy is superior to the married estate, carrying a special merit with it. However, since the ecclesiastical requirement of a celibate priesthood is not a matter of faith, but simply a practical measure for better administration of the office, its evaluation rests on a different basis.

The Right of Sexual Relationship

One question still presents itself: if sexual relations and marriage are God's will, and are, therefore, moral obligations for all persons who have not been expressly called by God to some other way of life, what are those persons to do who by particular circumstances have been prevented from getting married? Shall we follow the Old Testament, where the problem is raised, for example, in the story of Lot's daughters (Gen. 19:30ff) or of Tamar, a woman who had been prematurely widowed (Gen. 38:6-30)? While this is an age-old problem it appears to be particularly pressing today.

Espousing modern naturalism, many people believe that sex is an absolute necessity for life, and that every sexually mature person has the right to engage in sexual activities. Their arguments may be reduced to two: the one is purely biological, the other more metaphysical. The former view holds that life-long continence is harmful for a sexually mature person, and that, in the long run, is bound to engender both physical and psychical troubles. The other view points out that since every person is a member of one of the sexes he or she can never become a real person until his sexual destination is fulfilled. His life would be a failure if he had never experienced sexual intercourse with a person of the opposite sex.

At first sight it seems that the first argument could be refuted easily. Is it not a well known fact that there are many persons who have never had sexual relationships but yet enjoy good physical and mental health? However, their experience is counterbalanced by the considerable number of people whose undoubted sexual difficulties and troubles make them a burden for their environment and the best source of income for the psychotherapists. It must be admitted that sexual repressions are today the major cause of nervous and mental disorders. If these results are not generally existent in the life of the Catholic monastic orders it does not follow that for a person's health it makes no difference whether his sexual life is actualized or not. The Catholic experience only proves that the function of sexuality is not confined to its physical expression, and that given a strict spiritual discipline the usual harmful consequences of the suppression of sex can be successfully averted. The biological argument may be effectively refuted by the following reasoning: though human life is incomplete without sex, sexual intercourse is not, under all circumstances, necessary for the fulfillment of life since sexual desire is no ultimate but points beyond itself. To the metaphysical argument we object that the things of the world about us, including sex, are good gifts of God and, therefore, we have a God-given right to use them (1 Cor. 8:8; 1 Tim. 4:3ff). However, our freedom as the children of God demands that we remain unfettered by them and should use them according to God's plan.

Freedom means, that I am under no physiological necessity or moral obligation to submit to my sexual desires in every circumstance, but must bear in mind that the other person has been assigned to me by God as my neighbor. There are instances where two persons feel strongly attracted to each other yet where the stronger one is under obligation to withstand his own and his partner's sexual desires. The Christian service which we are called to render to one another will entail that under circumstances in which marriage is impossible people who are in love with each other should forego the possibility of sexual relations. Such a freedom from sex presupposes a willingness to subordinate one's whole life to the purposes of God. Hence the Bible recognizes no general and unlimited right to sexual intercourse. If ever I encounter a partner with whom I may enter into a sexual relationship comformable to God's will I may accept this as a divine gift. Nobody has a natural claim to find a suitable partner. The Creation story expresses this beautifully. It says that it was God who gave Adam a companion. While it is our privilege to pray for the fulfillment of our desires, nobody has a right to steal what God has withheld from him.

Undoubtedly the sudden termination of a married sexual relationship by the death of a spouse, by divorce, or a long involuntary separation creates a serious mental strain. However, the New Testament's more profound concept of sex shows these afflicted persons how they may still lead a satisfying life. For instance, there was a special office of widowhood in the early Christian congregations (1 Tim. 5:3-10). In the light of faith the widow was admonished to accept her loss as a divine suggestion to dedicate her entire life to service in the Christian congregation. When otherwise the sexual desire would become too intense, or the sense of the loss of her spouse too oppressive, then caring for others would help to dispel the excessively egotistic concern with self. This experience is still valuable today, though our congregations lack special institutions and organizations for such cases. Paul realized however that serious temptations might afflict persons not yet fully established in their faith, even in this kind of service. Therefore, he fixed strict requirements for the office of widowhood, and repeatedly advised young widows to remarry.

We should keep in mind, however, that the sexually perplexing situation in which a great number of adolescents and marriageable women find themselves in our time is not their own fault. The nations must collectively share the blame for a situation which they have created through warfare, revolutions, or mass dislocations. The responsibility for the difficult situation and the sexual chaos in which the people thereby afflicted find themselves must therefore be assumed by society as a whole. Unless we seriously attempt to alleviate their difficult lot God will make us accountable for their guilt. Through the vexing pressure of unfulfilled desires, which is so symptomatic of our age, God reveals to us what hardship people and nations place upon each other. In the sinful and inconsiderate pursuit of their interests and goals they fail to realize how their egotistic endeavors will affect other lives. Nations wage wars, start revolutionary upheavals, and try to amass great fortunes, with little or no thought for the anguish of the people who must bear the dreadful consequences of their exploits. Would God we would heed the severe warning that the Lord gives to us by revealing the chaos we have brought about in sexual matters through the pursuit of our legitimate national and economic interests! We see his judgment in the fact that God leaves us in our perplexity. Sociologists, educators, and psychologists are garrulously speaking and profusely writing about these problems, but without any noticeable success. If, as Christians, we accept our confusion as a divine sign then we'll realize that this calamity of unfulfilled desire and all of its accompanying evils and troubles are a burden laid vicariously upon these women and young people for a guilt in which all of us share.

XIII. SIGNIFICANCE AND VALUE OF MARRIAGE

The Origin of Marriage

The previous chapters were devoted to a rather general discussion of sexuality, sexual intercourse, and sexual fellowship, with only an occasional and incidental reference to marriage. This, of course, is not due to an intentional undervaluation of marriage but rather to respect for the basic facts. Obviously sex is a more elemental and universal factor in the history of mankind than the marital relationship. Yet there remains the question: does marriage have any special significance that is not already implied in sexual life, and are there any particular standards applicable to marriage beyond those already previously discussed?

Marriage is a lifelong mutual bond between a man and a woman based on sex. However, its nature as a permanent bond is not derived from the sexual desire which rather recoils from limitations. Paradoxically marriage has its origin in the problematical nature of sex itself. It is its temporary character and the resulting inability to impart an ultimate meaning and fulfillment to life that has led to the establishment of marriage as a necessary social institution. Any attempt to derive marriage from sexual or personal love's desire to last forever is a bit of romantic reverie; as though mankind had to elevate marriage to the status of a social institution for no other reason but that human beings might be able to demonstrate to each other their mutual love for the rest of their lives. On the contrary. There is always an element of mistrust implied in the marriage contract. As a publicly formed alliance, marriage is intended to bind the partners together even against their own will. Erotic love, on the other hand, may become a threat to marriage, and under certain circumstances serve to disintegrate it. F. W. Schlegel keenly observed that erotic love is bound to be faithless precisely when it attempts to be genuine, for it does not love the other person but only his physical presence. Because every person's individuality is limited and expresses only a certain aspect of human nature, erotic love passes fleetingly from one person to another if the presence of the first partner becomes boring or unsatisfying.

In Lutheran ethics, as we have seen, marriage is considered an "order of Creation" implied in the origin of man. The proof texts most frequently cited are Genesis 2:24 and Matthew 19:4-5. But Jesus' application of the Old Testament passage shows the ambiguity of the concept of order used in this case. For our Lord understood the co-ordination of the sexes not as a divine decree that must be obeyed, much less as an injunction that needs to be enforced. He pointed out that since the correlation of the sexes is a basic fact of Creation reverence for God's work should prevent mankind from undoing it. There is nothing in this view that would warrant our considering the social institution of marriage as such an order of Creation.

There is no Biblical commandment establishing marriage as an institution or demanding marital faithfulness. Rather marriage is considered a social arrangement enjoying a divine sanction because it incorporates mutuality and for that reason adultery and the profanation of marriage are prohibited. But these demands originate, as has been indicated, in the dignity of sex. The religious meaning of marriage lies in the fact that it is a divine gift. By itself it does not belong to the realm of things commanded. Only indirectly, then, with reference to the abuses of the divine gift, it became necessary to apply moral commands to marriage.

Originally, the institution of marriage was probably set up by social groups as an arrangement to insure the order, stability, and permanence of group life. From the very beginning, then, it was not a private arrangement of individual men and women but was a form of social life prescribed by the group. It is likely to be a bond imposed upon the men in the first place in order to insure the life, safety, and rights of women and children. Man's desire for property and his jealousy on the one hand, and, on the other woman's sexual dependence and her need for protection were probably factors which facilitated the enactment of such regulations. Thus it is the very instability of sex itself which tends to replace the loose ties of sexual attraction by the more stringent bonds of institutional customs and law. For our purposes it is immaterial to know whether monogamy or polygamy was the original form of marriage.

The value of marriage is not depreciated by tracing its origin to more or less selfish instincts, or to considerations of personal advantage. The fact that marriage is an universal institution makes it clear that, although men are concerned only about their own happiness and advancement, God uses human weakness as a means to achieve His purposes. Though people may regard marriage simply as a social custom and legal form, yet it serves to protect the divine meaning of sex. The mere existence of an external marriage bond makes it more difficult for the partners to betray their sexual mutuality than if they lived together on a voluntary basis only and without binding obligations.

Except for the institution of marriage society would quickly be reduced to a state of complete sexual and social confusion and anarchy. It is true that in Africa and Melanesia, notwithstanding abundant premarital sexual promiscuity, community life is exemplary in many respects. But the fact should not be overlooked that even such free associations are formed according to definite rules and that they grow out of the background of a community with fixed forms of marriage. From a biological viewpoint sex is a more urgent necessity than marriage, for without sexual intercourse mankind would cease to exist. But persons endowed with sexuality attain the true meaning of their sexual life through marriage only. Therefore, marriage has a particular dignity beyond that of sex.

The Dignity of Marriage

What then is the special significance that marriage possesses, in contrast with all transitory and free sexual associations? First of all, an erroneous idea frequently encountered in modern books on marriage needs to be dispelled. They speak very confidently of sublime, ideal, model, and happy marriages, and from this supreme ideal of marriage they seek to derive its general meaning. But such loftly flights of the imagination mean little to the average person. Equally mistaken is the notion that love alone imparts value to marriage. It is fortunate that the Bible, avoiding such idealistic speculations, simply accepts marriage as a universal institution of social life. Consequently the commandment not to commit adultery is impartially applied to the most idealistic as well as to all the dull, stunted, or bungled marital relationships. The value of marriage is not primarily determined by what people make of their marriages but by the fact that a divine gift was imparted to the couple when they entered this estate.

According to the Catholic Church marriage is a sacrament that mediates a special divine grace. However the Catholic theologians have great difficulty in showing what the foundation of its sacramental character is. On the one hand, they teach that the unity intended by the spouses by means of a voluntary sexual act forms the basis of the sacrament, in which case marriage would not differ essentially from any other voluntary sexual alliance; on the other hand, according to Catholic teaching there can be no sacrament if Christian faith is not present. Although Protestantism has refused to recognize marriage as a sacrament yet it appropriately designates matrimony as holy. Plainly, the theological differences are the result of divergent understanding of the nature of a sacrament. According to Catholic teaching any sign instituted by Christ as a means of grace is a sacrament, whereas the Protestant interpretation designates as sacraments those ceremonies only by which we participate in the redeeming grace of Christ. This redemptive quality is absent in sexual union, and even in a Christian marriage there is nothing that would transmute the divine gift of sexual union into redemptive grace.

What then is the gift God imparts to mankind in marriage which is not found in sexual unions? In the latter relationship masculinity and femininity already obtain a very significant positive function as a result of their correlation. The man is masculine for the woman's sake and vice versa. In marriage, or more exactly in the Christian one, a further element is added however. From the idea of Christ's marriage with His people, both spouses learn to interpret the unity of the flesh as implying their destination for a strictly personal fellowship in which the man assumes complete responsibility for their common life, while the woman becomes ready for dedicated service. Though these great possibilities are implied in any marriage, people without Christian faith are unaware of the depth of personal life to which their union may penetrate. Just as Christ's love for His Church is not only a fellowship of spirits, but extends into all of its practical and historical activities, so the personal union of the spouses is not confined to their common spiritual life, but permeates all the activities and events of daily life—in health and in sickness, in poverty and in wealth. This then is the divine grace manifested in marriage, that two people who are sexually attracted to each other are moved by God to enter into a lifelong alliance for better or for worse. Since no one knows what the future holds, marriage is always a venture. The validity of the marriage vow is not contingent upon the partners' mutual suitability to each other, although normally people select a marriage partner who seems to give the promise of an harmonious relationship. But since no one knows in advance how radically he and his partner may change in the next ten or twenty-five years, it is an evidence of divine grace that in spite of this great uncertainty the spouses should be ready to promise each other lifelong fidelity.

There are no exceptions to the statement that all marriages are made in Heaven. If some people make a hell out of their married life they only prove their unwillingness to use God's gift for the purpose for which it was destined. Thus, marriage is neither solely based upon sexual attraction or social requirements nor does God sanctify it in a vacuum, but rather He uses men and women in their actual condition to work for the attainment of His goal and theirs. Hence the Christian marriage is more than a mere social or ecclesiastical institution. Nevertheless it is not by itself holy but only when both partners accept it as God's way of bringing them together for a lifelong union. Its sanctification is therefore a constant process rendered possible by the fact that God provides all the necessary means and abilities to use His gift in understanding and obedience.

Christian esteem of the superior value of the institution of marriage should, therefore, not be based upon the defects of the unmarried estate and much less upon the moral dangers and the risks of venereal infection that attach to extramarital and occasional sexual relationships; nor is marriage to be thought of principally as a safeguard against sinful indulgence of sexual desire. Rather it is only through the Christian marriage that one understands that and why unmarried persons are unhappy and dissatisfied. Similarly it is from the benevolent results of marriage that one perceives the harm people inflict upon themselves by entering into extramarital relationships.

Notwithstanding the fact that mutual responsibility and dedicated service in marriage are not exclusively Christian virtues Christian marriage alone is holy, nevertheless, because within it these virtues are implemented by faith. From their relationship with God the spouses learn to live together in their marriage. This primacy of faith explains, in turn, why it is that an unmarried person, too, may find full satisfaction in life and why beyond the fellowship of marriage the spouses can be of real service to other people. Nevertheless, marriage partners are the recipients of a special blessing because there is no other relationship of life in which more varied and intimate contacts can be made. Therefore, celibacy or the unmarried state always implies a renouncement or loss.

XIV. THE BLESSINGS AND BURDENS OF MARRIAGE

The Transcendence of Sexual Desire

We can best understand the greatness of the divine gift which Christian marriage imparts to us by noting the dissatisfaction so frequently attending sexual desire and its fulfillment. True enough everybody does not experience it with equal intensity. It is a far cry from the momentary melancholy a boy may feel in the arms of his girl to the piercing clarity with which Strindberg speaks of the disappointments of the loving heart, or the mockery with which cartoonists constantly show up marriage. But people would not react so paradoxically to the satisfaction of their sexual desires were it not that at the bottom of their heart the vision of the love of God provided the standard by which they measured their experiences. Because of this love of God man realizes that the actual attainments of life never are ends in themselves, but rather point to the supreme goal for which he is destined. This love of God is the matrix in which all the other kinds of love originate. Thus it happens that, in spite of all disillusionment and painful experiences, people persist in entering into sexual relationships and in singing the praises of love.

This transcendence of sex assumes diverse forms according to life's various situations. Since it manifests itself, for example, as desire for genuine fellowship the woman, consonant with her role of Self-giving, will feel any separation or temporary interruption of sexual fellowship particularly painful. With the man it may be sensed in the tormenting experience that the dream-image of his beloved appears so much brighter and enticing than the real woman he lives with. This leads to the characteristic restlessness and infidelity of the male sex. Women seem to have less difficulty in reconciling the contrast between their dream-images and the realities in their lives—women are, as a rule, more realistic in matters of love—while in turn the absence from the beloved is generally less painful for the man because he finds comfort in the ideal image of her that emerges before him in all its enticing brightness.

Furthermore, the transcendence of sex may be experienced as a tension between the physical act of sexual intercourse and the disposition for personal life. The greater the passion the plainer it is that the sexual relationship cannot be completely one of person to person. This aspect of sex is the deepest reason why it appears so easily as something indecent, and why the woman can have the feeling that she is only a pleasure-object for the man's desires. True sexual fellowship requires a yearning for personal relationship.

Again, there is the inconstancy of sexual desire. While the desire itself is not directed toward a specific person but toward the other sex in general, yet any actual sexual relationship so profundly affects one's personal life that it makes people unwilling to serve merely as representatives of the other sex. Hence it is that the man, who assumes full freedom for himself in his sexual relationships, nevertheless expects complete faithfulness on the part of the woman. Nothing is so damaging to his sexual pride as a woman's reserve and irresponsiveness to his wooing, or her sovereign decision to terminate a sexual relationship. In her refusal it is not just his body which has been rejected but his very Self. Faced with the constant possibility of pregnancy the woman, in turn, desires security in the sexual relationship. She wants not only to be assured that nothing has happened, but also cherishes the wish for a husband and a home of her own. In them she feels herself acknowledged as a personality.

Finally, mental tensions are created by the fact that a dominant place in one's life is occupied by a sexual relationship with another person, and that, nevertheless, both sexual surrender and sexual possession lack an ultimate meaning. A temporary or brief sexual relationship raises the question of its worth-whileness—did one receive from the other person in proportion as one gave? In a permanent union it will easily happen that the man who pursues energetically the achievement of some professional or vocational goal is inclined to regard the woman as a hindrance to his plans. He finds that she takes up too much of his time, strength, and thought, and therefore he is torn to and fro between his love for her and the determination to end the relationship entirely. On the other hand, the woman having given herself completely to the man expects a proportionate return. Yet she knows that to possess the man completely is impossible. A man who did not divide his time between her and his spheres of male interest, but lived only for her, would not be a true man, and therefore would not be desirable.

Thus sexual desire directs the individual beyond himself in various ways, unaware of what it is driving at yet never fully contented either. Marriage only can resolve these tensions, and nothing but a Christian marriage will give complete satisfaction. This is the special blessing God has laid upon marriage.

The Blessings of Marriage

By divine arrangement, the lifelong union willed by the two people who enter marriage is the source of many blessings both in their personal life and in their social relations. The divine character of that blessing can be seen in the fact that it rests upon every marriage, regardless of the form in which it is contracted or its attendant circumstances, whereas it does not accompany temporary sexual relationships. People are instinctively aware of the divine blessing of marriage. A man expresses this by the fact that when he marries he leaves the parental home and thereby assigns a secondary position to his filial ties (Gen. 2:24). Likewise, a woman is firmly determined to have her man despite the dark picture of marriage others may have presented to her (Gen. 3:16).

What then are these good things that God imparts to married people? An American judge has recently summed it up as "aid, assistance, enjoyment, sexual relations, love, conjugal affection, companionship, felicity, advice, counsel, comfort, co-operation and mutual service." We can subsume them under the following five headings, keeping in mind that the above list did not specifically refer to Christian marriage but rather to an institution deeply influenced by Protestant ethics. They are: a fellowship of mutual service, expressed by a sense of responsibility and dedication; a mutual regard for personality; a sense of security; the promise of progeny; and the sanctification of their bodies.

To begin with, when two persons assume the mutual obligation to live together for the rest of their lives then the unity of the flesh is transformed into a life-long fellowship. Although the unity of the flesh becomes a reality at the first sexual union, yet it is only through the bond of marriage that its meaning and scope will be understood and experienced. The value of married life is not to be found in the opportunity of having a lifelong partner for sexual relations. Rather the couple experiences the paradox that only by serving another person can one truly become a Self. Individuality and dependence as realized in marriage not only do not exclude each other but mutually condition each other.

This experience engenders mutual helpfulness, consideration, willingness and effort to understand the partner, mutual esteem and reverence. The fellowship of marriage differs from every other relationship because it is based upon the couple's masculinity and femininity and upon sexual experience. But the common life experience of the couple is not the result of their sexual relationship; rather it originates in their determination to live with and for each other in the spirit of mutual obligation. Therefore, this mutual attitude does not change when sexual relations terminate. Even in old age married people will stay together not simply as good friends but as man and wife. A childless marriage is therefore not meaningless, even if the couple knew from the beginning of their marriage that they would never be blessed with children of their own. True marriage develops genuine fellowship and complete mutuality.

Secondly, there is mutual esteem. The spiritual confusion of our age may be characterized by the manifest mistrust people exhibit toward each other. Everybody attempts therefore to live his own life and avoids dependence on others. People are apparently unaware of the great treasures of fellowship. Typical of these attitudes is the romantic idea that marriage is an I-Thou relationship. It is assumed that an harmonious relationship between husband and wife is possible only when both have developed their distinctive individualities to the highest degree. If this were true then love between husband and wife would be nothing more than a regard for one's own worth, and for the spouse only insofar as he or she reflected that value. Mme. de Beauvoir expresses this misconception in a rather startling manner. According to her the ideal relationship of the sexes will be realized when both man and woman are conscious of their individual and personal values. In that case they will be able to live together in absolute freedom and without reciprocal obligations. But, as a matter of fact, such individual independence would defeat its very purpose. Though these two people would esteem each other as fullfledged personalities yet, with their desire to remain free, they would open the door to disunion in their relationship. Sex would then be something subordinate, like dining with another person. Since it lacked mutual obligation the Self would not be involved in such a sexual relationship. Sex then is simply a biological fate from which there is no possible escape. Yet, what a tremendous difference there is between the personal involvement in a sexual relationship on the one hand and noncommital partaking of a common meal at which people meet accidentally! The very freedom of such an association debases the woman to a source of pleasure for the man, and the man's tendency to live a fragmentary and self-contained life is abetted. Against such a fate, even supreme high-mindedness would prove to be defenseless.

In married life, on the other hand, sex is not an incidental factor, but rather a manifestation of the mutual lives of the spouses. Far from being a mere means for obtaining pleasurable experience it gives expression to the personal fellowship of the partners. By means of it the spouses learn to grant each other equal dignity and mutuality of esteem notwithstanding the differences of their sexual impulses and personal interests. Granted that such development cannot eliminate the tensions between married and professional life, but only a woman who fears marriage can imagine that in any profession or vocational occupation her womanhood would be more highly recognized than in marriage. Her husband's esteem and the close fellowship with him are of greater significance for a woman's personal development than any success in her job. The appreciation accorded to her professional achievement concerns only her work and her mind but not her Self as is the case in marriage.

Christianity has overcome the ancient Greek view according to which the woman has no soul. Since she is spiritually on a par with the man she demands regard be shown for her personality; this must not be done, however, to the neglect of her feminine nature and qualities. This is particularly obvious between the ages of twenty-eight to thirty-five years, when a woman becomes easily panicky as the door to marriage seems to be closing against her. Not having encountered a suitor yet she may then develop a feeling of inferiority which prompts her to accept as a last straw any man for husband in order to feel confirmed in her womanliness. Such an attitude does not result from excessive sensuality, but rather indicates an existential despair. Though in our days many unmarried mothers, who have been deserted by the father of their prospective child, seem to resign themselves to their fate, their experience nevertheless carries a deep disappointment with it. When a married man deserts his wife she derives a measure of satisfaction from the fact that as long as they lived together she was treated as a person; while the forsaken unwed mother must interpret her fate as exhibiting the man's disrespect for her womanhood. The question of the unwed mother's legal position in relation to the child's personal status and property has no connection with her mental and spiritual agony.

Thirdly, the woman as a sexual being harbors a deep-seated feeling of insecurity manifesting itself most plainly in her desire for a home. Very characteristically even the unmarried woman attempts to establish a home, as soon as circumstances allow, whereas the bachelor is satisfied to rent a room and have his meals in a nearby restaurant. However, a woman's feeling of insecurity is so deeply rooted in her sexual nature that she cannot be satisfied with the mere comfort of her home. Womanhood is not sufficient or complete in itself, therefore the woman is more open or receptive toward the other sex, and sexual experiences leave a lasting mark on her whole being. Hence she is capable of completely losing control of herself under the spell of sexual excitement. While a man who is deprived of sexual satisfaction may feel very unhappy he will not suffer from his being a man, because unlike the woman's case his Selfhood is not threatened by his masculinity.

In marriage the wife's sexual nature merges into a fellowship with her husband. Being able to keep the house for him, to be of assistance to him in a thousand minor things, and in general to make life pleasant and agreeable for him are effective means to bolster her sense of security. She is also assured that her husband's steadying influence no less than the constant awareness of the legal bond of marriage will protect her against other sexual enticements. While women suspect that the men are eager to exploit their weaknesses, their faith in their husbands far outweighs their mistrust. The very fact that he has become her lord provides protection for her. This trust in her husband's support against her sexual insecurity points to a more profound experience. Being more mobile than the man, she is more susceptible to influences that play about her, and she also has greater difficulty in making an independent judgment. Aware of the feminine nature the American business man addresses most of his advertising and promotional efforts to the woman. Marriage however has a stabilizing effect upon the woman's mobility.

Fourthly, since begetting children is dependent upon the sexual relationship, why should progeny be considered a special blessing of marriage? For an answer we have to differentiate between the biological fact of procreation on the one hand, and the place of children in marriage on the other. The child born to a married couple forms an integral part of their fellowship. Husband and wife are more than mere biological originators of new life. This is not just any child, but it is their child. By living in their midst it imparts additional meaning to their life. As the child grows up they realize that they are a generation. An heir of their life's efforts has been provided, and their perpetuation beyond death is assured. The responsibility parents have for their child is therefore not experienced as an oppressive yoke. On the contrary they feel responsible for what actually is a portion of themselves. At the same time it is through parenthood that they become the kind of persons whom the child can approach trustfully and lovingly, not on account of any special act of theirs by which they merited his trust and love, but simply because they treated this child as theirs. No institutional care, no matter how well arranged it be, and no pedagogy, not even the most advanced, can supply the good the child receives within the parent-child relationship. This applies equally well to the adopted child as to the child born within the family, since both belong to the family circle and will carry on its life. Although parents are often poor educators, yet the parent-child relationship endows the child with an heritage of mental and moral health incomparably more valuable than all formal training. For this reason parents have such great happiness in their children, while children reared in institutions or in orphanages feel instinctively the absence of the home's warmth and affection. It is hardly accidental that in a considerable number of Jesus' miracles children were restored to their parents, and that almost His last thought was concerned with giving His mother a new son (John 19:26).

Fifthly, marriage leads to the sanctification of the body. People have an instinctive feeling that the meaning of marriage transcends the natural relationship, and until recently entrance into marriage was universally connected with a religious ceremony. By imitating some of its religious forms, even the ceremony connected with civil marriage pays a kind of halting tribute to the transcendent nature of marriage. The same thing is true of the wedding banquet, or reception, which has replaced the original sacrificial meal. The varied Christian forms of contracting marriage are emphatic reminders that its meaning extends far beyond the ordinary transactions of life, and leads to a closer relationship with God. However, when Christians enter marriage they do not forsake the area of the natural, rather it is God who thereby enters their lives. Their bodies are sanctified by faith.

Christian ethics has given surprisingly scant attention to the importance of the sanctification of the body, although Jesus had emphasized that the new life brought by Him completely changes our total relationship to God, and thus exhibits itself in our physical lives, too. We are destined to become God's tools and helpers for His redemptive purposes in our entire personalities, our spirits and our bodies, in consequence of the incarnation of our Saviour. Since our complete sanctification is the goal of God's plans it necessarily includes our bodily life. Therefore, as far back as the Book of Leviticus, sexual sins have been considered under the aspect of holiness.

The holiness of our physical life was forfeited by sin. This is evidenced by the fact that sex, which was originally meant to bind two persons together, is now considered in the first place a means of providing pleasure. This attitude not only introduces an inner contradiction into sexuality but also affects our entire physical lives and thus our position in this world. The self-seeking of our bodily desires creates cleavages in mankind, for the fighting spirit and the lust to destroy are exhibitions of a powerful vitality. The undisciplined sexuality resulting from our physical vitality leads to unlimited self-assertiveness and an egotistic pursuit of pleasure. The sexual urge, in turn, will determine the place and direction of all the other manifestations of a person's life.

To mention a few things only illustrating the centrality of the sexual impulse. A perusal of the ads in some of our national magazines will teach the reader in a most drastic way to what extent our whole manner of physical care and culture, our concepts of health and sickness, or of the beautiful and the ugly are determined by the place sex holds in one's life. Even personal attitudes toward work and leisure, the joy of life, or the way of looking at nature and the surrounding world are reflections of one's sexual character. An inordinate pursuit of sex will foster a pleasure-seeking attitude in the individual. He will therefore despise labor or perform it simply as a means of making money for further pleasure. Since nature itself is encountered in the most impressive and intimate form in our own body and that of our sexual partner, our attitude towards sex is bound to affect our relationship to all the rest of nature. In view of the central place occupied by sex in our physical life, the naturalistic outlook which overlooks the divine purpose of sex, and the importance of its sanctification, betrays its utter lack of realism. Since it ignores the inner contradictions of sex any standards and rules derived from its superficial concept of sex must also be contradictory. Similarly those modern theologians who attempt to derive the ethics of sex from psychology and psychotherapy are guilty of misunderstanding its true nature. Notwithstanding the success psychologists and neurologists have had in removing pathologically disturbing mental troubles of a sexual nature, their methods fail to impart true meaning to the patient's sexual life.

Considering the decisive part that sex plays in life we cannot agree with the view that sexual life alone is sinful while all the other functions of the body are thought to be normal or neutral. The inner contradiction found in sex must rather be ascribed to the sinful will of the Self, which manifests itself in every aspect of life. Essentially, sex and sexual pleasure are, therefore, neither better nor worse than any of the other impulses and faculties of man. To be sure, the depravity of original sin is disproportionately more evident in sexual matters than in such emotions as hate, miserliness, or anger. The reason is not, however, that sex in itself is more evil but rather the fact that as the central manifestation of our will to live sex has a deeper and more enduring effect upon the total physical being than any other function or emotion. By the same token, however, sex is the starting point from which the sanctity of our corporeality can be restored. Paul emphasizes the fact that all other desires affect only one or the other portion of our life, whereas the sexual impulse operates upon our whole natural life (1 Cor. 6:13-18; cf. Gal. 5:19-21).

Sanctification of the body is realized in Christian marriage when the partner is accepted as united with us by God's grace. On this basis one is willing to treat the spouse according to God's will. Although Christian faith does not automatically lead to perfection yet it alters completely our attitude toward life. By means of marriage this change applies to sex too because it makes us conscious of our partner's sexual dignity. The husbands are therefore admonished to live with their wives according to knowledge (1 Pet. 3:7), i.e., according to the insights acquired by faith. Since sex is so important a factor in the life of the Self, its right use influences all other areas of our life also.

Sanctification of the body is not induced by the sexual act itself, but by the transformation of sex as accomplished by faith. Therefore, by their attitude towards sex, Christians can be the means of other persons' sanctification too. There are people who bear a kind of clean and wholesome atmosphere about with them that exerts a purifying effect upon the people in their environment. Impurity and lasciviousness flee before their presence, and the tension resulting from the chaotic nature of sex makes room for a free and joyous acceptance of sexuality.

By becoming one flesh, or one body, in sexual intercourse the santification of the one spouse affects the other too. Therefore, both Paul (1 Cor. 7:14) and Peter (1 Pet. 3:1 ff) reveal that the unbelieving spouse is sanctified by the believing partner. This idea, far from being the remnant of a magical mentality, is the keen observation of a psychologist schooled in faith. It has been pointed out how greatly the first sexual approach conditions the outlook of the partner. By a Christian marriage the spouses will be prompted to show consideration for each other and to let the partner feel one's esteem for his presence as God's gift. In this way then the sanctification of one spouse will, by inner necessity, transform the sexual life of the other, too.

On the other hand, the person with an unclean mind is not only a caricature of himself, but he also presents a positive danger to his environment, for his very existence and presence exude confusion of basic values that poisons everybody around him. For this reason, Paul deals in such an unequivocal manner with the incestuous person (1 Cor. 5:1ff). The apostle, in excommunicating him, does not seek to build up his prestige, let alone satisfy an unconscious sense of guilt. Rather he is deeply concerned about the future of the congregation.

The Burdens of Marriage

Since the blessings of marriage are such absolute realities, the Bible does not hesitate also to discuss frankly the burdens marriage imposes on the spouses. In this respect, too, there is no disagreement between the Old and the New Testament viewpoints.

Though cautioning people who are about to marry, the New Testament speaks as positively and confidently of the blessings of marriage as does the Old Testament, while the latter extols marriage in spite of the divine curse that will be felt in the burdens and troubles of married life (Gen. 3:16-19).

A special burden has been placed upon marriage. This is evident already at the inception of marriage. The two persons who want to get married face the risk that they know comparatively little of each other's life and character. Only under the relatively relaxed conditions of domestic life and only in dealing with the spouse will a person's real character come to light. Home is the place where the conventions and restraints of social life are thrown off so that a person forgets himself and lets himself go. For a time this may be very well, but in the long run it makes quite a demand upon the patience of the spouse. Then there is also the uncertainty about the way and the direction in which oneself and the spouse will develop over the years. A remarkable opportunity is offered our generation. Anxious to indulge in the love of adventures and the desire to take chances they could find no better opportunity than married life. Yet, oddly enough, these same people shun this encounter with the unknown and will not ordinarily face up to nor accept the realities of life. As time goes on there are added the necessity of living together not only in good but also in evil days with economic troubles, disappointments in one's work, and illness. All these burdens must be shared.

It seems that, as a rule, the woman more than the man is directly affected by the burden of marriage. Since marriage implies her willingness to have children, she must accept not only the pains and dangers of childbirth (Gen. 3:16) but also all the specifically feminine difficulties and mental crises that attend her sexual maturation and later the cessation of menstruation and the role of an old woman. Furthermore, quite apart from the special psychic problems of pregnancy, much of her time is spent in conserving her health, sometimes adversely affected by childbirth and the care of the children. Or think of the problems raised by her sexual dependence upon her husband, some of which may result from her jealousy and some from his marital unfaithfulness. There are also times when the wife has no sexual desire or is sexually irresponsive because she ages more rapidly than her husband, and is often weary from the work and activities of the household or from pregnancy. Her husband who does not share her predicament may then unconsciously feel imposed upon, and may be tempted to direct his attention to younger and livelier women.

Because the husband's sexuality does not so profoundly condition his physical life he will not feel the burdens of marriage as directly and with equal force as his wife. However there are difficulties of another kind in store for him. They are the result of tensions between his work and his sexuality (Gen. 3:17-19). No matter how much he may enjoy the blessings of sexual life they do not help him discharge his responsibility of carrying the economic load of the family's life. While the wife's burdens may be eased by her husband's tenderness and sympathy, or by the happiness she finds in her children, her husband's economic cares are unrelenting, even if she gives him the full measure of her love. Significantly, the burdens mentioned in Genesis 3:16-19 are directly connected with sex itself, therefore there is no hope that marriage reforms will ever lift them from mankind. In discussing marriage Paul refers particularly to the Old Testament doctrine of its burdens. In 1 Cor. 7:1, he emphasizes two things: firstly, a person who enters into a sexual bond with another person is divided in his aspirations (v. 34); and secondly, sexual bonds are inseparably tied up with difficulties in the flesh (v. 28). Sexual love prompts a person above all to please the partner (v. 33). For the sake of marital peace and contentment, a married person may give up his religious convictions and silence his conscience. In most mixed marriages one of the partners will eventually sacrifice his former religious faith. Similarly, a person may be willing to serve mankind by a life of self-denial, but finally he desists from his plans because he does not feel justified to make his family share in such sacrifice. What is reprehensible in such a decision is not the consideration shown for his spouse—that accords with God's will—but the fact that he is actually afraid of the world. Yet such dilemma cannot be separated from the sexual bond, for by affirming sex we affirm this world and its contradictions. For this reason it is inevitable even in a Christian marriage that the spouses seek to please each other. Upon such experiences as these Paul bases his judgment that it is good not to be married.

Modern critics of marriage discover another burden in the fact that in marriage the wife loses her independence. Paul expressly states that the woman is bound by the law (Rom. 7:2). If she takes her status seriously, her husband and children are constant concerns that condition her every activity to the point that she scarcely can choose what she wants to do. In this respect, marriage laws and regulations give the husband greater freedom. Nevertheless, the critics should realize that responsibilities are inseparably implied in the married fellowship. Even though they may be burdensome, there is no other way to receive the blessings of marriage except by a willingness to live for the family. The load that must be carried in marriage is not simply an accidental and avoidable admixture, but it is rooted in the very nature of this alliance. But God's promised blessing makes the burden of marriage light in comparison with the evils resulting from free or temporary sexual unions. In the light of his dignity and importance, the partner's weaknesses do not weigh too heavily, and since he means so much for us personally, any care and effort expended for him appear worthwhile.

The burdens of marriage, no less than its blessings, come from God. Where churches offer instruction for couples about to marry, the burdens that are in store for them should be duly stressed in order to counteract the rosy illusions most young people have about their common life. When marital unions of young Christians end in divorce this happens for no better reason than that they take the good things of marriage for granted instead of working for their realization. Likewise, they are unaware of the fact that the first misunderstandings or quarrels in their union are only an indication that married life must share the burdens of all earthly existence. But how should they form a true picture of marriage when the only reason presented for its superiority over extramarital sexual relationships is seen in the dangers and risks therein involved? For marriage, too, is not altogether free from the anxiety over unwanted pregnancies, and matrimony entails burdens of which unmarried life is completely unaware. For this reason many men shun marriage. But they overlook that over against any extramarital sexual relationship marriage has its own excellency in the divine blessing that rests upon it.

If marriage, nevertheless, is a disillusioning experience for many people, the reason is to be found in the passivity of their faith. People dislike the fact that the blessings of God may only be found and enjoyed when they are persistently sought (Matt. 7:7; Luke 11:9). Marriage is, therefore, both a gift and a task to be accomplished. Remembering birthdays and wedding anniversaries, presenting occasional small gifts, showing attention for the spouse's wishes and projects, and providing surprises are not just foolish sentimentalities, but are effective and highly important occasions to recollect the blessings God has granted to the marital union. For the same reason more than merely practical value attaches to the work the husband does about the house. The very fact that he should lend his wife a hand in the washing of the dishes or some other drudgery of the household will show his wife how intimately he is united with her daily life.

The Difficulties of Marriage

Just as the blessings of marriage are not obvious but must be constantly sought and discovered anew, so not all of its difficulties should be construed as God-sent burdens. Many marriage difficulties that the spouses bring on themselves could be averted, or their serious consequences could be avoided, if the couple would only take the trouble to treasure the blessings that they have in each other. Boredom, as the most common complaint of unhappy marriages, usually results from an overexpenditure of time and energy on the means that serve the married fellowship, rather than on the development of one's personal life and the personal contribution to the common life. The husband fails to realize, for example, that the large claim which the economic demands of the family make upon his time assumes more importance in his mind than his wife and children. Such men mistakenly believe that their excessive efforts for their family's future should merit special recognition, yet they forget that what makes them valuable in the eyes of their wives is the fellowship which they create rather than their being suppliers of clothing and housekeeping money. Yet no less frequently a wife will commit herself so intensely to preparing meals and keeping a neat home for the comfort of her husband that all her thought and energy is spent on these endeavors. She should not be puzzled that within a few years he prefers to spend his evenings elsewhere. Of course, any marriage becomes dull unless personal relationships are cultivated. In every marriage it must happen that, after some while, the habits and eccentricities of the partner have lost their edge, his unusual traits do no longer fascinate, and the repetitious rehearsal of his experiences and memories is boresome. In order to have a worthwhile married fellowship it is not necessary that the wife should take any special interest in her husband's work or profession because she wants to share his burden. When they come home from business most men are only too glad to leave the problems of the work-a-day world behind them. Yet husband and wife can have personal fellowship by engaging in common service for others, by sharing some mutual responsibility for other people, by cultivating common friendships or by developing some common interests.

A distinction should be made between the cares of marriage, which ought to be reduced to a minimum, and the inherent burdens of marriage which may not be cast aside without destroying the sexual relationship. The cares of marriage are of a more or less accidental character, and arise out of the confusing nature of this world; the burdens of marriage are inseparably connected with sex by divine decree. Thus, for instance, the wife has every right to demand the help of medical science at the time of childbirth, and a husband who refuses to obtain proper medical care to prevent undue suffering or the possibility of fatal hemorrhage, by referring to the ostensible curse which God had placed upon woman, is not conducting himself as a religious man but as a criminal. For the same reason, no sane objection can be raised against the use of anesthetics during childbirth. God's curse did not decree a certain measure of pain a woman must suffer in childbirth, but only that an element of pain and danger should attend all pregnancy and parturition. However, it would be sinful for a woman if she refused to enter marriage merely for fear of the dangers and troubles of pregnancy, or if she desired sexual pleasure, but would not accept the consequent pains and difficulties of child-bearing.

Similarly, the husband has the right and duty to take care of his family's economic needs and to make life easier and more attractive. A man in turn, who chooses to remain unmarried because he prefers the easier life of the bachelor, or who, after entering a sexual relationship, spurns his economic obligations for his wife and children, thereby clearly proves his disregard of God's will.

XV. STANDARDS AND FORMS OF MARRIAGE

The Purpose of Marriage

Marriage derives its meaning for Christians not from the function it has in social life, but from the blessing God has laid upon it. The failure to make this distinction accounts for the perplexity which the problem of marriage causes to the churches. The purpose of marriage has been sought, among other things, in the service thereby rendered to the state or nation, or in the happiness thereby provided, or in the procreation and rearing of children. Important as all these purposes are, they represent only certain aspects of marriage and never indicate its ultimate goal. Thus when given principal attention they inevitably lead to the neglect of other essential factors of marriage. Equally erroneous, however, is the romantic attitude in which the institutional character of marriage is ignored and sexual fellowship is interpreted as a goal to be realized by a striving for ideal love. Consistently, this view requires complete freedom in conducting erotic and sexual experiments until a suitable partner has been found with whom this high purpose of ideal marriage can be achieved.

In fact, however, marriage is based upon the willingness of two persons of opposite sex to establish an enduring fellowship conditioned by their sexual union. Christian marriage, in turn, is distinguished from all other types of marriage by the fact that the affection for the partner is determined by faith. This does not mean that Christians are intent upon attaining a purely religious purpose in marriage. Christian husbands and wives, too, possess the same sexual desires as other people. But they are also able to discern the divine pattern of their union. For them marriage is an alliance of two persons who, notwithstanding their physical nature and their sexuality, are members of the Body of Christ, and who therefore share the mystery of Christ's union with the Church. It is from this fact that the standards of a married life are to be derived. Of course, not all Christian couples are clearly aware of this mystery when they marry. We may even safely assume that the social function of marriage is uppermost in the minds of most couples who stand before the pastor. All the more important, therefore, is it that instruction concerning the Christian view of marriage should be given to confirmands and couples asking for a wedding if our generation is to attain to a renewed, deepened, and genuinely Christian understanding of marriage.

The Marriage Bond

From what has been said it is evident that every sexual union which has been consummated voluntarily implies a mutual obligation which must not be broken. By revealing themselves to each other the spouses have acquired a knowledge of themselves and the partner that continues to determine their bodily existence, even though they may not remember it, and perhaps most effectively in that case. Freud was not altogether wrong when he taught that sexual experiences that have descended beneath the threshold of consciousness form a prolific cause of neuroses. The objection is sometimes raised that it would be presumptuous on the part of the persons concerned to promise each other a lifelong fellowship. This objection would make sense only if the union of the two spouses were based merely upon an act of their wills. In truth, however, the Christian marriage vow signifies the willingness of the couple to honor the enduring relationship which God has brought about in their sexual union. For Christians, this union, far from being a merely biological fate, is a divine arrangement by which they are given an opportunity to express their faith even in their physical life. Therefore, marriage vows are exchanged not only in the presence of witnesses but before God.

Since the marriage bond is a permanent one and carries such important obligations with it, all kinds of attempts have been made to reduce the risks therein involved, for instance, by suggesting a trial period or a provisional freedom in sexual relationships before marriage. Free sexual intercourse before marriage is an accepted custom among many primitive groups. In the Western world, so-called trial marriages have been proposed, that is to say, sexual alliances which are entered into with the understanding that they may be dissolved after a certain time if they prove unsatisfactory to the partners. It makes very little difference whether such arrangements are entered into to determine the compatibility of the partners, or, as in some rural districts of Europe, to determine the fertility of the woman. For the provisional arrangements make no real contribution to genuine marriages since they lack the willingness permanently to be bound together. In turn marriages are rarely wrecked on account of sexual incompatibility; but rather the failure to co-operate constructively and to show consideration and respect for each other are the most common causes of unhappy marriages.

Sexual intercourse is completely shorn of its meaning when it is devoid of a sense of responsibility and obligation for the partner. For no person is an island and the unity achieved with his sexual partner in the first sexual intercourse implies a permanent tie. The decisive motivation of every sexual intercourse must therefore be the intention to establish a marriage in this manner.

The Standards of Marriage

Modern marriage law is almost exclusively concerned with the monogamous character of marriage, and penal law considers polygamy as the most significant and practically the only offense against married relationships. Over against this one-sided emphasis upon the defense of monogamy, the Bible presents a whole series of standards for marriage: lifelong duration of marriage; complete fellowship; reciprocity of personal contributions; the desire for children; and the exclusive character of the sexual relationship.

(i) *Lifelong Duration*

On account of the unique and indestructible effects produced in the lives of both persons, sexual union is meant to endure throughout life. When two persons marry, they enter into a station or an estate, from which they may not withdraw at will or at pleasure. The word "station" designates originally the place assigned to a soldier by his commander. One has to stay there and has no possibility of choice. Things would be different if the establishment of a sexual fellowship in marriage were dependent primarily upon an act of the partners' wills. Then it would be of a contractual nature like all other voluntary alliances. The partners would be obligated to remain together as long as the personal and material conditions existent at the time of wedding remained unaltered. Therefore, the opponents of the lifelong character of marriage are compelled to deny the unity of the flesh and must interpret the sexual intercourse as a purely incidental event.

Recently theologians have endeavored to temper the apparently over-rigid demands of lifelong marriage, obviously with the intention to provide a good conscience for Christians who terminated what seemed to be an unbearable married situation. Yet thereby two different matters are confused. There is the practical matter of the advisability of divorce on the one hand, and the question of the nature and the standards of marriage on the other. The marriage vows cannot be construed as being valid only for the time that the relationship between the spouses is a "real" marriage. They are meant to keep the partners together through good and bad days alike. The ontological basis of marriage—the unity of the flesh—persists in spite of marital infidelity and even when there is no longer any love for the partner.

Karl Barth has attempted to differentiate between marriages that are ordained of God, and are essentially indissoluble, and marriages that may be broken up since they were not established by God. But such distinction is not only theologically inadequate but also practically impossible to carry out. Assuredly, God is no more pleased with married persons who conduct themselves as though they were not permanently joined together by God than He is over any other infraction of His will. While these people ignore God's purpose, yet we may never presume to say that God was not originally involved in their union. Above all, who then would be in a position to determine whether a marriage was simply a human affair, or had been concluded by God?

Moreover, the Old Testament, acknowledging the permanent union effected by marriage, prohibits its arbitrary dissolution, and for the same reason Jesus condemned divorce altogether. For divorce is a denial of the divinely ordained purpose of sexual life, and a refusal any longer to accept the abiding blessings which God has conjoined with sexual intercourse. Hence Jesus interprets the permission to divorce his wife which the Old Testament grants to the husband as a divine concession to human weakness which is unnecessary in the age of the Spirit. Even if the recognition of immorality as a reason for divorce, in Matthew 5:32; 19:9, is traced back to Jesus (but it is a well-known fact that the parallels in Luke 16:8 and Mark 10:12 omit it), the case is not fundamentally altered. The married woman who plays the prostitute is actually no longer living with her husband in marriage; and the purpose of forbidding divorce—lest the woman might be tempted to have sexual intercourse with other men—is already effaced by the very fact of the wife's conduct. In a mixed marriage of a Christian with a non-Christian it may happen that the latter refuses to live any longer with the Christian spouse. In such a case there is no objection to separation (1 Cor. 7:15), because the couple lacks the common spiritual basis, on which the wrongness of divorce can be shown. However, in such a case the Christian spouse is not free to marry again (1 Cor. 7:11).

People frequently object to the New Testament view of divorce that it is unrealistic, since in many cases a person might be more likely to find the blessing of marriage with another person than the first partner. Might not the first marriage have been contracted upon a misunderstanding of its nature, or in ignorance of the partner's incompatibility? Suppose now that a person has been found with whom one agrees: should it not be permissible, or even a duty, to obtain a divorce in order to actualize the purpose of marriage? This line of argument is based upon the fallacious assumption that the meaning of marriage depends upon natural factors. However, what is required in such instances is a Christian faith which sincerely strives to lay hold of the treasures of God, and by means of them to render the common life purposeful. Had this been done in the first marriage it would have yielded what is now sought from the second.

Certainly, a second marriage must not necessarily turn out as unfortunately as the first; but we ought not to assume that the failure of the first marriage was caused by unsatisfactory circumstances or the evil intentions of the other party. The couple would never have married if they had hated or detested each other at the beginning of their marriage. If, from the outset, both of them had made a serious effort to understand each other and to lead a common life they would have found a solid basis for their union.

A divorce of a Christian couple is bound to have severe repercussions upon their personal life. Having originally decided to live their lives in mutual responsibility their striving is now stamped by their divorce as an ultimate failure. For the remainder of their days they will be burdened with the gnawing sense of having failed at a critical point in their lives. On the other hand, had they earnestly striven to remain together they would now be blessed with a sense of definite triumph.

All this applies only to Christian spouses, however. Not every marriage contracted between members of a church is a Christian marriage. Divorce will probably have less serious repercussions upon people whose reason for marrying was simply the wish to obtain a suitable sexual mate or social companion. The levity with which many so-called Christian couples enter marriage should teach the Church not to inveigh so much against the possibility of divorce or its frequent occurrence, but rather to endeavor to create a true understanding of marriage among its members.

(ii) *The Life of Fellowship*

Marriage and home belong together; for the best expression of the complete union of a couple is a home in which they live a common life of their own. In order that the newly married groom might "be happy with the wife which he has taken" (Deut. 24:5), the Law of Israel exempted him from military service and other public duties for a one-year period. It is characteristic of Israel's legal system, which in all other respects subordinated the individual to national interests, that it should show such a deep concern for the nature of marriage.

Both spouses need each other's physical presence first of all as a service that must be rendered to the partner in consideration of his weakness. The Bible repeatedly stresses the ease with which a person may succumb to temptations of license and infidelity (e.g., 1 Cor. 7:2). Since a long separation may be dangerous to the other person it should not be undertaken without good reasons. Although one of the spouses may have complete confidence in his ability and strength to withstand temptations, he cannot be sure that the partner will have equal strength. This truth was frightfully evidenced during the last war. Adultery was common in both sexes, not because people no longer loved their absent spouses but because they felt unable to endure any longer the strain of separation. The legislator correctly assumes that a long and baseless voluntary absence of a marriage partner from the common home evidences his indifference toward the marriage ties.

Domestic fellowship requires privacy, and hence demands at least one room in which the couple can be by themselves. The present housing shortage in our large cities and around the Army camps that compels two or more couples to share one room as sleeping quarters is incompatible with the nature of true marriage. Christians should therefore support every effort to provide adequate living space for married couples.

(iii) *Reciprocity*

In the union of married life the difference of the sexes is not submerged. Hence it is incorrect to speak of equality of the sexes since either of them has its specific function in marriage. However, the unity of the flesh, as this is understood in the Christian faith, generates a reciprocity of rights and duties. The spouses are completely obligated to each other with all they have and are, as this is perfectly exemplified in the reciprocal relationship between Christ and the Church. The Lord loves nothing in this world except the Church, and the Church has nothing that it may rightly love except Him (Eph. 5:25). The same attitude should exist between married people. Out of the correlation of the sexes the wife is engaged in the service of her husband, and he assumes the responsibility to care for her. In order to curb the husband's arbitrary interpretation of his superior position, the

Old Testament explicitly states that under all circumstances the husband owes his wife food, clothing, and regular sexual intercourse (Exo. 21:10).

Paul's statement that neither spouse has the right to withdraw sexually from the other person for a long period of time, and that only the need for meditation and devotion may be a reason for even temporary denial, also indicates this full reciprocity of the relationship. The apostle expressly denies the existence of independent rights for either of the partners, since bodily they belong to each other (1 Cor. 7:4-5); he reminds the husbands of their special responsibility and admonishes them to deal intelligently and understandingly with their wives in sexual relations (1 Thess. 4:1; cp. 1 Pet. 3:7). Evidently he thinks of consideration to be shown to the physical and mental condition of his wife whenever intercourse is envisaged. The sexual obligation, however, is not limited to the duty of occasional intercourse. Both spouses should treat each other as "in the Lord" (1 Cor. 7:39), i.e., as persons who are called by Christ to be God's children. They are, therefore, sovereign beings, in spite of their social or biological dependence. Consequently, they must mutually recognize each other's right to have his distinctive characteristics and habits. This is not an easy requirement. It is not enough to allow the partner to have his own way granted only he reciprocates. The unity of the flesh is meant to result in a vital fellowship. In marriage more than in any other relationship neither of the persons owns anything, but all things—not only possessions, but time, strength, all the joys and sorrows, hopes and cares—are held in common. This fellowship is not built upon the expectation of a reciprocal service; rather every service in marriage is freely rendered without hope of return. Marriage partners have no legal claims upon the spouse's person and rights (1 Cor. 7:3). On the contrary a spouse who would give less than himself would rob his mate. But, paradoxically, the more devotedly a married couple renders mutual service, the greater is the freedom they grant each other.

(iv) *The Desire for Children*

The Bible shows clearly that the immediate purpose of marriage is not the begetting of children, but rather the formation of a fellowship of the partners. However, in view of the fact that children are a divine blessing promised to the couple any sexual union in which children are not wanted cannot be considered a genuine marriage, notwithstanding its ecclesiastical consecration. Does this mean that marriage is impossible if either of the partners is anatomically or physiologically unfit for begetting children? Not necessarily, since even with normal people the mere wish to have children will not always lead to its fulfillment. Yet, a childless couple is not barred from living in a true fellowship. However, such couples should accept their inability to have children of their own as a divine sign to satisfy their desire for offspring by adoption or by caring for orphaned or homeless children.

In our days children are not simply accepted as an unmitigated divine blessing, but rather people will ask to what extent it is justifiable, or even obligatory, to limit the number of children. The so-called population explosion and the resulting fear of an overpopulation of our globe have given increased actuality to this question. Even Christians recognize that in certain instances it is desirable or necessary not to have children. The principles of heredity no less than social studies substantiate this view. The only difference of opinion concerns the conditions in which such a renunciation to have children should be made. While some advocates of the biological view stress the absolute necessity of healthy descendants, others are satisfied with a majority of healthy children and are ready to accept also a number of physical and mental misfits as may be expected according to the laws of heredity. From the sociological standpoint, some believe that some measure of economic need benefits the development of children, and only in cases of actual want should the number of children be restricted. Others insist upon a certain material prosperity of the parents as essential to the rearing of healthy children with well-developed minds and bodies and are in favor of small families in general. Obviously no hard and fast rules can be applied.

However, Christians are deeply divided on the question of what should be done to prevent undesirable offspring. Some contend that on moral grounds total sexual abstinence is the only acceptable method of limiting the number of children. Others point out that serious mental and psychic troubles may result when total sexual abstinence is practiced in marriage, and, therefore, they recommend the use of contraceptives. The opponents of this position hold that the use of any contraceptive method is an unnatural interference with the normal processes of the sexual function. In sexual intercourse it should be left with nature whether or not the sperm and the ovum find each other and a child develops.

This argument is inconsistent, however, because its advocates overlook the fact that man is constantly interrupting and changing the course of nature. Nature is not destined to be left unaltered. Man's dignity lies in his ability to transform it and shape it toward definite purposes. The Roman Catholic law of nature runs in this instance aground on its own inner contradictions. Sometimes the term designates the actual order of that which really exists, whereas in other instances the term refers to a teleological order. Thus it is not surprising that on the question of avoiding conception the Catholic Church's official attitude is ambiguous. In general, she advises sexual continence, and condemns the use of any contraceptive methods. At the same time, however, she not only permits but recommends confinement of sexual intercourse to the so-called safe days, i.e., to those days between the monthly periods when conception is least likely to occur. Yet such a restriction of sexual intercourse is also a means of preventing conception, and people who follow that method deliberately and definitely manipulate nature in their favor. Yet the moral question is not whether a Christian has a right to use contraceptives, but rather whether he is allowed to interfere at all with the process of fertilization in the act of sexual intercourse. It should be obvious that the ethical issue is not dependent on the means used for that end. For whether conception is prevented by the use of contraceptives, by the interruption of the sexual act, or by limiting intercourse to the safe days, there is an evident action of the will whose purpose is to prevent conception. One cannot argue in favor of the Roman Catholic practice that even on the safe days there is a chance of conception, for it is the intention and not the means used which determines the moral quality of an action. The real question, therefore, is only whether the intention to practice birth control is sinful in itself and under all circumstances.

The Roman moralists must assume the principal blame for the confusion in the discussion of the problem. In their ethical thinking they start from the individual sexual act, whereas the ethical view of the Bible is concerned with the whole sexual life of the two persons in their marriage relation. The crucial question, then, is whether a couple is fundamentally ready to recognize parenthood as a divine blessing, but not whether or not each sexual act is performed in conscious awareness of it or with the wish to have children. The ethical value of each single sexual act must be decided by the couple's concept of marriage. An act of coition is sinful when the spouses disavow all intention of becoming parents, but so is their refusal to have offspring even if they have no sexual relations, for such an attitude proves that they disdain the blessing God has placed upon their union.

In certain circumstances, however, pathological, social, and economic conditions may seem to be in conflict with a couple's willingness to have children. Would they, nevertheless, have a right to sexual intercourse? The theologians who in such cases advise complete continence seem to be unaware of the difficulties which would result in the life of the couple. The sexual relationship is not confined to the sexual act itself, but pervades all their bodily contacts, expressing itself in glances, furtive touches, small acts of fondling, and embraces. Since such contacts may lead up to coition, however, the advice to exercise continence would require complete bodily separation. No longer sharing the same bed, would not suffice; they would have to live in different places. For while a couple, though living together, might refrain from intercourse, they would under normal circumstances not be able completely to suppress the joy they find in each other and that would naturally call forth excitement and desire. In most instances the repression of their desire would produce harmful mental effects. On the other hand, if we were to go so far as to advise the couple to refrain altogether from caresses and all expressions of affection their marriage would be hopelessly impoverished because it would be reduced to a union for the pursuit of practical ends. Marriage is a fellowship of body and mind. On the other hand, no ethical superiority attaches to a marriage merely because all methods of birth control are avoided. There are not a few instances in which the natural way is merely the expression of uninhibited sexuality. The husband is selfishly indulging his pleasure no matter what the consequences will be for his wife and the rest of the family. Social workers testify that very often the origin of a very large family is to be found in the father's irresponsibility and addiction to alcohol.

It is contended that the use of contraceptives tends to stifle the normal desire for children. Yet though the use of methods of birth control is rather common in this country, statistics do not show any decline in the general birth rate, or in the number of births per marriage. On the contrary, it seems that early marriages encourage larger families, even though contraception is practised in the incipient stage.

Finally, a word needs to be said about the question of abortion of the foetus. Although it is not pertinent to our discussion here whether abortion constitutes legal murder, as the Catholic moralists contend, this much is significant, that it implies an outright refusal of the divine gift. While the spouses are free to use methods of birth control, they have no right to destroy new life which by the grace of God issues from their union. A medical verdict for an abortion as an absolute necessity for saving the life of the mother is the only exception. The actual life takes precedence over the potential one.

(v) *Monogamy*

Marriage attains its fullest meaning only in lifelong monogamy. Its necessity is frequently contested, however, because it stands in the way of people's desire for pleasure and freedom. Though there is no particular commandment of monogamy in the Bible, its superior dignity is attested by the images of God's Marriage to Israel and Christ's Marriage to the Church. The fact that both Testaments like to present the covenant relationship with God as a marriage is an indication of the high esteem in which the monogamous marriage was held by the Biblical writers. Therefore, we may conclude from the exclusive way in which Israel's relationship to God was interpreted that the same exclusiveness was demanded for the marriage relationship of Israelites.

Monogamy derives its place as the true form of marriage from the mystery of sex. All other reasons which have been adduced in favor of its normative character fail to do full justice to the pertinent historical and psychological facts implied in marriage. Idealism, for instance, favors monogamy as a means of preserving the dignity of personal life in sexual relationships. At best, however, this would demand that at no time should a sexual relationship be carried on with more than one person. Bernard Shaw who advocated this principle pointedly insisted that it did not require lifelong association with the same person. Much less can the normative character of monogamy be established on a biological basis. The fact that, under normal conditions boys and girls are born in almost equal numbers is interpreted as an indication that monogamy is the most desirable form of marriage because all people of the same age would be given the same chance. But the same biological principle would require that when the male population has sustained great lossess as, for example, after a long war, polygamy should not only be permitted but made a political duty in order to restore the balance of population.

The real reason for the absolute superiority of monogamy is found in the fact that in sexual intercourse another person has unveiled to me the complete secret of my and his sexual existence. This mystery of sex is of a strictly personal character, and it would be profaned if others were made to share in it. Having mutually unveiled this secret the partners are thereby tied to each other. If either of them allows himself to be sexually known to another person he thereby spoils the dignity of the spouse, because the latter is thereby treated as a casual acquaintance rather than as the person God had assigned for him. One disdains the singularity and the uniqueness of the service rendered by the first partner. The fact that some people are able to love more than one person at the same time does not prove that polygamy is as valuable as monogamy but only that love can become shallow.

Moreover, it is obvious that what Jesus says about marriage implies monogamy. His condemnation of divorce can be understood only on the basis of the exclusive nature of the secret of sex. Even a lustful look cast upon any person other than one's own spouse is adultery (Matt 5:28), because it not only attempts to intrude upon the sexual secret of the other person but also shows disrespect for the mystery of one's own sexual existence. On the same basis, divorce is rejected because it exposes the spouse to remarriage which, during the lifetime of the spouse, must be adjudged as adultery (Mark 10:12). In the case of disagreements every effort should be made by the spouses to be reconciled rather than desert one another (1 Cor. 7:11).

The objection strongly expressed in the Apostolic period against the remarriage of widowed persons has a different foundation, as can be seen in 1 Timothy 5:14, where young widows are not only advised but almost required to remarry. Since one of the partners has departed there is no danger that a third party would share their mutual knowledge in a new marriage.

Adultery

Adultery was one of the rare offenses in the Old Testament that was subject to the death penalty (Lev. 20:10; Deut. 22:22). Presumably, the adulterer was considered a kind of murderer who robbed the husband of his Selfhood by usurping the place the husband alone has a right to occupy with his wife. Both the adulterer and the adulteress treat him as though he were nonexistent or dead. However, in the Old Testament the husband alone is considered as bearer of such rights. Jesus' concept of marriage marks a change by lifting into prominence the sanctity of marriage itself as the element that ought not be violated. Therefore, the man who divorces his wife is the real sinner and adulterer. He is all the more guilty because by divorcing his wife he exposes her to the temptation of remarriage, which, during the lifetime of the husband, is equivalent to adultery (Mark 10:10-11; Matt. 19:8-9; 5:32; Luke 16:18).

From a legal viewpoint adultery is usually considered a culpable violation of the other spouse's right to have the exclusive sexual enjoyment of the partner. Over against such outlook Jesus refers to the ontological basis of marriage—the unity of the flesh and the divine purpose of marriage (Matt. 19:4-6; Mark 10:6-8.).

The legislation of different countries and states varies greatly in what is recognized as a valid ground for divorce or for the nullification of a marriage. Jesus and the Apostles considered all the above mentioned requirements for marriage as being of equal significance, and, therefore, the absence of any of them was considered culpable. On the other hand, Jesus contended that, in the last analysis, a marriage relationship could not really be dissolved because it rested on an indestructible ontological basis; it could only be disregarded. Therefore, His rejection of divorce is absolute. In a related question, Paul, though lacking any express direction of Jesus, felt nevertheless certain that God did not want the spouse of a non-Christian to leave his unbelieving partner (1 Cor. 17:12-16). In the story of the woman taken in adultery (John 8:3-11) Jesus is described as proceeding from the exclusive nature of the marriage relationship, which forbids even the lustful look as adulterous. The story hardly implies that all the accusers of the woman had legally committed adultery. By proceeding from this new principle Jesus annuls as absurd the death penalty demanded by Old Testament law for a woman's marital infidelity (Lev. 20:10; Deut. 22:22). If all violations of the standards of marriage are of equal importance, practically every married person has incurred guilt at one time or another. Infidelity and the lack of true religious faith go hand in hand. Marital infidelity furthers the dissolution of character, whereas true marriage develops upright men and women at peace with themselves. Furthermore, since adultery is disregard for the institutional character of marriage, it produces further irresponsibility in social life and indifference to the fellowmen, and this disorder becomes one of the causes for the ascendancy of authoritarian and totalitarian governments. It would be a most intriguing endeavor to write a political history of mankind in the light of sexual mores.

XVI. THE VIRTUES OF MARRIAGE

Faith and Duty

What exactly do we mean when speaking of standards of marriage? Both by the teaching of the Church and the prolific enactments of laws in modern secular life we are accustomed to thinking that right conduct consists in regard for extant commandments. A similar condition obtained among the Jews of Jesus' time when the Old Testament Law held the central place in their religion. Paul, obviously interpreting Jesus, emphasizes the opposite viewpoint. "But now we have been rendered nonexistent as far as the Law is concerned, and dead in relation to that by which we were held captive, in order that we should serve in spiritual renewal, and not in the old way of the letter" (Rom. 7:6). Wherein does this freedom from the law consist? Jesus no less than Paul rejected their Jewish contemporaries' belief in the primacy of the Old Testament Law. They explained it as a manifestation of God's will which was accommodated to Israel's limited understanding of God. But they did not substitute a new law for the old one. On the contrary, they showed that God's purpose in issuing commandments was to make mankind disavow all belief in man's self-sufficiency and to teach him the need of a divine redemption. Therefore, in His controversy with the Scribes, Jesus refers to the creative and redemptive will of God which is the subject matter of all revelation, and which the law of Sinai, too, was meant temporarily to serve. Though Jesus occasionally put His message in the form of a commandment, thereby seemingly paralleling the laws of the Old Testament, He was not really referring to goals to be realized by man's own efforts, but rather to purposes which God wants to achieve through man. The imperative or hortative form served to remind Jesus' audience that the goal of human life was not a matter of free choice but rather had been assigned by God.

The vital problem of man, then, is how to identify himself with the will of God in such a way that the service he renders to God is utterly free and spontaneous. The difficulty in attaining this goal is indicated plainly in 1 Corinthian 6:11-20. Man's ultimate peril is his enslavement to things and to people. He imagines that certain things are absolutely necessary to his happiness, or that happiness and success in life are unattainable unless his actions are conformable to other people's. However, in this way he barters away his freedom.

The problem seems almost insoluble in the sexual relationship because therein the persons seem to lose their personal existence when they become one flesh. The New Testament writers emphasize that under these circumstances the only condition in which freedom can be enjoyed is in the marriage relationship. Unlike extramarital sexual relationship which is occasioned by the compulsion of forceful sexual impulses, marriage originates in a reciprocal willingness of two persons to assume responsibility for each other. Therefore, the wife can, in substance, be obedient to her husband "in the Lord" (Col. 3:18), i.e., she is free when in living together with him she works for the purpose for which God established their relationship. The fact that both partners lose themselves in each other in sexual intercourse has no adverse effect upon their fundamental relationship of personal responsibility. Likewise, the husband, despite the power of the sexual urge, will also be able in his love to assume responsibility for his wife (Col. 3:19).

Without faith, it is impossible to attain to that level of true life which was made manifest in the life of Jesus Christ. In turn, however, faith imparts the assurance that in the new life God has personally called me to participate in the redemption of the world, and that through His Spirit He grants me the necessary powers and means to express this renewal in my actual life. In marriage this regeneration manifests itself in the Christian virtues of reverence, love, fidelity, naturalness, and purity.

Both in Thomism and in Christian idealism the development of the Christian virtues has been confused with a striving for a set of ideals. The hope to reach the lofty goal is then wrongly established upon the belief in one's own innate goodness. In a truly Christian life people depend entirely on God. They grow by constantly asking for His forgiveness and for His stimulating their willingness to be transformed into likeness with Jesus.

A genuine marriage is not immediately or automatically realized, rather it grows up. However, since Christians envisage the goal for which they are destined, they can give expression to their determination by embracing social institutions, because these help to preserve the gains people have made in the pursuit of their goal. Likewise, they will respect the social prohibitions and laws which serve to combat what is incompatible with the idea of marriage as held by the community to which they belong. Of even greater significance is the fact that they are conditioned by their being members of God's people, because as the historical organization of God's people the church is a powerful force that makes for righteousness. Unfortunately, many Protestants do not realize that church attendance and participation in church activity contribute greatly to the success of a marriage, and they are therefore surprised when, in spite of their faith, their marriages turn out so unsatisfactorily. Actually, however, they failed because they relied exclusively on their own strength and spurned the assistance God was offering them. More important, nevertheless, than these external supports of the Christian life are the Christian virtues because they are manifestation of the power of God's Spirit in the life of the people concerned. We shall now consider them in detail.

Reverence

Although hardly ever discussed in modern sexual ethics, the mutual reverence which the partners show for each other is of fundamental importance for the Christian marriage.

Christian reverence recognizes the greatness of the gifts two people impart to each other in their sexual union. The woman offers her virginity to the man, while he presents her with the gift of womanhood and therein implies the possibility of motherhood. On the part of the girl, the first intercourse means more than her allowing him to use her body for sexual purposes. She surrenders herself to him by sacrificing for him her virginity—an estate to which there is no return. From then on she is bound forever to the other sex. If the first sexual intercourse does not establish a lasting bond between the partners the experience is generally a constant torment for the woman. Although she may feel it intolerable in the future to live without a man she also knows now from her first disappointment that sexual intercourse will not bring about the complete solution of her personal problem.

Christian reverence reveals to the spouses the miracle of the sanctification of their bodies, teaching them that in their totality as human beings they are destined to live with and for God. Furthermore, Christian reverence discloses the divine blessing implied in the reciprocity of marital life. The beloved person is capable of setting free in the partner latent faculties which had lacked opportunities of development. All of us possess potentials which cannot be actualized in the unmarried stage, in part because they are tied up with our masculinity or femininity, in part because they can be developed only in the intimacy of a common personal life. Christian reverence shows itself not only as respect for the distinctiveness of the other but as a deep appreciation of the privilege of being a man for a woman and a woman for a man. There is real danger that under the burdens of marriage people should forget these privileges. When a woman is aware of her dignity and that of her husband, however, she will be able to break the tenacious grip which work or business have on her husband. It is in her power to bring him back to the life of the family, and, what is even more important, to revitalize his religious life. Similarly, the husband's reverence for his wife will help him to discover ways of restoring the fellowship of the family when she is in danger of being submerged by household chores or her responsibilities as a mother.

Love

Love commands the central place in Christian life. However, love can completely unfold itself in marriage only when the spouses have a mutual respect for their own and the partner's dignity, and the privileges of the married estate itself. The love commanded in the New Testament is not a new affection appended to natural love, but rather it is the same love, only lifted upon a higher level thanks to the Holy Spirit by whose operation the couple is able to see the true value of the partner and of their common life. Erotic love is not by nature opposed to Christian love. Yet, seeing things and people in a divine light, Christian love, as Paul shows in 1 Corinthians 13, is able to achieve immeasurably greater things than natural love.

Nygren's antithesis between Eros and Agape provoked a widespread condemnation of erotic love in Protestant circles. Yet experience does not corroborate his description of erotic love as a selfish emotion that seeks only its own good, happiness, bliss, and fulfillment. Outside of the Christian fold, too, it is possible to find instances of an unselfish love that endures privation and will even sacrifice itself for another person. Yet, it is true that love without faith is apt falsely to evaluate itself and others, and therefore not only may indulge in many silly actions but may often become harmful and destructive.

In married life Christian love means a readiness to live with all that one is and has for the sake of the partner (1 Pet. 4:10). Marriage is not only a bond between two spirits, but a union of two actual persons with bodies and minds, with all their problems, cares, and doubts; with their anxieties and joys; with their longings and needs for warmth and nearness and for mutual understanding. Furthermore, Christian love includes consideration and a sense of responsibility for each other. Unhappy marriages are not caused so frequently by infidelity and illwill as by selfish concern about personal happiness, unwillingness to make sacrifices, and lack of mutuality. One of the partners insists that the other should completely agree with his wishes and moods without granting him reciprocity. True love does not exclude a striving for happiness, but it must be a striving for mutual happiness.

Finally, since the partners are not only one flesh, but are also children of God, true love cannot exist without readiness to assume responsibility for each other. What a difference between love that finally reaches the point where two persons are constantly at the disposal of each other on the one hand, and the infatuation that causes two persons to lose themselves completely in each other! This latter attitude, so highly esteemed as the mystical apex of erotic love (cf. Abbé Prévost's *Manon Lescaut*), is really an obsession with one's boundless need for love. This is shown by the fact that under such circumstances persons are neither capable of giving guidance to the beloved, nor of setting limits to his passion. If we feel responsible for the partner we will fulfill his wishes as much as are in his own best interests, without yielding to them when they are unreasonable. However, love will take pains to make its denials understandable. Love's principal concern is to preserve the unity of the reciprocal relationship. Thus the personal influence one has over the other person is used as a means of serving him.

True love teaches trust and co-operation. Strong personalities are tempted to assume one-sidedly the whole responsibility for their marriage. Rather than ask the partner to perform certain services they want to do everything themselves and thus to get the full credit for the success of their common life. While it looks like sacrificial love, this is in fact a passion to dominate the other person. Hence such people are suspiciously fearful of the harmful effect the other person's independent action might have.

Likewise, Christian love is capable of bearing all the troubles and disillusionments that are inseparably joined with the sexual relationship; in fact, it grows and is intensified as it carries them. Tensions are inevitable in the sexual relationship, and opportunities for misunderstanding lurk everywhere in married life, so that the unity that God has established between a husband and his wife will rarely manifest itself in its whole glory in their fellowship. But Christian love is sure that God's work which brought the couple together is more real than are the outward conditions, and thus either spouse is not chiefly concerned with his own burden but with the other spouse's problems, and he will therefore help the other bear the load (Gal. 6:2). Surprisingly enough, the additional sacrifice and patience demanded to render such assistance do not increase one's own encumbrance, but actually diminish it. Only that part of the burden remains that exceeds the partner's load; and experience shows that our excess weight then seems comparatively light. Sharing the other person's burden makes us understand his true nature and condition, so that we are enabled to help him as God intends we should.

With such an outlook we are even capable of enduring the suffering he inflicts upon us. Far from making us doubt his love it rather becomes an indication that something is amiss in our mutual association, for no sane person takes joy in causing suffering or inflicting pain upon another person. Hence such conduct is invariably a sign that the other person feels neglected, or unjustly dealt with. Of course, even though our love will not permit us to retaliate for the injuries the other person has inflicted, and though we may try to uncover the possible cause of his irritation or anger, there is no guarantee that thereby the happiness of our marriage will be restored. True love may sometimes be a lifelong martyrdom. But if nevertheless we persist in our love we have the assurance that our life will never lack meaning. These painful experiences will enrich and deepen life by revealing how difficult it is for people to identify themselves with God's will, and to give visible expression to the unity of the flesh. By such a willingness our life becomes a living testimony to Christ Himself.

In sexual relations, Christian love is willingness to follow the sexual impulse in agreement with God's will. It therefore manifests itself in erotic love and Christian marriage does not demand the suppression of passion. Fortunately the time is over when a purely spiritual concept of love engendered fear of eroticism and hence neglect of the spouse's natural longing for physical love. In married life caresses should not be limited only to the loveplay that precedes coition but should have their legitimate place in the whole common life of the couple. Over against the viewpoint that sex dare manifest itself only occasionally and then solely in sexual intercourse, we must emphasize that all expressions of our sexual nature are of equal importance and value. On account of their passing character the happiness and excitement of sexual intercourse are of secondary importance to a happy marriage. Sexual intercourse alone is not fit to convey to the partner the assurance that our love is more than an impetuous desire to satisfy the sexual urge. Small but frequent daily attentions and the expression of tenderness and concern are evidence that one is aware not only of the spouse's presence but also that his masculinity or femininity is thankfully received. They are like a daily renewed wooing of the partner by which the spouses indicate that in approaching each other they are not claiming legal rights, but want to be united with the partner in a harmony of loving wills.

While not spurning the sexual impulse true love, nevertheless, sets definite limits for its manifestations. Love will prompt men to "dwell with their wives according to knowledge" (1 Pet. 3:7; cf. 1 Thess. 4:4) and thus to refrain from compelling them to have sexual relations. Neither spouse has the right to lay any sexual claims upon the other. The conduct of sexual life must not onesidedly depend upon one spouse's desire, but must be conditioned by the partner's physical and mental condition. For this reason, no general rules governing the frequency of normal sexual relations can be laid down. However, out of a sense of mutual responsibility the spouses will be careful not to provoke any physical or mental injury by an excessive or inappropriate indulgence in sexual activities (1 Cor. 7:3-5).

Fidelity

Love and fidelity go hand in hand. Whereas love's primary concern is the realization of the reciprocal relationship of the spouses, fidelity has to do with its lasting duration. Faithfulness is a readiness to do everything possible to maintain and preserve the bond established by sexual union. In Christian marriage fidelity implies the couple's constant recollection of the fact that God has brought them together, and that He expects their alliance to last during lifetime.

The basis of fidelity is not to be sought in the marriage vows. For these can easily be interpreted as excepting all kinds of unforeseen eventualities and developments such as lifelong invalidism, mental illness, or commission of crime by the spouse. Faithfulness must be undergirded by an unwavering trust in God's promise that He will preserve the unity of the flesh, and it must be accompanied by a daily willing acceptance of God's gifts and blessings. All attempts to derive fidelity from natural love are doomed to failure. Because natural love wants extensive evidence of one's being loved, and thus many lovers, fidelity is popularly considered an impossible virtue; neither is it generally regarded a necessary and inevitable concomitant of the marriage institution. Though from a sociological and psychological viewpoint marriage is generally to be preferred to all types of free sexual relationships, the institution of marriage does not render it necessary to live together with the same person for life. Rather, the sociological interpretation of marriage demands a limited fidelity, that is for the duration of a marriage only. But that marriage may be terminated at any moment. Those alone who believe that God's guidance has brought them together in marriage can develop a Christian faithfulness which is willing to live with the partner for all of life. Fidelity is, then, an emotion which affirms the lifelong character of marriage. Fidelity is required within a consummated marriage only, not with reference to a contemplated one. People are therefore mistaken in holding that the death of a lover or affianced person should be interpreted as a divine sign indicating to the affected person that he or she must stay unmarried for the rest of his or her life in faithfulness to the deceased.

Since marriage is not only based on a contract but also on sexual attraction, fidelity implies the readiness to protect and honor forever the gift the partner imparts to us in sexual intercourse. Faithfulness is not confined to mutual respect for the gifts the partners have made to each other in their first sexual union, the girl sacrificing her virginity to the man, and he bestowing upon her the gift of womanhood. For God grants the gift of fidelity also to persons who prior to their marriage have lived in a sexual relationship with another person. This is the case not only in a second marriage but also when people had extramarital relationship with a person other than their spouse. Faithfulness originates in the fact that God moves two persons to dedicate themselves to each other, and it is God Who engenders their willingness to harmonize their fellowship with God's intention. In turn, a married person is unfaithful not only when he has sexual intercourse with a third party, but also when he endeavors to terminate the marriage bond. On the other hand, fidelity does not restrict the formation of intimate personal associations with others, but it does prohibit any other person from assuming the unique place of the partner, or from sharing that place with him. The deep suffering imposed upon a spouse by his partner's infidelity justifies his right of vigorous protest; but a jealousy that forbids ordinary social contacts and friendship with other people indicates that love is dead.

Not every person who is not unfaithful does necessarily practice Christian fidelity. The goal of fidelity is a joy in and enjoyment of the married estate which aims at enabling the partner to experience the goodness of God who has united them. There is nothing mystical or miraculous about it, it is realized in the sheer happiness of belonging to each other.

Accord with Nature

It may seem strange to call naturalness a Christian virtue and it would be if, with modern man, the term designated giving free rein to the sexual urge. If the term is understood, however, as meaning an attitude which is in accordance with human nature, such attitude is not even the natural thing to the natural or primitive man. Naturalness is an unsophisticated acceptance of sex as coming from God and serving a good purpose. The simplicity of Christian naturalness is the opposite of affected secrecy so frequently associated with sex. The Biblical writers speak quite openly and freely about sex, but since they consider it in its relationship to God's purpose it is a serious matter to them. Nowhere in the Bible is sex in danger of sinking to the level of the obscene. The modern film industry, in order to make sexy films acceptable, increasingly turns to the Old Testament for new subjects. But characteristically the script writer has to supply from his own imagination those scenes which are apt to attract a public desirous of sexual excitement. Similarly, when lascivious people leaf through the Old Testament in the hope of finding some sexually spicy stories, they should be informed that the *Decameron* or the average modern paper back novel are more likely to fulfill their desires.

Paradoxically, however, nothing in the history of the Church has given so much offense as the Biblical naturalness. The influence that Hellenistic ascetic philosophy and gnosticism had upon the church, completely perverted the Biblical perspective. Sex was regarded as being by itself evil and thus to be shunned by earnest Christians. Of course, when sex, as such, is considered sinful naturalness appears to be levity and frivolity, and people wrongly identify it with the licentiousness of Naturalism. Yet the lack of inhibitions characteristic of that attitude contrasts characteristically with the concern and reverence of the Christian virtue.

Naturalness prevents a suppression of sex which would upset the mental and psychic balance of a person and in the practice of it never loses sight of its divine purpose. Paul admonishes overanxious Christians to form their principles in accordance with the nature of sex. If a married pair, for instance, were suddenly and for a long period of time to interrupt their sexual relationship, Paul says, they would lay themselves open to the temptations of Satan (1 Cor. 7:5; cf. 9:36). Instead of striking off the chains of sexuality, they would find themselves obsessed by sexual thoughts, or else a peculiar type of sexual frigidity might occur as a result of which one would cast doubt upon the partner's love or question the meaningfulness of natural life. In other instances where a couple shares the same home voluntary continence practiced for a long period of time might change their love into bitterness and hate. Instinctively sensing the lack of joy and satisfaction engendered by this kind of life people are tempted to seek the fault in their partner and thus are inclined to make life difficult for him and devoid of joy. Christian naturalness differs from Naturalism by the fact that a person views his natural life as destined for fellowship with Christ. Therefore, any sexual relationship by which one would be turned away from that goal is unnatural. Consorting with prostitutes, for instance, since militating against the holiness of the body is incompatible with Christian naturalness (1 Cor. 6:13-20). In such associations a Christian is unable to serve God with his whole corporeal life.

Christian naturalness is averse to all sexual perversions. Although naturalistic sexual ethics has not thrown out the notion of perversions it uses the term merely as a classification. Perversion then designates a deviation from the statistical norm. Take the Kinsey report for example. Since Dr. Kinsey's tables indicate the relatively frequent occurrence of homosexuality many young people no longer consider it a perversion. Christian naturalness and Naturalism agree largely in what they classify as sexual perversions but are at odds in their evaluations. For our purposes it will suffice briefly to enumerate the more common types of sexual perversions. Sadism and masochism are contrary to the nature of sex, for, even though a certain measure of pain is a constitutive element of sexual pleasure, the infliction of pain or the desire to feel pain and suffering must not be allowed to be the tie that binds two people together. In such relationship the partners are so concerned with seeking their own satisfaction that they are utterly indifferent to the other person's experience.

Likewise, sexual self-abuse (Onanism, masturbation) is unnatural. Physicians may be completely right in maintaining that such acts are no more deleterious to health than other sexual activities, and it may therefore do more harm than good to instill into young people the fear of possible ill health as the reason why they should avoid the habit of self-abuse. But the moral aspect of the problem lies on an entirely different plane. Onanism is a vice because it violates the law of mutuality in sexual life. The Onanist attempts to solve the sexual enigma for himself by imagining the presence of a partner, while actual fellowship is required. Since the imaginary partner is always available, Onanism leads easily to excessive frequency of sexual activity and to an immoderate overemphasis placed upon sex. Onanism is not only futile, because in this way one can never enter into the sexual secret, it is also a sin against society, for it is sexual activity without the possibility of love. It serves therefore to strengthen the egotistic tendency of the individual.

Homosexuality is another form of disregard for the interrelation of the sexes. Since in such a relation a person of the same sex assumes the sexual function of the other sex the result can never be an understanding of what manhood and womanhood signify to each other; these people attempt to accomplish a union for which they do not possess the natural qualifications. However, in judging homosexuality a sharp line of demarcation should be drawn between its moral condemnation, on the one hand, and its legal prosecution, on the other. Since in most instances this perversion is the result of a wrong psychical development in infancy, it seems to be more advisable to place these people in the hands of a physician than assigning them to a court of law. That in most of the countries in which homosexuality is a legal offense male homosexuality only should be punishable, while the equally prevalent female form should be disregarded, seems to be an indication that lawgivers, too, are occasionally guided by idiosyncrasies rather than by principles.

Unnatural, and contradicting the meaning of sex, are finally those cases of sexual intercourse in which the natural presuppositions for the unveiling of the inner secret of sexual existence are absent. This happens when an adult has intercourse with a sexually immature or imbecile person, or when sexual activities take place amongst children, who are mentally and emotionally incapable of sexual love. Experience proves that while infantile sexual acts do not promote knowledge of the sexual mystery they stimulate, nevertheless, sexual sensuality.

Chastity

Sexual purity or chastity is the crowning sexual virtue. Chastity is respect for the sanctity of the sexual mystery. From sexual reverence, as described above, chastity differs characteristically. Whereas the former is related to the dignity of manhood and womanhood, and therefore of marriage, sexual purity is reverence for the sanctity of the sexual mystery. Chasity is thus concerned with that side of sexual life which most profoundly differentiates human sexuality from that of animals. Therefore, unchastity is regarded as the height of revolt against the divine standards of sexual life.

In this light we may understand Jesus' extremely harsh words: "If your right eye causes you to sin, pluck it out and throw it away! If your right hand causes you to sin, cut it off!" (Matt. 5:29 ff). While Jesus hardly expected a literal observation of His commandment, it will not do, either, to get rid of its rigorism by explaining it as the fruit of the common oriental love for exaggeration. Jesus insists that one must dissociate oneself radically from every activity and desire that militate against purity. Since our outlook in sexual matters profoundly affects our whole attitude towards our earthly existence we cannot take the question of chastity and purity too seriously. Paul observes that since unchastity practically denies the deeper meaning of our bodily existence it annuls our membership in the Body of Christ (1 Cor. 6:15; cf. Eph. 5:3). An unchaste person not only acts as though no fundamental difference existed between man and animals, but also, for instance, in obscene speech and indecent behavior he displays an unholy joy in desecrating the sexual mystery.

By virtue of his being created in the image of God man's bodily existence has acquired a sanctity which no beast may share. God's redemptive work sanctifies the whole man, in body and soul, and destines him for fellowship with his Creator. Hence the body no less than the spirit is the temple of the Holy Spirit (1 Cor. 6:19), and the knowledge a person acquires in sexual union is not simply an understanding of the mystery of his manhood as destined for a woman and vice versa, but also of the fact that his fellowship with God embraces his sexual life and relationships, too. Therefore, chastity as we understand it is one of the Christian virtues that can be obtained only as a gift of the Holy Spirit. Though the ideal of chastity is held in high respect in many quarters outside of the Biblical religion, too, it differs from the Christian virtue both in function and goal. As a gift of the Holy Spirit, chastity determines not only the individual's activities but also exerts a deepgoing effect upon his total attitude toward life and people and controls a person's wishes and desires. Chastity requires more than refraining from extramarital sexual relationships or acts of self-abuse. Since mental sensuality, lustful thoughts, and the play of imagination are as significantly expressive of our attitude toward the other sex, as are the physical acts, chastity can be defined as that attitude toward the other sex which declines to have anything to do with unclean things. Therefore, Jesus stamps the lustful look cast upon a married woman as sinful (Matt. 5:28) because just as a sensuous contact with or a pleasurable touching of another person's body it covertly aims at sexual union.

Purity is not to be identified with the childlike innocence that is still unaware of sex. Like all Christian virtues it is not an inborn disposition but is a gift contingent on spiritual regeneration and appropriated by the believer in the course of his life. This explains why in many instances sexual purity is not a mere affirmation of one's congenital innocence but it is rather acquired in the struggle with temptations to which one may even have succumbed. This fact, in no way, contradicts the contention that purity is a gift of the Holy Spirit. Christ came to redeem sinners, and, therefore, all His gifts serve the development of a new and holy life contrasted with our original life of sin.

However, this fact has sometimes been responsible for a distortion of the idea of chastity. It was depicted as a purely negative virtue, namely abstention from immorality, and/or extramarital sexual relations. As a result of this misunderstanding sexual education has been largely negative, issuing warnings and laying down prohibitions. However, the more respect for the sanctity of the sexual mystery is exhibited in daily Christian life and institutions the more natural will it be for the younger generation to view sex with pure eyes. More however is required for that purpose than objective medical or scientific information about the sexual processes. As has been pointed out, the fact that sexual matters are presented to young men and women in the armed services of most countries under the viewpoint of preventing and curing venereal diseases has a destructive influence upon their sexual morality and mores. Young people are thus impressed with the idea that sexual intercourse as such is justified whenever the opportunity presents itself.

Sexually inexperienced persons act in a chaste manner when in spite of the sexual impulse they are willing to remain pure, that is to say to wait patiently for the true unveiling of the secret of sex. However, since young people are not outstanding for patience and the ability to wait, this poses an extremely difficult problem which is still aggravated in the case of those young people who had already some prior sexual experience, no matter how slight or imperfect it was. Moreover, a young person is steadily affected in his physical, mental, and spiritual life by the gradual development of his sexuality without being able to understand its meaning. He is therefore in constant danger of impairing his sense of chastity by an inordinate curiosity. Ignorance of the meaning of sex weighs so heavily upon adolescents that they are tempted to seize the most unlikely means of gaining sexual knowledge. Novels, books on art, and anatomical tomes are read not so much as sources of objective information but rather as stimulants of sexual imagination.

Of course chastity implies for the unmarried person a willingness to forego sexual activities. However, the motivations for such abstention is not that sex is something evil, but that the young person feels some intimation of the sanctity of the sexual secret which renders him willing to wait for its proper revelation. Thus understood the Biblical view of chastity might usher in the development of a new ideal of virginity in Protestantism. Until recently, Protestantism has retained the Old Testament concept of virginity, which simply meant the physical intactness of the girl's hymen. Of course, the anatomical fact was taken as a guarantee that the girl had not had sexual intercourse before her marriage. This is an inconclusive proof of a girl's chastity, however, because she might allow a man considerable sexual freedom without any damage to the physical evidence of her virginity. From the modern viewpoint of equality of the sexes it would seem unwarranted, furthermore, to lay more stringent requirements upon women than upon men in the matter of chastity. In large circles, however, the upshot is not an equal demand for chastity on the part of the man but the assumption that the quest for virginity was inappropriate, and the demand is made that prior to marriage both men and women should have the right to engage in sexual relations with persons of the opposite sex. A general change of mind in these matters is hardly to be expected until people adopt a renewed appreciation of the nature of patience and self-control in solving the sexual mystery and a new reverence for the dignity of sex.

Chastity is not required of unmarried people only. Although in marriage the mystery has been revealed to the partners it has lost none of its sacred character. Therefore, the mutuality of the spouses requires respect for the limits within which their secret may be shared with other people. Even though the knowledge of their mystery need not necessarily be restricted to the spouses care must be taken not to profane it through thoughtless communication. Of course, divulging details of their sexual lives to another person does not by itself destroy the mutual relationship of the pair. There may be situations even in which it is necessary for a spouse to reveal the intimacies of his sexual relationship to a physician or a pastor. All depends, however, on the spirit in which this information is given. Women's indiscriminate gossiping sometimes has a way of disclosing to other women the secrets of the marriage bed, and men sometimes boast in an irreverent way about their exploits with women in conversing with comrades at the inn, in the barracks, or around the campfire. In such instances chastity is violated no matter how impersonally objective the accounts are given. Sexual matters are not on the same plane with the commonplace recitation of children's antics or the details of a hunting trip or a recent business success. Chastity also refrains from all sly questioning and spying upon others in order to enter into their sexual secret. Nevertheless, prudery, though it dares to speak of sexual matters only under the cloak of greatest secrecy, yet is no more devout or pure than unchastity, because it is not rooted in sexual respect, but in aversion to and fear of sex. Sexual purity is not preserved by maintaining complete silence about it, but by speaking of sex matters only at the appropriate moment and with propriety.

How far is it legitimate to make a distinction between the moral and immoral in works of art? One thing is certain. A work of art is not immoral simply because a painting depicts the naked body or a book describes sexual relationships. But we must not assert that the treatment of sexual matters in a work of art is beyond the reach of an ethical pronouncement for the single reason that it is a work of art. The difficulty of subjecting it to a moral judgment lies, however, in the absence of satisfactory objective criteria. It is the pure person who can see clearly whether a work of art is intended to heighten sexual feeling, or whether it is executed for the sake of artistic effect. There can be no doubt, for instance, but that the modern so-called confession novel is frequently used by the author as an opportunity, by means of a literary production, to purge himself of some risqué or distressing phases of his own sexual past or imagination. There is no objection against doing this, but it should be done in the privacy of the consulting room of a physician or psychiatrist. Unfortunately, however, the readiness of some modern writers and publishing houses to use this type of literature for big financial gain reflects pathetically not only on public taste but also on their disregard for the dignity of sex. For the fact that such writing portrays the intimate manifestations and practices of sex with daring frankness does not render it either artistic or moral. On the other hand, the fact that unchaste or immature minds may be confused by some aspect of a work of art is hardly a reason for calling it immoral. For in a similar manner we avoid references to our sex life before our children, not because such discussions are immoral but because they are, at the time, inappropriate for them.

XVII. THE DISCIPLINE OF THE WILL

Faith and Will

Our discussion of the Christian virtues may seem to repeat the error of Idealism. Are not virtues attitudes of the personality to be attained by an effort of the human will? There is this difference, however, that the Christian virtues are God's gracious gift. His Spirit not only provides the incentive for developing them, but his operation also enables the natural faculties to grow into virtues. It was therefore detrimental for the Church, whenever people believed that man could become good and grow in grace solely by his own efforts. The Spirit of God operates in his own way, and cannot be pressed into the services of our own aspirations.

The spiritual stimulus is intensified when we make use of the resources which God has provided for our growth in Christian grace, particularly the Bible, the community of believers, and prayer. Yet no mere mechancial reading of the Bible is sufficient; we must perceive God Himself speaking to us in His Word. Similarly any perfunctory attendance at the church service is inadequate. Our ears must be attuned to the preaching of God's Word, and we have voluntarily to expose ourselves to the example of mature Christians by participation in the congregational life of prayer and the service of love. All of these activities foster our growth in the life of the Spirit. How frequently do people consult with their pastor about their sexual difficulties, without realizing that the present crisis would never have arisen had they participated in the fellowship and work of the Church!

A word needs to be said here about the wedding ceremony as a means of grace. Protestant theology has replaced the purely legalistic interpretation of marriage according to which it is a publicly concluded contract by the concept that marriage is a voluntary union, which implies both mutual surrender of the bodies in sexual relation and a willingness to establish a permanent union. Hence Christians may live together in a true married relationship without receiving the official consecration by a minister, and the wedding ceremony in the church does not form the indispensible foundation of marriage. Nevertheless the benediction pronounced by the pastor is no mere formality, or simply a nice looking appendage to the civil ceremony as many a young couple seems to think. In the church ceremony the spouses publicly affirm their membership before the congregation, and thus they confess that they regard their union an expression of their Christian lives and of their desire to live them according to the Biblical understanding. The Church's prayer and benediction form the congregation's response to the couple's declaration. The wedding ceremony, therefore, is not a mere public proclamation of the divine blessing promised to a Christian couple but also a valid offer of the great and real blessings that by God's will the Church has to share with the spouses. The minister communicates to them the portion they have in all those gifts of the Holy Spirit which they need in order to make theirs a Christian marriage. Though Christians do not act immorally when they live in a common law alliance they nevertheless thereby betray the immaturity and shortsightedness of their faith because they deprive themselves of the blessings available to them in the fellowship of the congregation. Married life is in constant need of prayer, both personal and common; for it is by the exercise of prayer that the Christian life is furthered and developed. The Christian life does not start from a perfect condition of spiritual maturity, and its development demands continual effort and diligence, rather than mere passivity. God's gifts are obtained by those only who take the trouble to secure them. Belief in the once-for-allness of Christ's work is but the beginning of the Christian life. But the Christian virtues do not grow up in the believer automatically. They are granted to those only who desire them as the indispensable evidence of their vocation, and who therefore pray persistently that they should be imparted and increased to them.

Self-Discipline and Commandments

The Saviour's entrance into human life not only exemplified but also assured to His followers the new life of the spirit. A sincere desire to possess the gifts of the Holy Spirit marks, therefore, the first and most important step in the life of faith. There is complete assurance for the fulfillment of such a sublime aspiration. The fact that the Holy Spirit is at work in every believing heart means that every believer is on the way to making his sexual life completely meaningful. The Holy Spirit has the power to purify and regenerate our hearts, and thus gives a new perspective and direction to our life. Our past is no obstacle to the Spirit's work. The well-known fact that prostitutes were numbered among Jesus' followers should encourage those whose past lives have been a barren waste. But if the Christian life is confined to formal prayer, Bible reading or church-membership it can never be anything but a nondescript generality. To be sure, these means can deepen the insights of faith, and can release some feelings of mystical piety, but no effects are evident in daily life. However, since these forms of spiritual life are widely held to be normative, many people conclude that faith is completely disrelated to actual life and experience. Therefore, many Christians turn to erotic love as the only effective solution of their sexual problem, hoping that it will do for them what is impossible for faith. Yet, as has been pointed out, erotic love, in itself, is not only incapable of setting limits to sexual desire, but also lacks the respect required for true appreciation of the mystery of sexual unity. But the opposite attitude is hardly more satisfactory. Experience proves that in sexual matters little can be effected by issuing commandments and prohibitions. With the decline of authority characteristic of our age, many young people will also question the right of their seniors to tell them how to behave. Others who want to comply with these commandments fall prey to fear neuroses, or else they lapse into a state of self-detestation when the questionable nature of their past lives and the possibilities of discovery loom before them.

These imperatives are bound to fail not because they lack an appeal to the will, but because thereby the will is not directly related to faith. When we look at sex with the eyes of faith we are humbled because we realize that our sexual life has not yet reached the high level for which God has destined mankind and for whose attainment he has granted us the Christian virtues. But faith also renders us thankful by teaching us that already the present level of our sexual life, no matter how spotty and imperfect it may be, is the work of the Holy Spirit. It is one of the fundamental principles of the life of faith, that real progress can be made only when the gains achieved are held fast and preserved (Rev. 3:11). This is not an unattainable ideal provided that the will is disciplined and that it is sustained by the mores and morality of the Christian fellowship.

What a disastrous folly to believe in complete sexual freedom! The result has been the dissolution of personal character, of the institution of marriage, and of the total structure of society. However, those who posed as the guardians of the Christian tradition must assume a large share of the blame for this development. Being ignorant of the Biblical view of sex they have failed to direct attention to the values in sex which on account of their God given character can serve as most powerful stimuli upon the human will. Therefore, the educational efforts of the church should not be directed one-sidedly against the sins of sex but should rather emphasize the blessings and gifts of sexual life and thus develop their joyful and thankful acceptance at the hand of God. Where this gratitude is found people will be inspired to remain on the level achieved, and they will be anxious not to put obstacles in God's way which would render it impossible for Him to lift them to a still higher level. In God's perspective, our readiness to grow in faith is a response to His command which requires of us to express true thankfulness for His gifts. This is the function not only of the Old Testament Law, but also of the countless admonitions of the New Testament which enjoin us to flee unchastity, and to hold marriage in honor. So understood, the divine commands are not heteronomous authorities which confront our wills from the outside, but they describe what the mature expressions of our Christian self-determination will be like.

Modern people seem to have a strange aversion toward ethical imperatives, and loathe to be reminded of sin. However, this resentment shown toward "the eternal talk about sin" should not rashly be interpreted as a symptom of insincerity and frivolity. People resent the vague generality with which theologians often refer to man's sinfulness. This is proven by the fact that evangelists who attack sin head-on attract large and attentive crowds from all classes of the population. Others repudiate the validity of commandments in the sexual sphere on account of their apparent arbitrariness. Hence it is of greatest importance to show that the commands of God contribute to the preservation of goods whose value is evident.

It should be recognized, however, that a discipline of the will that is confined one-sidedly to sexual matters will be difficult to put into practice. We resent so strongly any curtailment of our sexual desire that a direct attack is least likely to succeed. While sheer discipline of the will can effect stern personal restraints, it will not engender the equally important regard for the partner and the other sex. Because of the peculiar and unique nature of sexual pleasure, a self-centered person resents the suggestion to curb it, and the very suggestion to fight the impulse will make him prize its pleasures with renewed zeal. Therefore, any one-sided concentration on the problem of sex would disarm him in the very heat of battle. It will be more appropriate to cultivate the spirit of service, love, and reverence in other areas of life where it does not conflict so passionately with our desire of happiness and pleasure. Since the Christian life is a unity, not only every fault in one area of life affects the whole of life but also by the same token, such a shortcoming can be healed by strengthening a corresponding virtue in another sphere of life.

Of course, a disciplined will tends to avoid overt sexual temptations. If a person exposes himself to conditions that are conducive to sexual licentiousness, such as brothels, low taverns, certain dance pavilions, and amusement places, it is no wonder that the assaults of temptation prove too powerful for him. Moreover, any girl who accepts a drink or two at the invitation of a stranger or slight acquaintance exposes herself to danger, for such invitations are usually meant to break down her sexual resistance. Similarly, the defenders of heavy petting and necking should realize that when young people indulge in such familiarities they will hardly be able to withstand the temptation to go a step further and have sexual relations with each other. Such experiences, in turn, reaffirm the positive and constructive values inherent in membership in the Christian community. The kind of fellowship enjoyed there will effectively combat the temptation to indulge in questionable entertainments and amusements. Likewise when young people are in love, and one of them is well-grounded in his faith, he will be able to restrict the excessive sexual desire of the partner. Thus also one should not underrate the help which young people derive from cultivating common interests in sports, literature or art, and even scholarship. Experience shows that the less they take an interest in such activities, the more easily they are driven into thinking that sexual pleasure forms the only source of happiness. While those other activities are no substitutes for the kind of satisfaction offered by sex, they are apt to protect people against the temptation of prematurely indulging in sexual relations.

Without undervaluing the power of the disciplined will Protestantism nevertheless assigns less importance to it than Catholicism, because it is more interested in the motivation of action than in the mere transgression of commandments. Protestantism follows in this respect, Paul's example. In the counsel the apostle gives to married couples not to abstain from sexual intercourse for long periods of time (1 Cor. 7:5), he teaches them that once sexual desire has been aroused it can only be allayed by the power of Christian virtue, yet that doing so is not a self-acquired quality but rather the result of the Holy Spirit's work within us. The unaided human will, even though disciplined, is on the whole unable to withstand the temptations of Satan.

Mores

From a practical point of view, the customs regulating sexual life are far more important than the principle of self-discipline which has been greatly overrated in Christian education following an individualistic conception of the nature of man. Life in a fellowship with a fixed set of rules and customs tends effectively to support the efforts of self-discipline. For this reason the requirement of continence has been found possible among the clergy and the religious orders of the Roman Catholic Church. A person is greatly helped when he does not have to stand alone against temptation, but lives in an environment that holds the same convictions and ideals and seeks the same goals in life. By means of its customs a community expresses its sense of responsibility for the cultivation of certain values. The custom serves to exclude or repress all attitudes and behaviour patterns that conflict with the values recognized by the community. This goal is attained mainly through social sanctions for those who violate the custom. Thereby custom limits drastically both the incentives and opportunities to disregard or destroy these treasured values. If the community shows contempt for the adulterer as a person without honor, the offense itself occurs comparatively seldom. The relative uniformity of conduct demanded by custom precludes thoughtless and arbitrary conduct which results so easily when strictly personal decisions are demanded. Since this kind of support is of utmost importance for all people, it is presumptuous for any individual to insist on a life altogether of his own.

Unfortunately, however, modern society is divided into many small factions and units, and thus the readiness to live in accordance with established customs encounters today considerable practical difficulties. Formerly, Christianity and national life worked together for an integrated pattern of conduct. Today the individual is confronted with conflicting claims due to the fact that he is a member of a number of independently co-existing special interest groups and social organizations. There are but a few Christian leagues and fellowships and some professional organizations left that produce a special type of conduct of the older type among their constituencies. The situation is further aggravated by the fact that recent events have created purely masculine organizations which were free to develop their own life patterns. We mention in particular life in the army and in work camps. Their style of life clashes with feminine custom which is still largely based on the concepts of home and family and the specific needs of the women. The tension between these two elements was less perceptible in past generations because then the men were not separated from their wives for long periods of time. But in our time millions of men have been under arms, in distant places of work, or in prisoner of war camps for many years and the habits acquired under these conditions are not easily shed or forgotten. Moreover, the presence of large numbers of troops stationed outside their countries tends to prevent a synthesis of masculine and feminine attitudes. Since the young women and girls, generally, yield to the aggressive masculinity of soldiers, the young civilians in turn are compelled to adopt the same aggressiveness towards women. This development is strengthened by youth's powerful urge for independence. Not only has the older generation loosened its grip on youth in recent years, but also the economic development of our time has compelled the young people independently to assume responsibility for their own lives.

Finally, the egalitarian tendencies of our age have removed the support which the customs of an hierarchical society had given to the conduct of young people. This change submerged the chivalrous attitude toward women, and the rigid requirements laid down for the social standing of girls of the upper classes. This is all past history now, not only because the social classes that maintained these customs no longer exist but because women themselves refuse to claim privileges for themselves.

Compared with this universal and radical revolution in custom the recent attempts to introduce new customs, such as made, for instance, by the youth movements and related groups, reach but small circles. The absence of generally recognized custom has made the press, the motion picture, the television, the radio, and the theatre powerful media for the formation of public opinion. The average man argues that anything allowed public presentation must therefore be right, and that relative frequency of occurrence is tantamount to normalcy. Whereas formerly custom exercised censorship over literature and art today both create conventional life attitudes, which, more or less effectively, supplant established custom. However the modern conformism is no true custom because the latter originates in the concerted evaluations of identifiable groups and group consciousness, which either give recognition or condemn the conduct of their members. This is nonexistent today. The individual conducts himself as all others do not because he desires identification with the group but because he is utterly perplexed. The chaos of the last three decades has smashed the old values, and the absence of established standards commends adaptation to public opinion as the second best policy.

While some congregations still cling stubbornly to the customs of the past there is little hope of a general return to the mores of the seventeenth or even nineteenth century. Yet the very fact that the Church on the whole still believes in objective values dispels discouragement. The church still has the resources which can form the nucleus around which new patterns of conduct may evolve some day.

The State and Marriage

Next to the individual's free self-discipline and the demands of custom, it is the State that determines the form of marriage. However, at all times Christians have asked themselves the question: what right does the State have to legislate in marital matters? Since according to the Protestant view marriage is founded upon the voluntary union of a man and a woman, who are held together by their permanent devotion, every outside encroachment seems to contradict its very nature. Yet the fact cannot be denied that marriage is not a purely private matter. As a social institution it owes its origin to its social usefulness and it is protected and supported by social customs. In turn, marriage as the foundation of the family makes a decisive contribution to education, custom, and the economic life of a nation. It is, therefore, important to determine what the right relationship of Christianity and the State should be toward the institution of marriage.

The far-reaching social consequences implicit in the nature of marriage make it desirable to have it publicly acknowledged. However, if the State's recognition of marriage is conditioned by certain provisions irreconcilable with Christian faith, it is the Christian's privilege to forego public acknowledgement of his marriage, even at the risk of casting the slur of illegitimacy upon his children. This happened to the Huguenots in Southern France after the revocation of the Edict of Nantes, and is happening today to Protestants in Spain. In both instances, public recognition of these marriages has been made dependent upon solemnization by a Catholic priest. A different situation obtains in the case of civil marriages. In most countries of the Western world public recognition of marriage depends upon State registration; and in many countries the church wedding may not even precede the civil ceremony. In some countries the Roman Church has chosen to make this a matter of principle while at the best it was a question of prestige. The order of the two ceremonies is not a serious matter, unless the civic ceremony interferes with that of the Church. It is true that by the solemnity attending the civil ceremony some governments have attempted to create the impression that the wedding before the magistrate is the real thing, while the church ceremony assumes the place of a kind of beautiful after-piece to the main event. However, the fact that many people have this impression is not the fault of the government but of Christians to whom the church ceremony is a merely social affair.

A real conflict occurs, however, when the laws of the State view marriage as a temporary alliance only. This reveals the operation of non-Christian forces in the modern State, over against which the Church must maintain its Christian interpretation with forceful clarity. Nevertheless, the Church would be misguided if it directed its efforts against the laws of divorce. Rather, following her Master's example, she should instruct her members that not everything that is permitted by the lawgiver is in accord with the aims of the Christian life. An incipient alienation in a marriage cannot be healed simply by denying the couple divorce but only by attempting to reconcile the spouses. They should be shown that the Christian faith is the only means for effectively resolving the tensions and conflicts of married life.

Governments have no right to prohibit inter-racial marriages. Such a prohibition is a denial of the unity of the human family established by the fact that notwithstanding racial differences God has called all mankind to salvation. Whether or not one should actually conclude an inter-racial marriage is a question of expedience rather than of principle. It seems, for instance, that in not a few cases marriages between whites and colored people in the United States encounter special difficulties, since the colored community looks upon the white person as an intruder while the colored person is shunned by a section of the white group. However, the difficulties of this problem might conceivably motivate some Christians to enter deliberately into such a marriage in order to relieve some of the existing prejudices.

The laws of many countries attempt to give equal status to the unwed and the married mother. This is done for two closely intertwined motives: the desire to shield the child from suffering for the deeds of his parents, as well as a certain disregard for the institution of marriage. Existing laws disclose the obvious conflict in these motives. Naturally, the bosom of the family is the child's best refuge, but the more closely the legal position of the unwed mother is assimilated to that of the married mother, for instance, by letting her share in the estate of the child's father, the more seriously the family as a legal institution is threatened. If the illegitimate child were granted a full share in the father's inheritance this would be a practical legalization of polygamy. From a humanitarian viewpoint, modern society's tolerant attitude toward the unwed mother marks a progress over against the time when the girl had to bear her shame alone, while society allowed the man to go scot-free. But, notwithstanding the unwed mother's improved social status her child is not safe from embarrassment. Therefore, in order to assure a life for the child within the circle of the family, many unwed mothers give out their children for adoption. This is definitely to the child's advantage, but the ease with which it can be done in this country has certainly removed another restraint from extramarital relations.

A final question proposes itself: has the Church any right to demand that the Christian understanding of sex and marriage be made the basis of public legislation; and should the Government extend any special protection to Christian marriage? Let us remember that Christian marriage is not a special kind of marriage, but rather the way in which Christians from time to time have implemented the existing institution of marriage in their country. But our faith does not demand that the marriage legislation of the Old Testament be adopted by modern legislators, for in their specific requirements these laws reflected the historical conditions of ancient Israel. They cannot be treated as absolute principles.

For instance, no person today would think of appealing to Leviticus 20:10ff, as the basis for demanding the death penalty for adultery, or for sexual intercourse with a blood relative, with boys, or with animals. But the Christian citizen of today has every right to insist that proper legal and police protection be granted to all citizens, especially to women and children, against any peril in the sexual sphere, for instance, by the suppression of immoral publications, prohibition of public solicitation by prostitutes, and the detention of sex-offenders. Should the Government tolerate the propaganda of un-Christian or anti-Christian views of sex? We believe the State acts in its own best interests by furthering the Christian evaluations of marriage, and the Church must insist upon its right publicly to proclaim its interpretation. However, the strongest defense against un-Christian concepts of sex is to be found in Christian marriage. The light of faith shines to all in the house. By way of conduct Christians demonstrate the superiority of their ideal of marriage. Where it is lacking all prohibitions against adverse propaganda are valueless, because the Christian ideal seems to be of doubtful value to its own advocates.

Part Three

THE WAY AND THE GOAL

XVIII. THE PROBLEMS OF SEXUAL RELATIONSHIP

Sex in Married Life

Many modern books on marriage leave the impression that by means of marriage all sexual problems, if not all human problems, can be solved. This viewpoint represents a highly overidealized concept in which the actual difficulties and conflicts of married life are ignored. In spite of its high esteem for marriage, the Old Testament has nothing in common with this idealism, and it speaks realistically about the shortcomings of marriage. The New Testament, too, is aware of disturbing factors in marriage, and it describes therefore the unity of sex, love and marriage not in terms of a harmony already achieved, but as a unity which can be apprehended only by faith. There are three factors that create problems in marriage: the necessity of living together in marriage engenders one set of problems for the spouses; further, marriage as an institution is not capable of solving the personality problems of the partners; and, finally, the common life may be further complicated by the presence of pseudo-sexual problems.

The blessings of marriage may be experienced in any kind of marriage; and couples who regard their union in the light of Christ's redemptive purpose will always be in a position to grasp them. However, the fact that the spouses must live together permanently, and that they depend on each other exclusively not only in their sexual relationship but in most of the affairs of their daily lives, creates special problems and dangers.

In the first place, the diversity of the sexes remains after marriage and can neither be destroyed nor altered. Indeed, the necessity to live closely together day by day makes the differences between man and woman more oppressive for the spouses than for the same people in their premarital relationships. The husband will discover that in spite of the unity of the flesh his wife is often an incomprehensible and occasionally tormenting enigma. Among other things, he has difficulty in appreciating sympathetically the dependence and attachment which characterizes his wife's relationship to her mother, and which creates the mother-in-law problem. Or he fails to understand the existent tensions between his wife and his mother or between his wife's mother and himself. His own expressions of kindness and meekness may prove to be insufficient to eliminate this problem. The same thing holds true for the unique bond of attachment that exists between his wife and her children, because she alone has borne them, and she, more than anybody else, was responsible for raising them. Further, since his masculine nature is a stranger to her kind of thinking and feeling the husband can scarcely realize what it means for his wife exclusively to surrender her body to him and to be bound with him for all her life, for there is no corresponding experience on his part.

This gulf which separates the sexes is an occasion for never-ending perplexity to the husband because he can never be certain that he is treating his wife as she expects him to do. Correspondingly, the wife feels easily misunderstood, and considers that she is not taken seriously enough nor fully appreciated. The family usually takes for granted the housewife's labors in keeping an orderly and nice looking home, to say nothing of preparing the meals, and generally caring for the assorted needs of her family. She receives little recognition and scant praise for her painstaking care in maintaining her household and for her daily sacrificial service, while she is freely censured when things do not go well.

The modern wife generally resents her economic dependence. Many young girls today are self-supporting by working at a job or in a profession, and thus, when married, chafe under their dependence particularly in money matters. No wonder that without any pressing economic need the number of married women who are gainfully employed increases constantly. But while they acquire economic independence thereby the human tensions multiply too. She enjoys a realm of her own yet outside of the home. She is unable to make a real home for her husband and her children, though her added income permits her to furnish her rooms more elaborately and to go more frequently on a journey than the woman next door. In a good marriage, where relations are not strained and where the spouses share sufficient common interests, this strangeness of the sexes will rarely be noticed, although no marriage is entirely immune against the sudden appearance of the gulf.

The sexual intercourse of the couple may become another disturbing factor. While the turbulence of sexual desire is abated by regular sexual intercourse in marriage, it nevertheless usually remains a powerful force right into advanced years, so that irregularities or disturbances in its satisfaction are apt to produce far-reaching difficulties. A husband may be inclined, for instance, to consider the incidence of pregnancy, illness, or fatigue of his wife as infringements upon his sexual rights. In such a case, some will react with an attitude of bitterness toward their wife, whereas others may withdraw into a martyr complex, or seek sexual satisfaction with other women. Then again, there is the problem of the sexually insatiable wife, particularly if she has been unable to bear children (Pro. 30:15). She may either hold her husband in contempt for his unwillingness or inability to comply always with her sex hunger, or she may lapse into infidelity. However, even regular conjugal sexual intercourse has its dangers. Couples often take their mutual possession of each other for granted and fail to appreciate the mystery of their union. Since the former interplay of wooing and offering resistance ceases, their sexual relationship to each other becomes a matter of routine and, eventually, boresome. But continuing to be husband and wife they transfer their feelings for each other from the area of the purely sexual to that of personal relationships. The husband becomes a tyrant about the house, who boasts of his authority, while his wife's resentfulness makes her unbearable and quarrelsome.

Furthermore there are situations in which children are not

wanted, or would be an unbearable burden economically or physically. Because complete continence after a period of regular and frequent sexual relations is psychologically disturbing to many people they resort to various methods of contraception. But since none of these guarantees complete effectiveness the wife is in a constant state of worry over possible pregnancies that may even lead to a neurosis. The husband, too, may develop a fear neurosis, especially when he interrupts the sexual act; but most of all his feeling of self-reliance is shattered because he must approach his wife with a certain reserve. No less important for the sexual relations of the couple is the fact that marriage in itself is no effective barrier to the sudden development of a passion. While a person may be able to bridle his desires no cure for passion has ever been discovered. Passion is like an incomprehensible magic spell that may break unexpectedly into anyone's life. The passion which suddenly overtakes a marriage partner causes a much greater conflict than in the case of an unmarried person, because the other spouse is made to suffer under the partner's passion also no matter what effort the affected person makes to remain faithful. Finally, living conditions may also seriously affect the marriage relationship. It is much easier for a single person to make a smooth and ready adjustment to unexpected changes and difficult circumstances than for a couple, especially with children. Housing shortages, the working wife's absence from home, or the turmoil of international and domestic political uncertainties can be almost intolerable burdens for married persons. Conditions beyond his control may render it impossible for the husband to discharge his responsibilities towards his family in a satisfactory manner. The wife, immersed in tasks beyond the limits of her strength and time, and faced with an unpromising future, is unhappy, since everything she does for her family seems purposeless. To be sure, not every marriage must face all or even any of these problems, but neither is any marriage totally certain to be spared the problems that arise naturally out of the marriage relationship itself.

Personality Problems

Another group of marital problems originates from the fact that marriage partners are not only sexual beings but also persons. Since individuality differentiates people all personal relationships are fraught with tensions. Conflicts of personality, rather than being resolved by sexual love, are accentuated by the marriage relationship. Most other relationships permit a mutual evasion when conflicts arise, but not so in marriage where people do share the life of every day. Furthermore, in marriage more than in other relations, there is the temptation to drop all self-control and to let one's self go. In public life there are many compelling reasons for showing our best side in order to maintain pleasant relations with other people and for trying to hide our weaknesses. This demands a certain effort of will, particularly when fatigue and physical indisposition renders us irritable. But since the private lives of husband and wife are not conducted in public view, and without the restraining judgment of other people, the spouses are tempted to submit to their weaknesses. In a measure this explains some of the frequent disillusionment that follows the honeymoon. A spouse may suddenly exhibit a number of previously unnoticed but distasteful or objectionable traits. The Old Testament makes a pertinent reference to the contentious woman (Prov. 19:13; 21:9,19; 30:23), but if we could hear the wife in old Israel today she would probably complain with considerable acrimoniousness about ill-humored, miserly, suspicious, hard-hearted, and brutal husbands too.

Disturbances of the self-consciousness, such as the sense of inferiority, defeat, or fear, and lovelessness, are also apt to place a greater strain upon the marital fellowship than upon any other personal relationships. Although marriage itself does not produce these disturbances, yet the burdens and difficulties of conjugal life provide fertile soil for their growth, even to the point of producing a pathological condition in those persons who are constitutionally and emotionally so disposed. The intimate terms under which married persons must live familiarize them with each other's personal traits but especially their faults. How great then the temptation to get rid of one's own unpleasant sentiments by charging them to the partner! Thus, for an exhibition of his superiority, one spouse will humiliate the other, make impossible demands, or vex and domineer the other. In that way the partner serves as a scapegoat who must bear the blame for one's own unhappy and unbalanced state. One wants to punish the spouse for alleged injustices, or to show contempt and thus resorts to some form of marital infidelity, or to sexual frigidity. These are not sexual problems, however, but personality conflicts which can be resolved only from the center of the personality.

Furthermore, in most people the personal life encompasses a wider circle of interests than are covered by the marriage relationship. Therefore, married persons can never completely suffice to each other. They need to cultivate other persons and associates with whom they may converse and receive stimulating suggestions. Generally speaking, the law of the psychological triangle applies to all paired relationships, not to marriage alone but also, for instance, to friendship or the teacher-pupil relationship. Necessary as the third person may be for an effective paired relationship, yet the psychological triangle is also a threat to marriage on account of the reciprocal relationship of the spouses. Naturally, a spouse who finds no stimulation of his interests in his partner, may seek a close association with a friend of theirs. Yet the satisfaction gained from that companionship of common interests can appear so valuable that it eventually develops into love for the third person. This may be harmful for the marriage relationship.

From the foregoing it is plain that for the sake of the unity of the flesh the spouses must be ready to share each other's interests. It is apparent that no marriage can for long be satisfactory on a purely emotional basis and without a real fellowship of interests. The reciprocity requires that the partners have a common love of many things. This fellowship must exceed a mere joint involvement in movements, programs, or objective values. It must extend to personal interest in other people chiefly in the family and in each other's friends.

Pseudo-Sexual Relationships

All the relationships between persons of different sexes are not of a sexual nature even though they imply a feeling of sympathy, or a longing for it. Take, for instance, the father-daughter and the mother-son relationships which the Freudian school all too generally interprets as an unconscious and disguised sexual relationship. We must go even a step further. There may be intercourse between the sexes that is devoid of a sexual desire, and in which the sexual pleasure is simply a means of relieving a feeling of listlessness or unhappiness. This probably explains the strange phenomenon that girls and young women, who thus far had lived a modest life, are willing to enter into sexual relations when they are transplanted to a locality, where they feel lonely. A similar explanation applies to many cases of Onanism. Similarly a good deal of sexual familiarity among young people is not aimed at sexual intercourse but is done in search for some compensation for motherlove and affection denied to the young person.

Our age seems to be unaware of the fact that the more trying and insecure external circumstances are, or the more a young person feels unhappy, the more does he or she need the security of the nest, and the warmth of motherlove. Most parents lavish abundant caresses upon a very young child, but are reluctant to give the ten or eleven year old child similar proofs of their affection. This is the case not only where on account of housing conditions family life lacks privacy or where the family's economic needs demand the mother's employment outside the home, but also where under normal economic conditions the mother is too selfish or too negligent to spend much of her time with her children. But the modern father perhaps even more than the mother neglects his normal role in the life of the family. When the sense of insecurity is strongest, at puberty, the father is called upon to occupy a most important place in his son's life. He is destined to represent the grown-up mature person to his children, and to be the one who takes their immaturity seriously. He is meant to be the authority that asserts itself lovingly, and stands ready to prove itself. However, if the father has no time, or is disinterested in the development of his children during the insecurities of that most difficult period of puberty, there is no balancing factor. No wonder that young people upset by that experience seek compensation in sex.

As a result, a boy wanting to show his superiority may take a sexual interest in younger girls. A mother's withheld affection is obviously also one of the main causes for a boy's indulgence in masturbation, i.e., a pleasure sensation caused by exciting the sexual organ but without sexual significance. Masturbation has wrongly been called the safety valve for the pressure of sexual desire, for it is practised by many boys who are too young to feel sex as pressure. In the case of the maturing girl masturbation is found but rarely. However, if she is suffering under a real or imagined withholding of her mother's love or her father's attention, she may give herself to any man who will show her the consideration and friendliness she needs.

Another type of pseudo-sexual relationship is that of the person who in self-abandonment suffers under the meaninglessness of his life. This type is rapidly increasing today, because by the dependence on radio, press, and television, and by purely passive participation in sports the individual development of the creative powers and faculties is gradually blocked, so that life becomes increasingly emptier and duller. In competition with alcohol and narcotics youth turns to sexual pleasure as an easily accessible source of momentary satisfaction. Of course, this type of pleasure-seeking requires and exhibits no personal interest in the partner, and people change frequently from one partner to another. In contradistinction to the satisfaction of genuine sexual desire, for which there can be no substitute, this type of pseudo-sexuality desires merely pleasurable feelings, regardless of their specific nature. Such a person will pursue any personally acceptable highly charged experience. His unbridled sexuality is a symptom of pathological addiction.

As has been shown, pseudo-sexuality is not confined to marriage. Nevertheless one can imagine the disastrous effect upon a marriage when one of the spouses exhibits such tendencies while the other spouse is unable to help him develop a healthy sexual life. A husband, for instance, may be unfaithful not because he wants a new sexual partner but because he wants to be mothered —a desire which his wife may fail to recognize. For the same reason the psychological triangle may develop into a sexual relationship with the third person. Originally, one of the spouses felt drawn to him or her without any sexual implication, merely on account of the spouse's irresponsiveness to some side of his or her nature. Although in every life there is a positive need for a companion or for someone with whom special interests may be shared, it is not necessary for that purpose to enter into a sexual relationship. Rather people succumb to the temptation of the opportunity created by increased familiarity.

To be mentioned in this connection is the queer type of faithless lover who breaks off his sexual relationship with a girl but at the same time begs to retain her friendship. He came to the sudden realization that what attracted him to her was not his desire for a spouse in marriage but his need for a companion to comfort and encourage him or for a friend to cheer him in his loneliness. Similarly, a girl or a woman may associate with a man in the hope of finding understanding or moral support, or because she wants somebody to admire or to mother. She believes she may more securely bind him to herself by granting him the privilege of sexual relations.

It is apparent that marriage not only does not provide the solution of all sexual problems but that it may actually raise new problems and aggravate existent difficulties. This, of course, does not mean that every marriage must necessarily be unhappy but that a happy relationship in marriage does not automatically result from the fact that two people were deeply in love at the time of their wedding.

Sexual Relationship, Disturbed or Unfulfilled

Married couples are not the only persons whose sexual lives may be disturbed. Sexual relationships which are not meant eventually to lead to marriage generate a whole set of problems of their own. In marriage sexual difficulties affect both partners in different ways but with equal severity, whereas the extramarital relationship throws a heavier burden upon the woman (Isa. 4:1). The same is true in the case of a woman who has lost her companion through death or divorce. Whereas a man is able to find compensation for his loss in the company of other men, a woman is vexed by the oppressive feeling that her life has lost all meaning.

What renders the alliance with a man so important for a woman, and its severance so painful, is not the social status conveyed to her by her companion but rather the recognition which her womanhood receives through her association with a man.

This is proved by the way a woman reacts when she has been deceived or forsaken by a man. Many girls who have been jilted, after having gone steady with a man for a long time, fear to fall in love again with some other man. They have experienced that their feminine dignity depends in a precarious way on a male partner. The first lover's faithless disregard of her womanly dignity makes such a girl apprehensive of repetition. Unhappy as she feels in her abandonment, yet she lacks the courage to take another chance on love. What in this case grieves and humiliates her is not the thought of having surrendered herself to him, but the feeling that he so lightly esteemed the unity of the flesh. For this she now assumes the blame in her unhappiness.

On first thought the single woman who was never married would seem to belong to a different category. While among the single women there may be not a few who had a chance to marry but declined it, nevertheless, women are not, as a rule, completely unconcerned about their unmarried plight. No matter how many friends of their own sex they may have, they feel that without a husband or at least a male friend something is missing in their lives. Invitations to social affairs are usually extended to couples while the presence of single women is felt inconvenient. This situation explains why an unmarried woman, as she approaches the thirty year mark easily becomes panicky. In her effort to prove to herself that she is still attractive she may easily be willing to have an affair with the first eligible man, only to discover that in this way she will encounter neither marriage nor happiness.

XIX. OUR SIN

The Sense of Shame

People today discuss sexual matters with greater freedom and less reserve than their grandparents, but that does not mean that their attitude toward sex has become more natural or that its problems have diminished in this generation. On the contrary, it looks as though the constant talk about sex and the prominent place assigned to it in modern literature and the movies were symptoms of a deep-seated uneasiness, which people are at pains to shake off. For instance, is not the fact that modern man discusses sexual problems in a scientific manner a thinly veiled device to hide one's own concern behind the generalities of science? Similarly, the eagerness with which people turn to the presentation of sexual subjects in motion pictures, or novels, is a circuitous road to viewing one's own problems objectively by means of their reflexion in a work of art. The advantage of probing oneself in the artistic presentation lies in the fact that it imposes no obligations upon the onlooker or reader. However, the excessive interest in sex indicates that it is anything but taken for granted or considered natural in modern life.

Sexual problems are of such a highly personal nature that they may be discussed only with trusted persons; but even then a frank and free discussion is difficult. We betray our discomfort and uneasiness, to say the least, by our efforts to conceal or excuse, magnify or extenuate the individual details of the case. If sex were as natural as eating, drinking, or sleeping, the psychotherapist would not have to employ such varied and unusual techniques and psychological tricks to lay bare his patient's troubles. The fact is that sex is the part of the Self of which we are ashamed. But the sense of shame is a complex phenomenon, and unless we understand its various aspects and treat them adequately, all manner of ills, and even pathological states of overintensification may be the sequels; or through a false sense of guilt or superficial attacks upon prudishness people may destroy not only a false sense of shame but also all reverence for the mystery of sex.

The sense of sexual shame is a reluctance to reveal our personal sexual life and experiences to others. It shows itself under three forms, as modesty, a feeling of being ashamed, and a sense of guilt. They are related to three different aspects of sex: the mystery of sex, the seemingly inferior value of the sexual organs, and personal lapses in sexual life—none of which is peculiar to any degree of culture, or to any form of religion. Sex is so indissolubly related to our physical nature and our personal self that every person has some intimation of its nature and basic standards. However, the development of moral consciousness and spiritual depth are most valuable helps to a clearer understanding of our sexual life.

Sexual shame exhibits itself first of all, and in the most general way, as modesty. Concomitant with the first awakening of sexuality is the awareness of its mystery. Hence the realization of one's sexual nature fills a person with awe and the wish to protect the mystery from profanation. According to the Bible, the first man and woman perceived their nakedness only after they had eaten of the tree of knowledge of good and evil, and then they made fig-leaf aprons for themselves (Gen. 3:7). So sexual modesty makes it first appearance only after the first man and woman had attained mutual knowledge. Originally, they were not ashamed of their nakedness (Gen. 2:25). A young child, who has no understanding of the nature of sex, is unembarrassed by his nakedness. However, whereas full sexual knowledge is gained only at an age when the meaning of responsibility and mutual interdependence can be understood, modesty makes its appearance at a much earlier stage. In view of the fact that the whole bodily system of the woman is affected by her sex, modesty concerns a larger area of the body and manifests itself more vigorously in the female sex than in man.

Frequently confused with modesty, but basically different, is the feeling of being ashamed of the sexual organs. The little girl especially is taught in earliest childhood not to expose herself to strangers. However, this restraint has originally nothing to do with sex. Like the inhibition people have to uncover their buttocks this feeling is related to the excretory functions. Man is ashamed of being a child of nature. The instinctive feeling of uncleanness, associated with the urinary and bowel functions, and later with women's menstruation, is transferred to the parts of the body that serve these functions. Inasmuch as these bodily parts are also sexual organs this feeling of shame is easily associated with sex itself. Some people, therefore, consider their sexual parts as ugly, repulsive, or ridiculous and eventually transfer this contempt to the sexual act itself. As distinct from modesty, which is a positive attitude destined to guard the mystery of sex, this sense of being ashamed is a negative attitude towards sex.

Quite different from these two forms is the sexual shame. It is caused by the sense of guilt felt by a person who has transgressed the standards of sex. Unlike the perplexity called forth by a violation of modesty or the unpleasantness associated with the excretory functions this sense of guilt is hatred of oneself on account of the disregard one has shown for the very standards with which one has identified one's self. Although this experience is formally the same in all cases of moral transgression, there is a special after-effect in our relation to sex. Since we are inseparably joined to our physical nature, this kind of shame may affect one's attitude toward sex and the evaluations of the sexual organs by ascribing a sinful character to both.

For the most part this reaction results from the fact that the first initiation to sex is usually given to a child by a person who has himself violated the reverence for sex. The secretive manner in which such a person talks about sex impresses the child with the idea that sexual matters constitute a subject not to be discussed in the presence of parents and other authoritative people. The child naturally infers that sex, as such, is indecent and therefore not permissible. Hence, it is not surprising that a child should protest violently against the suggestion that his parents had ever indulged in anything as immodest as sex. Occasionally when such children have accidentally witnessed the sexual relations of their parents, or have discovered that their mother's pregnancy was caused in this way, they are thrown into psychical troubles because their mental image of the parents excludes all indecency. In not a few cases, these infantile associations of sex with guilt are never replaced by a healthy view of sex. As a result, there are women, especially in the Western world, who feel defiled after the wedding night. Also, it is probably the association of sex with guilt that accounts for the fact that sex is so often veiled in the symbolism of our dreams. For the sake of psychic health and a genuine fulfillment of our lives, it is therefore highly desirable to disentagle these misguided associations and to replace them with a true reverence and a sound naturalness in sexual matters on the one hand and, in the case of transgressions, with a genuine sense of guilt on the other.

The Knowledge of Sin

As has been pointed out, sex, too, notwithstanding its close connection with our physical life is subject to divine standards. In their light the first two forms of sexual shame are dissociated from the sense of guilt. Modesty can develop positively, and the worth and depth of sex can be accepted and enjoyed without restraint. Furthermore, although the instinctive disregard for the excretory functions and their organs is normal, yet when they are kept distinct from sex the divine purpose of sex is safeguarded.

On the other hand, this purpose compels us to acknowledge the necessity of feeling guilt when the standards of sex have been transgressed. Therefore, the sense of sexual guilt cannot be dismissed as a mere misinterpretation of the other two forms of sexual shame. The intrinsic standards of sex are directly evident. They manifest themselves as an impulse to respect the nature of sex. This inner voice disturbs the average man's attitude of self-righteousness who boasts that he did never commit sexual crimes or open adultery, it dispels that sentimental toning-down of moral judgment which calls any action good because it is done out of love. Nevertheless, many people find it easy to silence that voice because they identify sin with outward actions. They feel good because they have not committed any serious sexual sin or crime, but thereby they disregard their countless sins of omission. Furthermore, we associate sin with acts of deliberate malice, which the average person rarely commits, but fail to discern the sins of folly, rashness, or blindness so common in sexual matters. Finally we are so exclusively concerned about our individual relations with other people that we lose sight of the fact that as citizens and members of the Christian congregations we share the responsibility for their mistakes and derelictions too.

Aware of these shortcomings, true faith will feel contrition not only for the transgression of commandments but also for the indifference of our hearts which disregard God's gifts, and for the lack of faith characteristic of our past. Before God's Spirit lifted the veil of darkness from our life we arrogantly considered our personal freedom to be autonomy though already then we surmised dimly that true life must be essentially superior to what we were. However, measured by the image of true humanity that the Spirit forms in us, our conjugal faithfulness is only faithfulness conjoint with, and in spite of, unfaithfulness; and even an unmarried man though he has never been intimate with a woman, and has never practised self-abuse knows that he is far from clean. Somewhere within every person there lurks a secret pleasure in impropriety; at some time disorderly desires are felt in every heart. Let everybody test himself before the mirror of his dreams. Measured by God's standards scarcely a single adult person is without sexual sin.

We do not, thereby, imply that every adult person has lived a sexually disordered life, and trampelled sexual decency under foot. In fact, it makes a great difference for the health of social life whether we control ourselves in sexual matters or not, whether our thoughts and speech are chaste or salacious, whether our lustful desires are allowed to issue in acts or not, whether or not we deceive ourselves about the guilt of our sins by moral callousness; but before God none of this makes any essential difference. Before Him the crucial question is whether or not we have maintained the sanctity of sex. However, the sense of our sinfulness must never be construed to mean that sex and the pleasures of sex are sinful by themselves. That we should experience sexual desire is as natural and as morally irrelevant as the sensations of hunger or weariness. On this point we agree with the Naturalistic interpretation. Rather, sin consists in our yielding to desire in disregard of the image of human life that the divine Spirit has set before us. The sin of our sexual desires consists in their aiming at wrong goals, for instance when the imaginary portrait of a partner fools Onanists, or the perverted image of a spouse is pursued in homosexuality; but also when we desire another's spouse or seek satisfactions that are incompatible with the true goals of sex, for instance in sexual perversions or by indulging in obscenity and indecent pleasures.

Our consideration must take us still a step further. Jesus taught plainly that a sinful act is not confined to the performance of a deed but rather is rooted in the initial impulse of the will, for instance, a covetous wish, an impure thought, or a lascivious glance. Furthermore, we are constrained to agree with Paul, that approval and toleration of sin is no less culpable than its actual commission (Rom. 1:32). In this respect modern Christianity has incurred a grave guilt. Our congregations have failed effectively and articulately to protest against the widespread glorification of sexual sins, and have been guilty of serious negligence by enduring the degradation and scorn heaped upon the Christian virtues by the radio, the motion pictures, television, and the press. We have no right to plead excusable weakness. Our toleration is a sinful disdain of the divine insight granted us; and thus we are no less reprehensible than those who committed gross sexual sins. Our indifferent and tolerant frame of mind shows plainly that we do not only consider these portrayals of sexual sin unimportant but that we actually give them our inner approval, or even find them desirable.

Since sex is essentially a relationship with another person we also commit sin when we throw temptation in the way of others. This is not only done when our evil attitudes and behaviour set to him a bad example but also when in flirtation and coquetry we go so far as to arouse sexual wishes and desires in others. While we may be unwilling to satisfy them, we thereby may excite him sexually to the point where he will look for satisfaction elsewhere. Notwithstanding their narrow perspective, the Pietists rightly suspected that there is a kind of dancing for instance that is sexual in nature. Then there are also those instances where the unity of the flesh is violated. It is not a rare occurrence today that a couple will not enter marriage, even though they have reciprocally unveiled the mystery of sex and thus created a relationship that cannot be dissolved. Likewise, does it not happen all too frequently that married couples fall short in their reciprocal relationship, which alone gives a perfect meaning to their sexual union! Indifference, selfishness, contempt of the partner, unwillingness to live for him or to let him share in one's personal life, are no less sinful than adultery. Our standards of what makes a genuine marriage have deteriorated to the point that we are more seriously concerned about unhappiness in marriage than about regard for its standards. However the quarrels, humiliations, mistreatment, and the frigidity and vexing disaffection of an unhappy marriage constitute spiritual problems because they prove that at least one of the spouses has failed to understand the meaning of marriage. The unwillingness to help the offending partner toward bettering the married relationship is just as sinful as the wrong he does. Considered in the light of faith not all of the causes of marital infidelity are on the side of the unfaithful partner. For this reason the injured partner should seriously scrutinize his heart in order to discover whether it was he who had failed to live up to the promises made to the partner at the time of the wedding. To be sure there are some marriages which from their very beginning were doomed to disintegrate on account of the absence of good faith of one of the partners even though the other partner would give his full measure of love and faithfulness. Such instances, however, are extremely rare particularly in our age when marriages are no longer arranged by parents or relatives.

Again we act sinfully when we refuse to accept the mutual responsibilities that Christians owe each other. In many instances we have to share the blame for the ills of our fellowmen. A case in point is the dissolution of the power of time-honored custom during the last century and a half. It is not merely the result of changing economic and social conditions but it is also indicative of a crisis in modern faith, inasmuch as the modern Protestant seeks to be his own lord in matters of faith rather than looking to the church for direction in his spiritual life. This inevitably had a powerful influence on the whole area of sexual relationships. Since this individualistic outlook has dissolved the fellowship of the church the young person of today lacks the sure footing that custom, respectability, and the fellowship of the congregation used to offer. For a similar reason, the problem of the single woman in the Christian congregation has become acute. In modern Protestantism each person seeks the fulfillment of his faith in himself and therefore fails to note the responsibility he owes the other members of the congregation. However, since every member is destined to make his own peculiar contribution to the life of the congregation his masculinity or femininity are included. We sin against these solitary women when we do not provide ways of so integrating them into the life of the congregation that they are given an opportunity as women to meet the other sex. Since the women's organizations engage in work that women can perform without any male assistance they cannot render this service. Thus far our congregations lack forms of social life which provide adequate opportunities for uniting the men and women of the congregation and in particular the unmarried ones in joint undertakings.

These unfortunate situations are not inherent in the nature of manhood and womanhood as such but are caused by our failures. Neither in personal nor in group life do we permit manhood and womanhood full opportunity to develop along the lines that God intended. Therefore, these unsatisfactory conditions show no less contempt of God's will than unbridled lust or unchastity. Sexual continence, for instance, is not in itself a virtue. Many times it may be nothing more than a complete indifference toward the opposite sex. Even an unmarried woman is destined, however, to express her femininity, for example by evidences of motherliness, and the men might courteously and helpfully assist wronged and injured womanhood. Or consider those chaste women whose repressed sexuality expresses itself in a desire to harm, injure, or degrade persons of the opposite sex. All of these must be accounted as sexual sins unrelated though they are with a sexual act.

A sexual relationship that is devoid of a true spirit of reciprocal giving and receiving is also sinful. Despite a lot of unqualified talk about love, that is supposed to render sexual life ethically perfect, love without the spirit of reciprocity is counterfeit. Take, for instance, those persons who accept the other person's love as though it were a reward for their own goodness and service, and whose pride will not allow them to receive it as a free gift.

The Consciousness of Sin

Not every person feels guilty when he violates the intrinsic standards of sex. Even the Christian conscience must be trained to grasp the breadth and depth of a true sexual relationship, and to perceive how easily we fail to impart to the partner all that he has a right to expect on our hands. The consciousness of guilt admits that as persons we are responsible for our evil attitudes and deeds. We are not simply the products of inherited tendencies and natural forces, nor mere victims of circumstance. Since we are endowed with the power of choice we must assume responsibility for our lives. Of course, people may feel the pressure of an uncontrollable fate that creates situations in which escape from sin is impossible. Take, for instance, the fact that during the last twenty years military service and mass expulsions of populations have exposed many millions of young people prematurely and against their will to sexual reality. But while they could not be held responsible for this manner of sexual initiation these same young people wilfully entered then into acts of license and vice, for which they alone must bear the blame.

The awareness of guilt is not only readiness personally to assume responsibility for our evil deeds, but is also a recognition of our total inability to rectify them. Under the influence of erroneous pagan ideas late Judaism and the Church of the Middle Ages taught that good works would compensate for evil deeds. However, this view does not recognize that the perpetrator of a wrong is powerless to undo the evil results of his misdeed and its contagious nature by which still others will be perverted. In the sexual sphere this is most obvious in cases of seduction, rape, and adultery, as the most flagrant and irreparable desecrations of the sexual mystery; but even a man's lustful look at a girl, or his thoughtless indifference that begets or deepens a solitary woman's sense of inferiority, are sins that work permanent damage. Furthermore, sinful deeds, like contagious diseases, contaminate their environment. The fact of my own wrong-doing may eventually convince another person that he too has the right to do the same thing although he may have struggled for a long time against this temptation. Therefore, persons in positions of authority and trust in the community have an especially large responsibility toward everyone. Rightly do people expect the minister to exhibit extraordinary zeal in keeping the moral law. Or take the role the high schools play in the evaluation of sex and sexual practices. It is almost proverbial that one student's immorality gradually infects his fellow-students. We are not always completely aware of the fact that our fellowmen know more about us than we think, and thus, even though we may not wish it, our sexual sins discolor our surroundings.

When the gravity of guilt is taken seriously it produces such profound results in our personal life that it is most important to prevent the development of a false sense of guilt. Many Christian people have no clear understanding of the three forms under which sexual guilt is manifested, and therefore they endure unnecessary torture from certain scruples concerning their sexual attitude. Because of the close emotional relationship between parents and children in the early years of their lives, disobedience to some parental prohibition, such as not to play with their sexual parts, may be interpreted by the children as serious sexual sin. Since such things are done in secret and no opportunity exists for the child to resolve his tensions a guilt neurosis may develop; and in the case of a person reared in a religious home this may be religiously interpreted. It is evident that the immense emotional weight of the neurotic sense of guilt is apt to block the development of a genuine guilt-feeling. The same thing holds true of the conflicting rivalry of mother and daughter for the father's love. If no effort is made to explain to the girl that the attraction she feels for her father is a normal stage in the development of her sexuality, in which the father furnishes the features of her wish-image, she may fall into the obsession that she desired him as her lover. In that case the sense of guilt and the ensuing wish for self-justification may lead to open hostility against her father. All such cases involve great mental torment because, owing to the widespread depreciation of sex, the sense of guilt weighs particularly severely upon such a person. It is, therefore, important for those people both to know whether they have incurred a genuine guilt, and whether or not it is really connected with sex.

The Burden of Sin

It is a widespread error to believe that sexual sins are more blameworthy than other sins. The reason for this view is obvious. In the truest sense the standards of sex apply most perceptibly and vigorously to our bodies. The only other parallel is found in political life. Just as the will of the authorities in the body politic so our sexual impulses compel us in the totality of our physical-spiritual life to make certain decisions. Moreover, our sexual activities exert a deep-going effect upon our total physical life. As a result the nature of sin is more impressively evidenced and realized in our sexual lives than in other spheres of life, even though sexual sins are not by themselves worse than any others.

The dreadful nature of sin is particularly pronounced in sexual life. God punishes sin with sin. Exery sexual experience, from the smallest desire to the completed act, stamps its ineradicable traces upon our lives. The sexual experiences of childhood and early youth persists in a person's mind right into old age, and his development is consciously or unconsciously influenced by them. These first experiences occur at an age when the child is not yet able to understand their meaning or their dangers. It is therefore not a mere romantic sentimentality, but an experience supported by the Christian faith that for many persons the attainment of the first sexual knowledge is tantamount to being driven out of the paradise of youth; for in most people's lives the acquisition of sexual knowledge has implied guilt. These first experiences are most disturbing when the sexual impulse is aroused at an age where it is not yet connected with love, and so lacks respect for the secret of sexual reciprocity. As such persons grow up their loveless impulse engenders ever new images of the object of their desire while these unfortunate people are unable ever to find real satisfaction. They are the pure type of unsatisfied persons.

Since sins against the sexual fellowship damage and destroy the ability to love, therefore, from a psychological viewpoint any suggestion of unlimited sexual intercourse without moral responsibility is absurd, for in proportion as the restriction is diminished the ability to love vanishes. Unrestrained sexual intercourse renders life empty and unsatisfactory, and tends increasingly to isolate a person.

Of course, it is not always true that violations of the divine standards of sex result in severe psychic and physical illness. Nevertheless, according to modern psychological theory more neurotic and psychic troubles are sexually induced than was formerly held. But more serious is the fact that sexual sins, to a greater extent than all else, impede our knowledge of God and weaken our faith. Paul states emphatically that adultery and immorality make it impossible for a person to enter the Kingdom of God (1 Cor. 6:9-10; Gal. 5:19-21). That is to say, although they do not preclude spiritual life altogether, they deprive us of the use of those resources by means of which the Holy Spirit establishes harmony among people, and hence we lack the power to build up a new and constructive fellowship. Assuredly, we would be guilty of an unjust interpretation of Paul's statement if we were to inject the heathenish inference that certain reprehensible sins have the ability absolutely to exclude anyone from fellowship with God. Rather, Paul envisages the direct connection between the mental state of the adulterer and the new life called forth by the Spirit according to the redemptive will of God. According to Paul, adultery and immorality rule out the possibility of love, because they result from a wrong egotistic concept of human life that is incompatible with the divine mind. Since Christ approaches us through our fellowmen, any person who does not truly love his fellowmen cannot love God (1 John 4:20).

Sexual sins not only make man's life burdensome, but are also impediments of his attempts to do what is right. Every sexual act establishes a permanent bond between the two persons (1 Cor. 6:16-17), and imposes reciprocal duties upon them. Consider the countless instances, however, where premarital intercourse was had with another person than the spouse, or where married people have entered into some sexual relationship with another person. For those who deny the significance of moral laws in sexual life the matter may end with psychic conflicts and troubles. But the Christian deludes himself by thinking his conduct is justified simply because it was motivated by love. Does not the sexual bond morally obligate him with the third person to the same extent as with his spouse? But how can he fulfill his responsibility to the one without dealing unfairly with the other? Moreover, since sexual sins so profoundly determine our whole self for the rest of our lives no hope can be entertained that by exercising or strengthening the will we can throw off their dominion over us. To be sure, in the course of his life a person may be able to resist temptation by the exercise of his will and a deepened understanding of God's will, but neither the past guilt nor his memories can be blotted out and they continue to stimulate his desires.

But how strenuously man fights against the acknowledgement of his condition! Are we really so helpless? What remains of man's superiority if we are not only powerless but also do not even have the possibility to attain the good? Nevertheless, God will not spare us the painful recognition of our nothingness. He does so in order to condemn our pride which deluded us into thinking that we might be able to find a meaning for our lives apart from His revealed will.

XX. THE GOSPEL OF FORGIVENESS

The Flight from Guilt

Positivistic psychologists find fault with the Christian religion primarily because in it the distinction between good and evil is basic. They suggest that human conduct be measured solely by the standards of expediency. But experience shows that one cannot move very far in that direction until one has to postulate objective values as the basis even of expediency. While it should be admitted that confused Christian teaching on the subject of sex is responsible for false guilt complexes, the attitude of those psychologists shows that they are unable to deal with genuine feelings of guilt on the part of their patients. The distinction between good and evil is of the very essence of man. But while it is impossible for people to ignore their guilt there are many attempts to silence the accusing voice or to minimize the gravity of sin. There is, for instance, the individualist *à la* Nietzsche who attempts to become greater than his guilt. But thereby he only betrays his ignorance of the true nature of doing wrong. In turn, however, what can a person do who has attained to a full realization of his guilt?

Since sexual sin is always an offense against human fellowship, we instinctively turn to our fellowmen for help and relief from its oppressive weight. Yet, the kindly interest and encouragement of a trusted friend, a physician, or a pastor, helpful as it is in restoring our faith in God, cannot lift the burden from our shoulders. Even though their sympathetic understanding may re-establish us into the life of the community, yet more is necessary. The specific nature of sexual sins is to be found in the fact that it is directed against the other sex. We need, therefore, not only the forgiveness of those persons against whom our sin was directed but also that of the other sex. This explains why some men believe their sins might be expiated by the love of a pure virgin because she would represent womanhood in its original state. On the whole, however, the need of forgiveness on the part of the other sex seems to be more easily understood by women than by men. Encumbered by their guilt women seek for a man who shows no sexual desire for them and in whose fellowship they hope to receive a priestly expiation or forgiveness of their sins. It is hardly by mere coincidence that prostitutes felt drawn into the presence of Jesus (Matt. 21:32). They saw in Him the representative of pure masculinity. His case shows, however, that, if sex is to be rescued more is required of the deliverer than to have a pure and healthy sexuality. Since our sexual sins are our own fault their burden is not removed until it is forgiven. People felt that Jesus had the power to dispense forgiveness. In theory we all know that sin cannot be pardoned except through Christ, yet how difficult to find the way of forgiveness!

Repentance

The remission of sins which God proffers to the believer is not the result of a general confession that definitely blots out our entire sinful past. Rather, a living faith is constantly aware of new transgressions of God's will, and requests every day afresh divine forgiveness. Let no one imagine that just because he believes himself to be saved, he is holy and that whatever he does in faith is summarily forgiven. But equally wrong is the attempt to escape the sense of guilt by holding that God, being aware of our weakness, will pay no attention to our sins. How absurd to believe that sinful acts can be adjusted by refusing to think about them. For guilt never forgets us because we are constantly under God's purview, and He continues to remind us that every sexual sin is an infraction of the order He has established in the relation of the sexes.

Repentance is a painfully perceived and unambiguous admission that, regardless of the pleasures therein enjoyed, certain actions of mine were contrary to God's will. The positive evaluation of repentance has been under vigorous attack by both modern psychology and theology. Psychologists have attempted to empty repentance of any religious significance by construing it as a re-interpretation or sublimation of the feeling of inferiority or the fear of the father's authority. Theologians have considered repentance as a refined but surreptitious attempt of the individual to gain the divine blessings by means of his own efforts. Realizing that their good works were insufficient to please God people would think that they could reach the goal by admitting their faults. We cannot deny that some forms of repentance accord with the psychologists' definition, and also that theologians have sometimes described repentance in a manner that rendered it a meritorious work. However, in both instances, the discussion is irrelevant to the idea of repentance as found in the New Testament where it designates a change of heart.

Jesus taught clearly that repentance is not a matter of measuring our lives against the demands of the moral law, or against our own ideals, but rather we feel it when we see ourselves in relation to the sublime purpose God has for us. As we look at Jesus we understand what man is destined to be, and how infinitely God loves us in giving us a chance to live such a life. However, repentance that is kindled by the offer of a new life can never banish the pain our guilt imposes upon us. It would be unrealistic to interpret our condition in a purely idealistic manner, by holding that our destinies would work themselves out automatically as a gradual development into perfection.

Our natural pride rebels against the idea that the meaning and value of our life should rest upon the pursuing love of God and the pardoning grace of Christ rather than upon our own personal achievements. But there is no other way left. By faith we experience in the long run that the acceptance of Christ's forgiveness is less painful and humiliating than the burden of our guilt. For the life He creates within us offers the only possibility to live in the truth. If it is too late for us to have an experience of genuine chastity and love, repentance at least enables us to face ourselves as we are in our relation to God. Repentance has nothing in common with prudery that vilifies sex because of its dangers, but it is just as alien to the superficial modern viewpoint which treats sex as purely natural while ignoring its intrinsic standards and the guilt of their transgression.

The Divine Forgiveness

People today find it hard to believe that God's forgiveness can really affect our way of life. They think of God's forgiveness as a kind of divine unconcern felt about our sins. They argue that a loving father could hardly be as stern as the moralists in dealing with our guilt and that he might be thought to be content with the expressions of personal regret. Such a sentimental view, however, is ignorant of what life in Christ is like.

The risen Lord is at work within the Church, both in its proclamation of the Gospel, and in its fellowship. If I accept its services I receive strength to overcome my sinful tendencies and to live a new life in spite of my sinful past. For this reason repentance and forgiveness are inseparable, although in actual life there are times when we emphasize the one or the other; yet it is the same Lord Who reveals His Will in the standards He sets for our life, and in granting the experience of the remission of our sins. Thus His forgiveness not only assures us that our sinful past will no longer rise up in accusation against us, but also offers us a new life in harmony with the divine will notwithstanding our weakness and guilt. The door of the Kingdom of God is open to all those who are naturally weak-willed, indecisive, and vacillating provided that they appreciate this possibility of a new life and humbly receive it as an unmerited gift. The forgiveness of God encourages us to be ourselves, and to see ourselves in the radiant light of His truth in spite of the faults of ours which, too, are thereby revealed. If psychoanalysis offers us a possibility to accept our life as it is by showing unconcern for our past, how much more God by remitting our sins!

The comfort of divine forgiveness is most real to those unfortunate persons who as the victims of an inexorable fate were plunged into guilt. While God does not ignore any sin, He does not confront us with the truth in order that by knowing it we should be knocked down and crushed. To those who despairingly look into their past and stare hopelessly into the future God promises a new beginning. The curse of a wasted life can be broken provided only we resist the danger of refusing liberation, because in self-pity we have come to love our fate.

Since faith is personal fellowship with Christ repentance is the beginning of the new life. Repentance is not an act of reflexion that compels us every time to wrestle with decisions until they become actual deeds. Rather, belief in God's forgiveness is an action in which we accept the new possibility which the grace of God provides. The woman who anointed Jesus in the house of Simon (Luke 7:36-50) is a wonderful illustration of what we mean. She felt instinctively that receiving divine forgiveness demanded not only a personal acceptance of God's gracious will but also outward expression. It is only by doing things that we can show our appreciation of the gift of forgiveness and its Giver. For this reason the new life is never confined to moral discipline or the development of one's personality. Accepting God's forgiveness requires a life of fellowship with the other members of Christ's body because it is through the Lord's presence in the Church that the redemptive grace is mediated to us.

As long as a person dare not venture to live by the grace of divine forgiveness he will be hunted by the demands of the moral law and thus be constantly in flight before sin. Since his main concern will be the struggle for moral betterment, he will never be able to live his own life. Being afraid lest his sex should triumph over his moral efforts sex is in his mind the constant source of temptation. The more we concentrate on the fight against sex the more firmly it grips us and the more severely it tempts us. On the other hand, if the supreme good we desire is the power of the new life we are relieved from the burdensome pressure of sexuality. Living by the grace of forgiveness we can again take an affirmative attitude toward sex. Whereas, formerly our attention was focussed on the sexual impulse and its problems it is now directed toward God and thus we lose our natural self-centeredness. We then experience in full happiness that this world is the place where God operates in all and through all. Thereby, the illusion is dispelled that life is worthwhile only when we have attained moral perfection. To live by the grace of forgiveness implies not only the assurance that God can make good use of our lives in spite of our misused sexuality, but also the readiness to leave it to Him to decide in what manner He will restore the meaning of our lives. Therefore while, in view of our sinful past, repentance precludes a good conscience it nevertheless presents us with a conscience that has been comforted.

XXI. LIFE IN TRUTH

The New Life

To judge from the definitions given by some modern theologians one might think that faith is but a true understanding of one's self, while it would bring no changes with it either within the individual believer or his environment. Although this description has brought to light an element of truth neglected both by the social gospel and by orthodoxy, yet in its one-sidedness, it, too, contradicts the New Testament picture of faith. That view is characterized by a new sight of reality, in which God's Spirit adds a kind of fifth dimension to our existence and a new direction of our inner will, or our Self, in which God's redemptive work is accepted as the supreme value. All non-Scriptural views of man have this in common that they regard only those things as essentially necessary to life that serve man's self-chosen purposes and needs. The Scriptural viewpoint, however, recognizes only fellowship with God as essential. Hence no life is meaningless merely because it has not realized its self-appointed goals, or has not contributed to the biological demands of its environment. As applied to our sexuality this means that life does not lose its meaning when the individual fails to find satisfaction of his desire, and that people can live purposeful lives without contributing to the perpetuation of their nation or race. While the supremacy of God must be obediently accepted man is not thereby coërced. On the contrary. Faith is the free affirmation of the impulse which God's Spirit gives to our lives. Through faith it is possible to increase and extend the human relationship in sex quantitatively and qualitatively beyond its initial stage.

The obedience of faith does not demand, for instance, that the solitary unmarried woman, the widow, and the divorcee should remain in their condition and marry under no circumstances. This would be a stoical attitude quite remote from the willingness of the believer to live his life for God. These women should rather be shown that even if they find no husband, they are able to employ their womanly qualities for good in their surroundings. In all conditions and in spite of all our sins the obedience of faith is possible because God will provide all the resources necessary for the goal He has set us. Therefore, hope and prayer are the most important ingredients of the new life. The believer must realize that in order to solve his sexual problems he must bring them before the Lord in prayer. Much marital unhappiness could be avoided if lovers would ask God's guidance in selecting their marriage partner, rather than depending only upon the intensity of their infatuation. Likewise, the believer who conducts his marriage as in the Lord will seek to make his marriage transcend mere sexuality by emphasizing his fellowship with God. Then the spouse is not only a sexual partner but also and above all a brother or sister in Christ. In this way the instinctive longing inherent in all love becomes real: our earthly lives are transmuted into lives with God.

The Fruits of Obedience

As compared with the deceptive and unrealizable possibilities of Idealism, the Christian has considerable advantages. In the first place, faith overcomes the inner contradictions of the Self by means of accepting the truth of God. Apart from faith man vaccillates between asserting himself as he is on the one hand, and aiming at an ideal goal irrespective of the possibilities of realizing it on the other. If, for many people, sex is a particular fertile field for psychic troubles the cause does not lie in sexuality itself, but rather in the contradiction between the function that God has assigned to sex, and the improper use to which we put it. The way of faith is the opposite of the violent solutions advocated by psychoanalysis, which are a real threat to true life. The patient is there persuaded to believe that his trouble is caused by a conflict between the Self and a Super-ego represented by the conventions of society, the admonitions of the parental home, or the moral teachings of the Church. He is assured that healing is possible if, after rejecting the demands of the Super-ego, he learns to be and to accept himself. His defiance of the demands of the Super-ego appears an unnecessary effort, since his present conflict is interpreted as an unconscious continuation of a conflict situation in which he had found himself with his mother or father in childhood. Although psychic difficulties are sometimes caused in this way yet the solutions offered by the Freudian school hardly pierce the surface of the sexual problem even in those cases. The original conflict would not produce such dire results in the patient's mind unless he thought that he had a natural right to satisfy his sexual desires as he pleased, ignoring thereby that a healthy sex life must be based upon the principle of reciprocity between the sexes.

God would not so persistently offer us forgiveness but for the fact that commonly we make a mess of our sexual lives by refusing to face the truth and to live by it. Instead we place either an unjustified confidence in our own ability to handle our sins, or we disastrously blind ourselves to the contradictions between our actual conduct and the divine meaning of sex. Or we are seduced into repeatedly committing a certain sin because we fail to see why it is evil. While our mind may not be aware of the disunity of our life, our Self feels it instinctively, and thus we are unhappy without knowing the reason. When faith recognizes this contradiction the Holy Spirit opens our eyes to the falsity of enticing temptations, and stops the effects our sins would otherwise have upon other lives.

The Christian family is a product of faith. It offers the matchless opportunity of suffusing every relationship of daily life with the Spirit of God. Since the spouses have to live together and are unable to escape each other, every moment of the day and every activity in the home form a challenge to live in common according to the divine purpose. While the social importance of the family is almost universally recognized, its usefulness is often interpreted on false premises. Important as certain social functions are, like the rearing of children, the legal regulation of inheritance, or the stabilizing of the social order, yet what makes Christian marriage so unique is the fact that there is no other force fit to engender that genuine renewal of social and political life that Christian marriage does. For here alone marital love manifests itself as the complete surrender to, and dependence upon, the divine will. The fact that Christ accepts us as we are does not mean that faith is not able to make basic changes in our lives. Surely the believer is not a sinless person, but on the other hand a wide gulf separates the sin of weak faith from unforgiven sin. In forgiveness our life receives a new direction and dynamic, so that in spite of its provisional nature sex is used by God to further His plans and achieve His purpose. Physical love and sexual relationships, rather than being incompatible with the nature of the Church, are the prerequisites for the fulfilling of the Church's purposes. It is upon Christian families that the fellowship of believers rests.

Likewise among Christians the crises of married life are not the beginning of its disintegration, as in the case of unbelievers, but serve to remind the couple that marital harmony is not a natural product. Rather, we must implore God for faith and strength if we want to reach that goal. Even so, God allows temptations to enter our lives for our training and development; not as though He were intent upon our downfall, but simply to warn us against the superficial belief that sex is a mere means of pleasure, without serving a higher end. Every weakness and difficulty of sexual life provide occasions for those in fellowship with Christ to test their faith and to implore divine aid for its strengthening. This fellowship with Christ is the most priceless treasure of our faith because it relieves us from the necessity to contend single-handed with the difficulties of our life. In Christ we are borne up and strengthened by the Christian fellowship. By means of its forgiveness the Church proves that it is the Body of Christ. Although the Church never dares take the sins of its members lightly, yet it never finds their sins a reason to exclude them from its fellowship.

Perhaps not all congregations have fully developed their forgiving function. Some are lukewarm and indifferent to the sins of their members, while others show a hardhearted and pharisaic attitude toward the fallen member and instead of offering help cast him out and forget him. Both types manifest a lack of appreciation of divine forgiveness on the part of such congregations. However, a Church that is aware of its living by God's measureless forgiveness will also be eager to show forgiveness to the individual member (Luke 7:47).

It is true that the Church is not constituted merely by forbearing the mistakes and sins of its members but by proclaiming God's will. She faithfully teaches and upholds the standards and virtues of sexual life and she admonishes and directs her members by exercising church discipline. In order to be effective the latter does not require expulsion from the fellowship of the Church. Much more important is the fact that the common life of the congregation develops custom which in turn serves as a standing reproof against the offending member. Modern individualism which believes tenaciously that the individual by his own power is capable of achieving a good life tends to depreciate the value of the Church, but in so doing he forgets that the Church creates the atmosphere from which we draw our spiritual nourishment. This is obvious in the adverse effects which life in college or in the armed forces or any other separation from the native atmosphere of congregational life has upon the spiritual growth of young people. Under these new circumstances, they find it difficult to continue their former practices of spiritual life, or to cling to the Christian ideas which they took for granted while they lived within the fellowship of their congregation and its youth organization.

Of all the resources that the church has at its disposal for strengthening the faith of its members the most neglected one is intercessory prayer. People seldom realize to what extent their lives are affected by the congregation's constant and united intercession in their behalf. How many dangerous temptations have been averted, and how much unexpected help have we experienced, not as a result of some chance combination of circumstances but of the united intercession of the Christian congregation! However, this fact underscores also the great responsibility the congregation has for the lives of its members. The Church possesses authority to act in Jesus' name and to announce and impart Christ's forgiveness to everyone. If it lacks this consciousness, or fails to exercise this unique prerogative, it closes the door of God's Kingdom against the needs of sinful men. Nevertheless, although individual congregations may be remiss in their duty, the believer has the constant comfort that the Church universal is greater than any individual congregation, and that if one congregation falls spiritually ill or dies other members of the Body of Christ will supply the needed help, strength, and comfort.

The Limits of Christian Obedience

The special privileges granted to the believers should not blind us to the fact that the Holy Spirit's activity upon us does not immediately make us perfect Christians. His first touch is only felt as an impulse to overcome temptations to sin. Moreover, since no person can isolate himself completely from all social relationships, we have to live in an environment dominated by sin notwithstanding our faith. No wonder we find it difficult to participate in the political and economic life of the national community without being contaminated by its sins. There is, finally, the fact that the divine forgiveness does not wipe out our past as though it had never existed.

For this reason Christian marriages, too, are not necessarily a success. A strictly legalistic application of Mark 10:19, that would absolutely forbid divorce among Christians might, in certain instances, contribute to driving the spouses into greater wrong. Sometimes a pastor has to realize that the only solution of a marital problem that is humanly possible is to counsel divorce. This does not mean that divorce is in accordance with God's will, but merely that such a step is most advisable because under the existing conditions a constant witnessing of parental dissension would work more serious damage upon the children than a divorce, while a divorce might at least give some assurance of an harmonious homelife. We are bound also to take a similar position toward the remarriage of divorced persons. Although Jesus rightly states that establishing a new marital relationship during the lifetime of the first spouse is a sinful deed, yet it is altogether possible that unlike the first one the second marriage might be a true fellowship. Of course, in cases of a second marriage of divorced people, the couple should forgo a public wedding ceremony in the church because the first marriage vow has been broken. Yet no minister has a right to refuse a private ceremony contending that there could be no blessing upon the second marriage. It is also a little short of presumptuous to think that Christians have it in their power so to alter circumstances and conditions that they could live in a sinless zone in which all temptations are removed. For instance, the Church cannot overnight so change its members that all of them will show a serious sense of responsibility for the plight of solitary women in the congregation, to say nothing of the impossibility to eliminate the excess of women in the adult population.

However, in spite of all these limitations, faith makes an essential difference in our lives because we are thereby enabled to live in the truth. Those who follow Christ do not pretend to be better than they are. But faulty and imperfect though our lives may be yet they can effectively bear witness to our willingness to recognize God's truth. Thereby our fellow-men receive some intimation of the mystery of sexual unity and the divine purpose of sexual life and they experience a purification of the sinful atmosphere in which they and we live.

Life in Christ

Without communion with Christ all attempts to bring our religious life to bear on sex will remain wishful thinking. Christ is the perfect exemplification of true life, and by the power of His sacrificial life we, too, are enabled in spite of our sin to live in the truth. To this end, two requirements are imposed upon us: we must practise forgiveness as we have received it, and must be ready to live our lives by divine grace.

Religious individualism believes that to receive divine forgiveness is sufficient for a life in truth. However, we do not conduct our lives in a vacuum but must live in the association of other people, therefore we double our guilt by not seeking the forgiveness of him whom we have wronged, also. People who desire God's forgiveness as a means of attaining personal purity or as an escape from the unpleasant results of sin betray their lack of understanding of faith. Such a person is what Jesus called a hypocrite. He is motivated by an ethically disguised selfishness. In view of the fact that all of our actions and attitudes affect other lives about us it is also essential that both the individual and the community that has been injured and debased by our wrong deeds should forgive us. Hence we have to ask their pardon, yet that cannot be done without previously confessing our sins to God and requesting His forgiveness. On that basis alone can we be frank toward other people. Apart from it the fear of losing my spouse's respect will prevent me from confessing my secret sins to him or her. Or in those instances in which the deceived spouse has detected the lapse of his partner the offender will attempt to muster up excuses or make flat denials of any involvement and thus make bad things worse. But if he has attained the peace of God's forgiveness he will also feel free to ask the forgiveness of his offended partner. Many marriages that were on the verge of disintegrating might have been saved if the offending partner had only taken a timely opportunity to ask his spouse's forgiveness. Maintaining silence and concealing guilt in order to shield the partner from the bitter truth only creates reticence and uncertainty that ultimately lead to a more painful estrangement than a full revelation of the truth once and for all would have done. Of course, after years of trust in his faithfulness it is difficult for the wronged partner to meet the other's confession of his infidelity; yet since his confession is a proof of his love, it also provides the basis and the opportunity for forgiveness and a new beginning.

Forgiveness, of course, does not denote an unconcerned and indifferent attitude toward the partner's guilt. Jesus did not refrain from speaking about the sins of the woman who was a sinner (Luke 7:36 ff), or of the woman taken in adultery (John 8:2 ff), nor should marriage partners gloss over each other's sins and guilt. A so-called broadmindedness that allows mutual freedom in the sexual lives of married persons has nothing in common with true marriage or genuine love. However, Christian forgiveness will never use the spouse's guilt as a pretext for estrangement or separation, since the guilt of one of the partners cannot destroy their mutually established union. Realizing this fact should move the injured partner, too, to forgive and to be reconciled. To forgive an acknowledged wrong is not only necessary as a demand of faith, but it also exerts a wholesome influence upon the one who forgives. The cause of many psychic disturbances can be traced back to a partner's adamant and unforgiving spirit toward an injustice he has suffered at the hands of the other. An unforgiving attitude begets an unhealthy frame of mind. Refusal to be reconciled destroys personal perspective, develops self-centeredness and self-pity, and blinds its possessor to his own dire need for forgiveness. Forgiveness releases us from an excessive concern about ourselves and restores us to real life.

Forgiveness must be exercised not only when the basic sanctity of marriage has been violated by adultery but must also extend to the social relationship of the sexes. How great is the burden of grief and bitterness that many solitary and lonesome women have called down upon themselves by an unforgiving attitude toward men and society in general, for having sustained the loss of their husband, or because no one has married them. They too must strive to live affirmatively and constructively by forgiving as they have been forgiven (Eph. 4:32; Col. 3:13). It is most important for us to realize that we live in a world of sinful people with whom we can live peaceably and constructively only when ready to forgive.

Finally, life in the truth requires an unfaltering willingness to trust in God's grace in the face of every adverse circumstance. We firmly believe that Christ has the power to permeate the whole life of mankind. But His might will not necessarily manifest itself immediately as moral progress in our lives. Despite his fervent prayers a believer may languish for a long while in the bondage to his desires; or an humble and forgiving solitary woman may have to seek for years for a congenial friend; or sincere and fervent love may prove to be powerless to prevent the breakup of a marriage. These experiences, however, do not contravert the reality of God's forgiveness, but only attest to the wisdom of the divine pedagogy. God's objective is not to render the individual happy but to offer all men the opportunity of a constructive fellowship with each other and with Himself. While we all know that repentance is the first step on the way to this goal, we are nevertheless easily deceived about the sincerity of our repentance. Very often what makes us regret our deeds is not that they are violations of the divine command but rather that they interfered with our desire for personal happiness, or that falling so deep hurts our pride. On account of such false repentance God may allow a sinner to languish in the misery of ungovernable impulses until he learns through the bitterness of his disappointments that he is not made for personal happiness and purity, but for God's sake. God wants us to understand the depth of divine love, which in spite of man's sinfulness, yearns to possess him for himself and to use him for His ends. Once we have realized that it is more important to submit to God than to realize certain ideals, we'll also be able to master our life.

When we live by divine grace we do not measure the goodness of our life by self-chosen standards but are rather willing to submit our lives to God's judgment, certain that it is a part of his redemptive governance although it cuts and burns away those tendencies and wishes that are unfit for His service. Since growth in faith does not depend upon our personal plans and programs, but follows entirely the way on which God leads and educates us, there is little hope for us directly to come to grips with our various sins. Our basic problem is not a moral issue but rather the spiritual confrontation with the sinfulness of our Self. We must therefore learn to live our lives from the center of our person toward its circumference, that is to say from trust in the divine grace to the implementation of faith by deeds. For in faith God affects not only some faculty of ours, be it understanding, will, or feeling, but rather the innermost depths of our being. If things are to improve in our lives, we must first of all comprehend that overflowing bounty of God's love out of which He sent Jesus as our Saviour, and grasp the celestial paradox that God sacrificed Himself for sinners. As long as we pretend that life is worth living because we are satisfied with our own deeds and think it intolerable that God should love us without ground or reason, we have not yet laid hold of the depth and breath of divine grace. The Lord calls us to become His children notwithstanding our past guilt, and our recurring lapses into sin. From God's fellowship not even the adulterer, the prostitute, and the homosexual are excluded. Although we constantly revert to old sins God's willingness to forgive is indefatigable. In our faith it is God's grace that works a strength made perfect in weakness, which purifies us and builds a new humanity out of our confusion and guilt. Because faith shifts life's center of gravity from the Ego to the will of God, sexuality appears in a new light, and it can be accepted without apprehension and full of thanks. God uses the physiological impulse of sex to unite His children most intimately, and the love of Christ empowers us to love our partner in true mutuality. Only by viewing sexual problems through the divine perspective of the giving and forgiving will of God can sex be considered with the earnestness it deserves. The Author and Finisher of our faith leads us on to the distant heights where the winds of divine truth blow free.

BIBLIOGRAPHY

During the last two decades the literature on sex and marriage has increased so rapidly that a complete enumeration would be bewildering rather than helpful for the non-specialist. It seemed to be wise to confine this bibliographical list to a selection from recent literature. The various headings are to remind the reader that our subject is not only of great complexity but also of a controversial character, since no general agreement exists as to the basic axioms from which the ethical evaluation is to start.

HISTORY OF SEX AND MARRIAGE

Derrick S. Bailey, *Homosexuality and the Western Christian Tradition,* London, 1955.

William Graham Cole, *Sex and Love in the Bible,* New York, 1959.

Ben Zion Goldberg, *The Sacred Fire: The Story of Sex in Religion,* New York, 1958.

Mary Esther Harding, *Woman's Mysteries Ancient and Modern,* New ed., New York, 1955.

David and Vera Mace, *Marriage East and West,* New York, 1960.

Bronislaw Malinowski, *Sex and Repression in Savage Society,* London 1927, reprint 1958.

Bronislaw Malinowski, *The Sexual Life of Savages in North-Western Melanesia,* 3rd ed., London, 1932.

Margaret Mead, *Male and Female: A Study of the Sexes in a Changing World,* London & New York, 1949.

Raphael Patai, *Sex and Family in the Bible and in the Middle East,* Garden City, N. Y., 1959.

Arthur Phillips, ed., *Survey of African Marriage and Family Life,* London, 1953.

Denis de Rougemont, *Love in the Western World* (Engl. tr.), New York, 1941, British revised edition: *Passion and Society,* London, 1956.

Kenneth Walker and Peter Fletcher, *Sex and Society* (Penguin Book).

Edward A. Westermarck, *The History of Human Marriage,* 3 v., 5th ed., London, 1921.

PSYCHOLOGY OF SEX

Edmund Bergler, *Conflict in Marriage: The Unhappy Undivorced,* New York, 1949.

W. G. Cole, *Sex in Christianity and Psychoanalysis,* New York & London, 1955.

Helene Deutsch, *Psychology of Women: A Psychoanalytical Interpretation,* 2 v., New York & London, 1944-45.

Havelock Ellis, *Sex in Relation to Society, being Studies in the Psychology of Sex,* London, 1946.

C. S. Ford and S. A. Beach, *Patterns of Sexual Behaviour,* London, 1952.

Erich Fromm, *The Art of Loving,* New York, 1956.

Walter M. Gallichan, *The Psychology of Marriage,* New York, 1918.

V. W. Grant, *The Psychology of Sexual Emotions,* London and Toronto, 1956.

Mary Esther Harding, *The Way of All Women: A Psychological Interpretation,* London, 1933.

George W. Henry, *All the Sexes,* New York, 1955.

Nikolai M. Iovets-Tereshchenko, *Friendship—Love in Adolescence,* London, 1936.

Karl A. Menninger, *Love Against Hate,* New York, 1942.

Oswald Schwarz, *Psychology of Sex* (Penguin Book).

Frances Strain, *The Normal Sex Interest of Children from Infancy to Adolescence,* New York, 1948.

Otto Weininger, *Sex and Character* (Engl. tr.), London, 1906.

SEXUAL ETHICS: NON-RELIGIOUS

Simone de Beauvoir, *The Second Sex*, (Engl. tr.), London, 1953.

Gerald Heard, *Pain, Sex and Time: A New Outlook on Evolution and the Future of Man*, New York & London, 1939.

A. Kardiner, *Sex and Morality*, London, 1955.

Benjamin Karpman, *The Sexual Offender and His Offenses: Etiology, Pathology, Psychodynamics and Treatment*, New York, 1954.

Ian Landau, *Sex, Life and Faith: A Modern Philosophy of Sex*, London, 1946.

SEXUAL ETHICS: PROTESTANT

D. S. Bailey, *The Mystery of Love and Marriage: A Study in the Theology of Sexual Relation*, London & New York, 1952.

Derrick S. Bailey, *The Man-Woman Relation in Christian Thought*, London, 1959.

Roland H. Bainton, *What Christianity Says About Sex, Love and Marriage*, New York, 1957.

Peter A. Bertocci, *The Human Venture in Sex, Love, and Marriage*, Association Press, New York, 1949.

Richard Clarke Cabot, *Christianity and Sex*, New York, 1937.

R. H. Charles, *Courage, Truth, Purity*, Oxford, 1931.

Simon Doniger, *Sex and Religion Today: Selected from the Pages of 'Pastoral Psychology'*, New York, 1953.

Arthur Herbert Gray, *Men, Women and God: A Discussion of Sex Questions from the Christian Point of View*, London, 1923, New York (1938).

Richard Bartlett Gregg, *Spirit Through Body*, Cambridge, Mass., 1956.

Seward Hiltner, *Sex Ethics and the Kinsey Report*, New York, 1953.

Seward Hiltner, *Sex and the Christian Life*, New York, 1957.

C. S. Lewis, *Allegory of Love: A Study in Medieval Tradition*, New York, 1936.

W. N. Pittenger, *Christian View of Sexual Behavior*, Oxford and Toronto, 1954.

Wilmor Henry Sheldon, *Sex and Salvation*, New York, 1955.

B. H. Streeter, *Moral Adventure*, New York, 1929.

SEXUAL ETHICS:
CATHOLIC

H. Jone and U. Adelman, *Moral Theology,* Westminster, Md., Rev. ed. 1957.

Ernest Charles Messenger, *Two in One Flesh,* 3 v., Westminster, Md., 1949-1952.

Vincent Wilkin, *The Image of God in Sex,* London, 1954.

SEXUAL EDUCATION

Charles E. Batten and Donald E. McLean, *Fit To Be Tied: An Approach to Sex Education and Marriage,* Greenwich, Conn., 1960.

Lester D. Crow and Alice Crow, *Sex Education for the Growing Family,* Boston, Mass., 1959.

Alfred Schneiding, *Sex in Childhood and Youth: A Guide for Christian Parents, Teachers and Counselors,* St. Louis, 1953.

Lewis M. Terman, et. al., *Psychological Factors in Marital Happiness,* New York, 1938.

Leslie D. Weatherhead, *The Mastery of Sex through Psychology and Religion,* New York, 1947.

MARRIAGE
JEWISH VIEW

David Robert Mace, *Hebrew Marriage: A Sociological Study,* London, 1953.

MARRIAGE
CATHOLIC VIEW

John R. Cavanagh, *Fundamental Marriage Counselling: A Catholic Viewpoint,* Milwaukee, 1957.

Herbert Downs, *The Meaning of Marriage* (Engl. tr.), New York, 1939.

Dietrich von Hildebrand, *Marriage* (Engl. tr.), London, New York, 1942.

George H. Joyce, *Christian Marriage: An Historical and Doctrinal Study,* London, 1948.

A. Keenan and John Ryan, *Marriage, a Medical and Sacramental Study,* New York, 1955.

John A. O'Brien, *Courtship and Marriage,* Paterson, N. J., 1949.

C. C. Zimmerman and J. F. Cervantes, S.J., *Marriage and the Family,* Chicago, 1956.

MARRIAGE
PROTESTANT VIEW

T. Bovet, *Handbook to Marriage and Marriage Guidance,* London & Toronto, 1958.

Henry A. Bowman, *A Christian Interpretation of Marriage,* Philadelphia, 1959.

Mario Colacci, *Christian Marriage Today: A Comparison of Roman Catholic and Protestant Views with Special Reference to Mixed Marriages,* Minneapolis, 1958.

Melvin D. Hugen, *The Church's Ministry to the Older Unmarried,* Grand Rapids, Mich., 1959.

T. A. Lacey, *Marriage in Church and State,* London, 1947, reprint 1959.

Gerhard E. Lenski, *Marriage in the Lutheran Church: A Historical Investigation,* Columbus, Ohio, 1936.

A. T. Macmillan, *What Is Christian Marriage?* London & New York, 1944.

F. Alexander Magoun, *Love and Marriage,* New York, 1948.

Arnold S. Nash, ed., *Education for Christian Marriage,* London, 1939.

William T. Thompson, *An Adventure in Love: Christian Family Living,* Richmond, Va., 1956.

Oscar Daniel Watkins, *Holy Matrimony: A Treatise on the Divine Laws of Marriage,* London, 1895.

MARRIAGE
NON-RELIGIOUS VIEWS

Frederick L. Good and Otis F. Kelly, *Marriage, Morals and Medical Ethics,* New York, 1951.

Mary Macaulay, *Art of Marriage* (Penguin).

André Maurois, *The Art of Being Happily Married: A Play* (Engl. tr.), New York, London, 1956.

Bertrand R. Russell, *Marriage and Morals,* New York, 1929.

Edward A. Westermarck, *The Future of Marriage in Western Civilization,* New York, 1936.

Edward A. Westermarck, *Three Essays on Sex and Marriage,* London, 1934.

MARRIAGE
SOCIOLOGY

E. Chesser, *The Sexual, Marital and Family Relationship of the English Woman,* London, 1956.

A. Deutsch, ed., *Sex Habits of American Men: A Symposium on the Kinsey Report,* New York, 1948.

Sidney Ditzion, *Marriage, Morals and Sex in America,* New York, 1953.

Winston W. Ehrmann, *Premarital Dating Behavior,* New York & Toronto, 1960.

Paul G. Hansen, et al. *Engagement and Marriage: A Sociological, Historical and Theological Investigation by the Family Life Committee of the Lutheran Church—Missouri Synod,* St. Louis, Mo., 1959.

J. Himmelhoch and S. F. Fava, *Sexual Behavior in American Society: An Appraisal of the First Two Kinsey Reports,* New York, 1955.

A. C. Kinsey and others, *Sexual Behavior in the Human Male,* Philadelphia and London, 1948.

A. C. Kinsey and others, *Sexual Behavior in the Human Female,* Philadelphia and London, 1953.

F. E. Merrill, *Courtship and Marriage: A Study in Social Relationships,* New York, 1949.

Franz Carl Müller-Lyer, *The Evolution of Modern Marriage: A Sociology of Sexual Relations* (Engl. tr.), New York, 1930.

Pitirim A. Sorokin, *The American Sex Revolution* (Extending Horizons Book), Boston, 1956.

MARRIAGE COUNSELLING

Alphonse Henry Clemens, *Marriage Education and Counselling,* Washington, D. C., 1951.

Arthur Herbert Gray, *Successful Marriage,* London, 1941.

George A. Kelly, *The Catholic Marriage Manual,* New York, 1958.

William H. Leach, *The Cokesbury Marriage Manual,* Rev. ed., Nashville, Tenn., 1959.

C. S. Mihanovich, Bro. G. J. Schnapp, and J. L. Thomas, S.J., *A Guide to Catholic Marriage,* Milwaukee, Wisc., 1955.

J. Kenneth Morris, *Premarital Counseling: A Manual for Ministers,* Englewood Cliffs, N. J., 1960.

Emily H. Mudd, *The Practice of Marriage Counselling,* New York, 1951.

Rex Austin Skidmore, et al. *Marriage Consulting: An Introduction to Marriage Counselling,* New York, 1956.

INDEX OF BIBLICAL PASSAGES

OLD TESTAMENT

INDEX OF SUBJECTS AND NAMES